Footsteps
in
Summer

Footsteps
in
Summer

Diary of an epic walk of discovery across Britain

Russell George

Matador
9 Priory Business Park
Kibworth Beauchamp
Leicestershire LE8 0RX, UK
Tel: (+44) 116 279 2299
Fax: (+44) 116 279 2277
Email: books@troubador.co.uk
Web: www.troubador.co.uk/matador

ISBN 978 1784620 547

British Library Cataloguing in Publication Data.
A catalogue record for this book is available from the British Library.

Typeset in Aldine401 BT Roman by Troubador Publishing Ltd
Printed and bound by CPI Group (UK) Ltd, Croydon, CR0 4YY

Matador is an imprint of Troubador Publishing Ltd

www.footstepsinsummer.com

This book is dedicated to everybody who played some part in my JOGLE adventure.

CONTENTS

FOREWORD

Cancer Research UK is the world's leading charity dedicated to beating cancer through research. We have saved millions of lives by discovering new ways to prevent, diagnose and treat cancer, and survival rates have doubled over the past 40 years.

We fund research into more than 200 types of cancer, from the most common – such as breast, bowel, lung and prostate cancers – to rare types of tumour and children's cancers; we support groundbreaking science that benefits everyone. We currently invest nearly £400 million annually into our scientific research programme.

Research is cancer's ultimate enemy, but our life-saving work relies entirely on the money contributed by our supporters, whether through direct giving, legacies, one-off events or volunteer fundraising. We receive no Government funding for our research, so without the dedication and generosity of our supporters, we wouldn't be able to carry out any of our life saving research.

One such supporter is Russell George, who undertook a 955 mile solo walk from John O' Groats to Land's End to raise funds for Cancer Research UK. Russell has now written this book to tell the story of his epic adventure, including the numerous challenges he faced during his journey, the people he encountered en route, and the places he passed through.

Thanks to Russell and all the incredible people who support Cancer Research UK we will beat cancer sooner.

Frances Milner,
Supporter Led Fundraising Director,
Cancer Research UK

You can make an additional donation to
Cancer Research UK by visiting:

JustGiving.com/FootstepsInSummer

INTRODUCTION

7.00am. Terminal 5, Heathrow Airport. In the vicinity of the departure gate for the Edinburgh shuttle, a throng of impatient business passengers is congregated. Suited citizens of the corporate world, tapping away frenetically on laptops, purposely scanning slick PowerPoint presentations and barking into mobile phones, they effortlessly assumed a mantle of self-importance as they awaited the boarding announcement for their flight. I speculated on their collective motives for the journey north – a crucial board meeting at the Edinburgh office; the final sales pitch to a major client; a quarterly visit from the London head office to the Scottish subsidiary; the delicate meeting with a key supplier; a critical job interview; or perhaps just a day out at an industry conference.

I had taken this early morning flight on numerous occasions over the years, but today was very different. I kept my distance, watching instead from the relative safety of the coffee bar. I no longer fitted in with the corporate crowd, I was conspicuous. My laptop shoulder bag had been replaced by a large plastic carrier bag. I had discarded my suit and tie for today, and was dressed instead in lightweight chinos, a striped polo shirt and, most visibly, stout walking boots. My motives differed from those of my travelling companions, but I too had a mission and my journey a purpose. Most of my fellow passengers would be returning from the Scottish capital later that evening, but my day would end in the northernmost reaches of Caledonia. My mission would begin on the following day and, for me, there would be no return flight. Today would be my last contact for several months with the concrete and clamour of the fast paced, commercialised world which the sterile Terminal 5 building symbolised.

Three months earlier, I had taken 'early retirement' after over thirty years working for the same company in the energy industry. I was looking forward with optimism to the new opportunities ahead of me, but I really wanted to mark this key event and the unprecedented period of freedom it offered by undertaking a life-changing project. I wanted to embark on a tough personal challenge, which would also provide the opportunity to raise a significant sum of money for charity.

In a moment of extreme madness, probably fuelled by the intoxicating lure of the great outdoors, I had committed to undertake a solo trek from John O' Groats in northern Scotland to Land's End in Cornwall (conveniently abbreviated as JOGLE, or LEJOG for the reverse journey). I was planning to complete this gruelling physical and mental 950 mile walking challenge in around eight weeks, staying in a wide variety of accommodation en route.

I should perhaps explain that I was not a long distance walker. In fact, I wasn't even a middle distance walker. At best, I could have been described as a casual rambler, who enjoyed the occasional mountain walk in Snowdonia or the Lake District, so this walk would be far more daunting than anything I'd done before in my life. However, finishing work provided the perfect opportunity to undertake a few months of rigorous training, so there was a reasonable chance of getting myself into slightly better shape. With a steely determination and a dash of recklessness, I convinced myself that I would somehow complete the walk within the allotted time.

As soon as I had started to inform colleagues and friends about my planned walk, the reaction of most people had been to ask why I was doing it. While they were always polite and sincere in their questioning, their body language usually portrayed unspoken words, which I interpreted as a challenge of my sanity. I took on the role of a fly on the wall.

"Mad fool, does he realise what's he's committing to?"

"Shouldn't he leave a journey like that to the professionals?"

"He'll never be able to walk that far!"

"Why doesn't he just drive from John O' Groats to Land's End instead?"

"He'd be safer retiring and taking up golf or gardening"

"He's risking life and limb! Why doesn't he get another job instead?"

They might well have been absolutely right, but I was never going to admit it to them. At the very least, I had to give the impression that I knew what I was subjecting myself to and to exude some degree of confidence that I could and would complete the journey.

To those prepared to listen, I tried to explain that there were three main reasons why I was undertaking the walk.

Firstly, although I was technically taking early retirement, I was far too young to don my carpet slippers and sink into my armchair. Proper retirement wasn't for me just yet, so I resolved to embark on a 'project' that would help me transition from my previous office-bound working life towards new and stimulating ventures in the future. This 'project' had to be a challenge, an adventure that would be both physically and mentally demanding, and potentially life-changing. I'm sure that some immediately interpreted this as a male mid-life crisis project (perhaps they were right again), although it was almost certainly not as dangerous, costly or frivolous as purchasing a

Harley Davidson or a fast sports car and definitely didn't involve wearing day-glow Lycra! I'd always enjoyed hiking and hill walking, albeit only carrying a light daysack, so it seemed like a natural choice for me. The inescapable fact that I'd never walked for more than two consecutive days merely added to the challenge!

Secondly, I really wanted to raise some funds for charity and to "give something back" after being fortunate enough to have had a secure and rewarding career for over thirty years. At university, I'd been actively involved with the Student Rag Week and throughout my twenties I'd regularly participated in fundraising for various charities, but career, marriage, relocation and the arrival of young children gradually displaced these virtuous activities. My 'project' would give me the opportunity to embrace others to help to achieve a significant contribution to a worthy cause, in this case to Cancer Research UK. I figured that family, friends and now former work colleagues would consider my 'project' to be sufficiently worthwhile to want to make a contribution and, hopefully, strangers I would meet en route would feel equally motivated.

Finally, I wanted to undertake the walk because I actually had the opportunity to do it. Finishing work at a relatively young age created the once-in-a-lifetime chance to do something that lasted for longer than the traditional couple of weeks' annual holiday, but I also sensed that I should embark on this challenge now, while I was physically able, rather than looking back from my armchair with regret in the years ahead, lamenting that I had too many unfinished entries on my 'bucket list'. I'd listened to too many people who had confessed to letting life's opportunities pass them by, and I didn't want to fall into the same trap.

Those friends and colleagues who had now started to

accept that I was forging ahead with my 'project' typically wanted to know why I'd opted to walk specifically from John O' Groats to Land's End. After all, there were plenty of other less demanding long distance trails in the UK, which might cure me of my affliction more readily. Beyond these shores, even more opportunities beckoned. Didn't I fancy traversing one of the many European trails, which would offer truly impressive views, a warmer climate and a broader cultural experience? What about the 'real' challenging journeys, such as trekking to the North Pole or climbing Kilimanjaro, adventures which I would genuinely reflect on in later years?

In truth, my choice of walk was probably the unconscious outcome of my accumulated holiday reading over a number of years.

In the previous summer, I had read a book called *End to End* by Steve Blease, a humorous account of his own walk from Land's End to John O' Groats, capturing the highs and the lows of this gruelling journey undertaken by a man who hadn't done any serious walking in his life. What I didn't appreciate at the time of reading the book was that Steve was taking a career break at the age of fifty, having worked behind a desk for over thirty years – you've probably spotted the parallels already!

However, *End to End* was only the most recent of a number of long distance walking challenge books that I had read over the years. The first was John Hillaby's *Journey Through Britain*, also from Land's End to John O' Groats. John (who was also fifty when he undertook the walk) was a veteran of long distance walking and his circuitous journey was completed almost entirely on tracks and bridleways. My original copy of the book was borrowed by a work colleague and never returned but, thanks to the wonders of Amazon, I'd recently been able to re-purchase a second hand copy!

Some years later, I came to read *Two Degrees West* by Nicholas Crane, who is more familiar to many as the umbrella-carrying presenter of the television series *Coast*. Crane walked along the line of the Central Meridian (to be precise, within a one mile wide band of the line) from Northumberland to Dorset. He encountered a cross-section of diverse landscapes and people, which was perhaps unsurprising as the route bisects both remote areas of rural England and the industrial West Midlands.

My next read was a variation on a theme. Peter Mortimer's *Broke Through Britain* recounts the author's walk from Plymouth to Edinburgh. Not an incomplete Land's End to John O' Groats, but a journey made without any money, relying instead on the kindness of complete strangers for food and accommodation. Probably the most political of the books on my reading list, he encountered life on the fringes and observed the widening gulf between rich and poor.

My final influencing book was *Two Feet, Four Paws,* by Spud Talbot-Ponsonby, which recounts the experiences of a determined young woman and her dog as they spent a year walking around Britain's coastline, raising money for homeless charities along the way. They slept in a fifteen year old camper van, which was driven by a large crew of volunteer drivers and faced innumerable challenges during the 4,500 mile journey. Tragically, Spud was later diagnosed with cancer and passed away in her early forties, leaving behind a young family.

The cumulative effect of these apparently innocuous holiday reads was now evident; their themes had been blended over time and etched into my psyche. On one level, the books shared a similar plot – a long distance walking challenge in Britain – but at a more subtle level, they all drew on the wide variety of landscapes and cultures encountered on their cross-sectional routes. This was Britain characterised in a single journey, from imposing mountains to remote beaches, from rundown estates to quaint chocolate box villages, from the industrial heartlands to sparsely populated farming communities. There was another common theme – each author encountered a diverse range of people en route, most of them complete strangers. Their observations of interactions with such people revealed yet another fascinating dimension of their respective journeys.

The prospect of walking in my own country appealed to me. Why did I need to leave this island when such diversity was on offer? What better way of experiencing such diversity than by walking along the longest diagonal slice through Britain?

So it seemed like a natural outcome. Inspired by Messrs Blease, Hillaby, Crane, Mortimer, and Talbot-Ponsonby, I would set out to walk my own cross-sectional journey through Britain. John O' Groats to Land's End. Top to bottom. End to End.

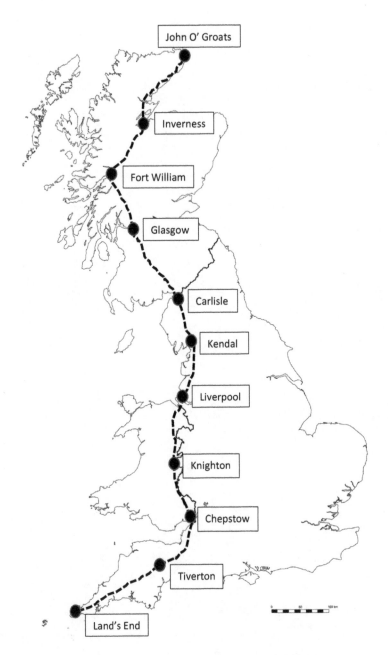

John O' Groats

Inverness

Fort William

Glasgow

Carlisle

Kendal

Liverpool

Knighton

Chepstow

Tiverton

Land's End

0   50   100 km

Ordnance Survey © Crown copyright 1999

CHAPTER ONE

The Road to Inverness

Day 0

The easy journey from home to Wick

My original plan had been to catch the 6.00am bus, which conveniently passes a couple of hundred yards from my front door and finishes its journey at Heathrow Terminal 5. However, at the last minute, my two teenage children both decided that they would like to travel to the airport with me, so my wife drove us by car instead. Even Daniel, who normally struggles to get out of bed for school, managed to dress rapidly and sprang downstairs with renewed vigour.

As I gazed out of the window on the flight to Edinburgh, I was preoccupied with the fact that this journey of little more than an hour would take me nearly three weeks to cover on foot. More disturbingly, the distance from Heathrow to Edinburgh represented only about a third of my overall journey. There was no hiding from the fact that 950 miles was a mind-blowing distance to contemplate, so I determined that it would probably be more sensible to consider it as a series of much shorter distances, which I would try to conquer one day at a time. On this basis, I would not be overawed by the enormity of the challenge, but instead would focus on ticking off each daily instalment.

My transfer flight to Wick was not scheduled to leave for a few hours, so I had time to relax in the departure lounge at Edinburgh airport. But something was troubling me. In the back of my mind, I had a nagging doubt that I hadn't packed the USB charger for my smartphone. I'd been using it late into the previous evening as I sent out my final e-mails and had knowingly left it as the final item on my kit list to be packed. Without a charged smartphone, my adventure would be severely handicapped – no phone, no texts, no blogs, no mobile photographs, no GPS, no electronic maps, no internet – so this pocket-sized gadget was a critical part of my equipment. I wasn't entirely convinced that I hadn't packed it in my rucksack after all, whilst on auto pilot, but as my rucksack was still in transit, I wasn't in a position to check. After a brief consideration of my options, I concluded that Edinburgh airport was probably the last bastion of retail civilisation I would encounter for at least a week and so I decided to invest in a replacement charger, thereby removing the risk of communication failure.

Opportunely, I was seated outside the airport branch of Dixons, but my joy was short lived. For all the wondrous gadgets they displayed on their shelves, they currently had no stock of USB chargers. My mind and gaze now turned to the Boots store across the concourse, as I recalled from a previous airport visit that they sold a wide variety of travel gadgets. I scoured their extensive range, which included travel adaptors, inflatable pillows and sleeping masks but, alas, there were no USB chargers. My heart sank and the prospect of a temporary return to the pre-digital age beckoned. As a last resort, I decided to try the WH Smith store, located at the opposite end of the terminal building. My luck was finally in! Amongst a smaller range of travel gadgets I pinpointed a single, white USB charger, which I grabbed from the shelf and purchased immediately. I was back in the digital era!

The flight from Edinburgh to Wick was delayed by an hour, which I overheard one of the check-in staff whisper was apparently due to the crew having the wrong security passes, although no official explanation was provided. When we finally boarded, I was surprised to discover that the flight was completely full, with most of my fellow passengers flying up for the Deloitte's 'Ride Across Britain' cycle ride from John O'Groats to Land's End, which was due to start two days later. Inexplicably, my seat at the rear of the plane was double booked, but more worrying was being informed by the stewardess that I would be responsible for opening the cabin doors if there was an emergency!

With the skies clear, there were fantastic views of the Forth Bridge and snow-capped peaks, but again I was translating the distance travelled into walking days. I engaged in conversation with Harry, one of the younger participants in the Deloitte's cycle ride. He explained that the event was largely undertaken by corporate teams – he was a member of the Cadbury's team, but was their sole representative from the factory floor. He wasn't confident about completing the 9 day ride and had only recently taken ownership of his bike, but I admired his determination. I was also rather envious of his large supply of chocolate bars, inevitably provided by his employer!

Just before we touched down in Wick, the UK's most northerly mainland airport, I spotted my bed and breakfast accommodation, which was situated about a mile from the town centre, a short distance from the end of the runway. It is officially named Wick John O' Groats Airport (John O' Groats is actually some 16 miles to the north), but I concluded that this was no more misleading than London Heathrow, which is 15 miles from central London, and much less misrepresentative than the deceptively named London Luton, London Stansted or London Gatwick airports, which are all at least 30 miles from central London.

My rucksack was one of the last items of baggage to be unloaded from the hold. Only one bicycle appeared to have been carried on the plane – most of the participants had arranged for their cycles to be transported by road. To protect the rucksack and its contents, I had carefully enveloped it in bubble wrap for the flight so, on being reunited at Wick, I rapidly had to unwrap it. I had secured the bubble wrap well, so removing it was more testing than I had anticipated and I soon found myself attracting unwelcome attention from other passengers in the terminal building. When I finally parted the bubble wrap from my rucksack, I tried in vain to wedge the bulky waste into one of the undersized airport litter bins, so eventually I had to discard it on the polished floor. At last, I could lift the load onto my shoulders for the first time, leave the diminutive airport building and take the short walk to the town centre.

The sun was shining and it was pleasantly warm. This was not the way it was supposed to be. When I'd been planning my walk during the dark winter evenings, I'd envisaged Wick to be grey, damp and depressing, so I'd prepared myself for a downbeat start to my adventure. With an hour or so to wait before I could check in to my B&B accommodation, I sat on the rocks overlooking the harbour and town, consumed my packed lunch and skimmed through the many good luck messages that I'd been sent on my smartphone. Listening to the lapping of the waves and the squawking of the neighbouring gulls as I relaxed in the sun's rays, I was soon lulled into vacation mood – it felt like the first day of a seaside holiday. I hastily had to remind myself that this was the start of a physically and mentally gruelling two months and that genuine moments of relaxation like this would be very limited.

Wick is an estuary town and a former Viking settlement, which was once the busiest herring port in Europe in the 19th century. It used to be two towns – Wick itself, and Pultneytown, just over the river, but they merged in 1902. My Bradshaw's Guide from 1866 described Wick as a "stirring town", where "multitudes from distant parts resort during the fishing season, when the town presents, especially on the days of success, a most wonderful scene of bustle and excitement."

Today's Wick, sometimes described as Aberdeen in miniature, has considerable character and it was evident during my short stroll around that re-generation funding had reached parts of the town centre. The lively harbour provided a picturesque backdrop, even if it was somewhat quieter than in its heyday.

One end of Mackays Hotel, a wedge-shaped building which reaches its narrowest point nearest the bridge, stretches the full length of Ebenezer Place, which appears in the Guinness Book of Records as the world's shortest street at just 2.06m in length.

I walked along the estuary footpath to the Impala B&B, which would be my base for the next two nights. My hosts Alan and Lynne, originally from Nottingham, were very welcoming and I knew immediately that this would be a very comfortable base from which to start my walk. I'd wondered why a bed and breakfast house in Wick had been named after an African antelope, not normally known to inhabit the highlands of Scotland. The simple, but less dramatic, answer was that the previous owners had originated from South Africa.

I strolled into town for my evening meal, but the holiday atmosphere had not subsided. I decided to eat at the local Wetherspoon's pub, where the service was remarkably efficient compared to others I had experienced in the South East of England. By coincidence, I bumped into Harry the Cadbury cyclist, who was also dining there. We shared a few beers and mulled over our respective journeys. We concluded that we would both experience much physical and mental pain during our expeditions, but that my pain would probably last six times as long!

Wick was bathed in a golden glow as I returned on foot to my accommodation. My final night of freedom was over and I was ready for my adventure to begin for real.

Day 1 – John O' Groats to Wick
Distance: 17.5 miles
Weather: Sunny

Underway at last, with a gentle introduction to a long walk

I awoke with the daunting realisation that the serious business of walking would start today. After months of talking, route planning, accommodation booking, equipment buying, training, fundraising and packing, my epic walk was about to begin. There was no going back now – my rucksack was packed, my route maps neatly arranged and my body hoping that the months of practice walks would equip me to keep going for 57 days.

After the second of many full English, Scottish and Welsh breakfasts to be consumed on my JOGLE journey (the first had been on the plane to Edinburgh!), my host Lynne kindly drove me to the railway station to catch the bus to John O' Groats. As I would be returning to the same accommodation for a second night, I had left much of my kit behind in my room, so that I would have the luxury of being able to travel lightly for my first day.

A 'Ride Across Britain' cyclist, without cycle, joined me at the bus stop. He informed me that all participants in the event were required to register at the start today, one day before the ride itself commenced. He seemed genuinely impressed that I was walking the route and observed that I would still be in northern Scotland by the time he arrived in Land's End. The single decker bus arrived on time and we shared the 40 minute ride to John O' Groats with a handful of other passengers, knowing that I would be retracing the entire journey in reverse on foot during the course of the day.

John O' Groats is no more than a handful of shops and cafes next to a small harbour, from which ferries run to the nearby Orkney Isles. It is not even the most northerly point on the mainland (that honour belongs to Dunnet's Head a few miles away), but it is the traditional starting point for the journey to Land's End. John O' Groats is visited by thousands of tourists each year, most of whom are not End to End travellers. It has been described as a "seedy tourist trap" and has won an award for being Scotland's most dismal town, but on this bright June morning it was bathed in sunshine and looked most pleasant.

I'd originally planned to stay overnight at the youth hostel in John O' Groats, only to discover from the Scottish Youth Hostel Association's website that it had closed down in the previous year, one of numerous hostel closures across the country. To compound matters further, the main hotel in John

O' Groats was being totally refurbished and the 'Ride Across Britain' cycle event, scheduled to begin on the following day, had clearly accounted for the remaining beds at the other hotels and guest houses. This predicament had resulted in my cunning plan – staying overnight in Wick, catching a bus to the start in John O' Groats, and then walking back to Wick for a successive night's accommodation.

I located the tourist shop which administered the official 'End to Enders' log book and duly signed it, knowing that there was no exit from my challenge now. A few steps away, I had my official photo taken next to the infamous direction finger signpost, as evidence that I had at least made it to the start. The photographer advised me that the same company managed the official signpost at Land's End and he wished me luck in reaching there a couple of months later. I took a few personal photos and strolled around the pretty harbour, then prepared myself for the start.

I'd made a laminated A4 poster, which read:

WALKING 950 MILES
JOHN O' GROATS
TO
LAND'S END
IN AID OF
CANCER RESEARCH UK
DONATIONS WELCOME!

I attached the poster in a prominent position on my rucksack, hoping that it would attract some attention from anybody approaching from behind or, more optimistically, from anybody I might overtake. It paid an immediate dividend when, just as I was about to embark on my journey, a couple of tourists rushed over and deposited my first en route charity donation into the collecting jar.

At 10.45am, some six months after first conceiving of the idea, I took my first tentative steps in the direction of Land's End. After the protracted build up and the many practice miles, it was a great relief to be walking for real, knowing that every step would bring me closer to my final destination.

Weather conditions were absolutely perfect – bright and sunny with a pleasant breeze. This was a real bonus and certainly not the climate that I'd prepared for when I was planning this part of the journey, when I'd anticipated driving rain and grey skies. I soon reached the official starting base for the 'Ride Across Britain' cycle ride – it was quite an impressive operation, with rows and rows of identical green tents erected in perfect symmetry and hundreds of finely tuned bikes waiting to be reunited with their owners for the start of their own journey to Land's End. In the distance the Orkneys were crystal clear across the blue shimmering waters of the Pentland Firth.

Back in January, an integral part of my planning for the journey had been to consult the exceedingly informative website *landsendjohnogroats.info* managed by a travel writer and web developer named Mark Moxon, who completed the same walk in 2003. The website is a minefield of information, from route planning tips, equipment guidance and accommodation advice, but also includes links to the blogs of other walkers who have undertaken the journey in recent years. The website provided me with sufficient confidence to consider myself capable of completing the journey and afforded hours of fascinating insights into the highs and lows experienced by other End to End walkers.

Before unfolding maps and plotting any daily routes, I'd

had to make a key decision regarding the direction of the walk. Would I journey from South to North, or North to South? Bottom to top, or top to bottom? LEJOG or JOGLE?

Most walkers take the LEJOG option, starting at Land's End and finishing in John O' Groats. There are a number of practical reasons for this:

- The terrain in the South West is flatter and much easier under foot than the more rugged terrain in northern Scotland, allowing the walker to build up stamina during the journey.
- Most walkers live nearer to Land's End than to John O' Groats, so it's easier to head for home if they have to quit in the early stages – apparently quite a few do.
- The prevailing winds generally blow from the south in the summer.
- The sun is more often behind you (when it actually shines!)
- Many long distance path maps and guides are based on south to north directions.
- Cornwall is much busier in the summer, so most walkers opt to start here outside of the holiday season.
- Spring in Cornwall starts earlier than in northern Scotland.

After digesting all of this practical data, I decided to buck the trend and chose the JOGLE option, from North to South. In part my decision was based on the same factors, but in reverse. My logic was that although the terrain in Scotland is indeed more challenging, I would rather confront this early in the journey and strike a psychological advantage, knowing that the physically most demanding part of the route was behind me. The sun, the wind, upside down map reading and congested Cornwall – I would have to learn to cope with all of these challenges. But in truth, my decision was largely not based on logic at all – it just felt right that my walk would start at John O' Groats, beginning at the top of the United Kingdom and finishing at the bottom.

Many others had undertaken this infamous journey before me. The first recorded End to End walk (which also followed a north to south route) was undertaken by two wealthy brothers, John and Robert Naylor, in 1871. They covered a circuitous route of 1,372 miles in 62 days and, some 45 years later, the surviving brother published a book of their walk under the catchy title "From John o' Groats to Land's End, or 1372 Miles on Foot. A Book of Days and Chronicle of Adventures by Two Pedestrians on Tour in 1871". It's an extraordinary tale and a fascinating read but, the distinctive writing style is somewhat protracted and the book is peppered with literary quotations and verses.

In 1960, Dr Barbara Moore completed a well-publicised north to south road walk in just 23 days. She was a colourful Russian-born health enthusiast who gained celebrity for her long-distance walking, being the first woman to cross the United States from New York to Los Angeles. Dr Moore held unorthodox views on nutrition and claimed that people could live to be 200 if they gave up smoking, drinking and sex. She planned living to the age of 150 herself, but sadly only made it to 73 when she died – perhaps she had succumbed to the very vices she had argued against!

Later in 1960, the entrepreneur Sir Billy Butlin, who founded the Butlins holiday camps, organised and sponsored a road walking race from John O'Groats to Land's End, an event which was considered to be a major publicity stunt. The race took place entirely on roads and started in late February, not the ideal time of year to undertake such an event, and there were calls from the authorities for the race to be abandoned. Of the original 1,500 entrants, 715 started the race, 170 dropped out during the first few hours, and only 138 eventually finished. The winning man, a Doncaster glass worker, completed the race in 15 days and 14 hours, while the leading woman, a hairdresser, took just over 17 days. One of the more amusing anecdotes from the race related to a search for stragglers during one particularly stormy night – the stewards found a man sleeping in a barn and subsequently dragged him to the nearest checkpoint, but he turned out to be a local tramp taking shelter for the evening.

In later years, Sir Ian Botham (twice) and Jimmy Savile (three times) would complete the walk for charity, so I was in both good and bad company.

To the surprise of many, there is no fixed official route for walking from John O' Groats to Land's End. The shortest route is just over 600 miles as the crow flies, but unfortunately most of this is across the sea, with a mid-point respite on the Isle of Man. The shortest route by road is 814 miles, but most walkers add to this by opting for more scenic (and less dangerous!) routes. There are walking routes which eliminate roads almost entirely, but inevitably these add significant miles to an already lengthy journey.

Ultimately, the route chosen is influenced by a number of personal decisions:

- How many miles will be walked each day?
- How long is available to complete the walk, including rest days?
- What balance of off-road and road walking is desired?
- Are specific destinations or footpaths to be incorporated?

I had spent a few January evenings reviewing the journeys of other End to Enders and was somewhat bemused by the sheer variety of routes followed – no two journeys were the same. The alternative options around northern Scotland and Cornwall were limited, but there was an almost infinite selection of routes in between. After some deliberation, I established the principles and parameters for my own walk:

- Due to holiday commitments, I had a window of just under two months to complete the walk.
- I would aim to walk for an average of around 18 miles per day. This was not based on any particular science, but it seemed like a reasonable distance to walk in the course of a day.
- I would incorporate a number of rest days.
- I would seek to utilise long distance footpaths, public footpaths and towpaths wherever possible, but not if they resulted in a significant deviation from my overall route. As a first contingency I would use minor roads and, if all else failed, I would resort to 'A' roads.

My own route was primarily designed around the inclusion of two long distance footpaths. Firstly, the West Highland Way, which runs from Fort William to just north of Glasgow and, secondly, Offa's Dyke Path, which mainly clings to the border of England and Wales from north to south. I'd walked a very short section of the West Highland Way when I spent a year in Glasgow as a postgraduate student and had always intended to walk the entire route one day. The choice of Offa's Dyke was influenced more by the fact that I'd holidayed in Wales since I was a small child and must almost have spent enough time there over my lifetime to qualify as an honorary Welshman, but I'd never set foot on Offa's Dyke!

With these two major long distance footpaths forming the main foundation of over 230 miles of my route, stringing together the rest of the route was reasonably straightforward. The first stage from John O' Groats to Inverness offered little or no routing choice. From Inverness I would take another long distance path, the Great Glen Way, to Fort William to link with the start of the West Highland Way which finishes near to Glasgow. I would then head for Carlisle, before skirting the Lake District and joining the Lancaster Canal to its finish in Preston (just beyond the halfway point of the walk) and onward to Liverpool, my home city. From here it's a short distance to join Offa's Dyke Path all the way down to Chepstow, then across the Severn Bridge near to Bristol. The final stages slice through Somerset and Devon, before passing through Truro and Penzance on the final stretch to Land's End.

That's around 950 miles in 57 days, including 5 rest days. Incidentally, the record for the journey on foot (running) is a mere 9 days! Faster still, a Kawasaki motorbike once completed the trip in 11 hours! But a McDonnell F-4K Phantom Jet demolished those records with a time of 46 minutes 44 seconds – about the time it would take me to walk three miles!

Today's walking route from John O' Groats was entirely on the main road, as there would be no alternative footpath routes for a few days. Despite this, the traffic was not an inconvenience – most of the vehicles appeared to be taxis ferrying the four hundred cycle ride participants to their registration point in John O' Groats. In the fine weather, the sea and moorland views were inspiring and the gently undulating hills blanketed in gorse and heather made for a benign and calming start to my journey. I soon realised that I could not have begun my journey in better conditions, but also noted with caution that this initial euphoria could not be present for the entire walk.

One of the few blots on the landscape featured a large diameter pipeline, which lay across the fields like a trail of elongated spaghetti. This was the location of a pipeline bundle fabrication site, managed by Subsea 7, a global leader in seabed-to-surface engineering, construction and services to the offshore energy industry. The Pipeline Bundle ingeniously integrates the flow lines, water injection, gas lift and control systems necessary for any subsea development and assembles them within a steel carrier pipe. At each end of the pipeline, the structures, manifolds, incorporating equipment and valves are attached, before the fully tested system is then launched and transported to the required location. The longest pipeline bundle length is nearly 8km – that's more than an hour's walk for me!

Apart from a handful of independent cyclists (who were either beginning their long journeys to Land's End or nearing completion in John O' Groats) and the shop assistant in Keiss who took payment for my lunchtime sandwich, I experienced no human contact throughout my entire 17 mile walk to Wick. A few houses were dotted along the roadside, but I could see limited signs of life as I passed by. I had already expected to be alone during the initial days of my walk, but hoped to encounter an influx of fellow walkers when I joined the first long distance footpaths after Inverness.

My arrival in Wick signified the completion of my first day's walk. I knew that it hadn't necessarily been a representative day, due in part to the euphoria of starting my journey and in part to the fact that I was carrying a half empty rucksack. Nevertheless, I was 17 miles closer to my final destination and it felt appropriate to place a large mental tick through the box marked 'Day 1'.

Back at the Impala B&B, I re-loaded my rucksack in readiness for the next day's walk and wrote up my daily blog. I hadn't originally intended to maintain a blog during my journey, but I'd been encouraged to do so by family and friends, so I relented. In any case, it would be a good way of capturing my journey and would allow me to keep my supporters updated on my progress. I dined at an Italian restaurant in Wick, then walked the now familiar route back to my accommodation.

Day 2 – Wick to Dunbeath
Distance: 20.3 miles
Cumulative distance: 37.8 miles
Weather: Cloudy, then sunny later

More miles, a heavier load and a first taste of loneliness

Lynne from the B&B kindly drove me to Wick town centre again, where I re-joined my route. Today's walk would be more challenging, with extra miles to be completed and a heavier rucksack to be carried.

Most of the route was on the A99 road, which followed the coast for much of the journey. The scenery was not quite as impressive as the previous day's. The terrain was flatter and much of the road as straight as an arrow, but views of the distant oil rigs in the North Sea added a different dimension. Gorse and heather dominated again, but there were very few trees to be seen, giving the impression of a barren landscape. The occasional farm building broke the monotony and a temporary electronic road sign captured the mood with the warning, "Frustration can cause accidents".

I usually walked on the right hand side of the road, which was much safer as it meant that I was facing the oncoming traffic. I could cope with oncoming traffic – vehicles were generally discernible from a distance and I could take steps to ensure that I was visible to them. The greatest challenge was spotting cars (they were always cars!) which approached from behind at great speed, using the right hand side of the road to overtake slower vehicles travelling in my direction. The overtaking drivers were typically focused on the road ahead and were less likely to notice the rucksack-laden walker to the right.

Although there was often a grass verge at the side of the road, I soon discovered that the most efficient way to walk was by following the white line on the side of the road itself. My logic for this was that the grass verge tends to be rutted, especially in dry weather, and longer grass can camouflage holes and obstacles which are subtly positioned to trap unsuspecting pedestrians. To counter the longer grass, the walking leg has to be raised higher, but this consumes greater energy, especially during a long day of road walking. So for the walker, the road surface is a more comfortable and energy preserving option, so long as vigilance for approaching and overtaking vehicles is observed.

During the five months of preparation I'd undertaken prior to starting my journey, I had accumulated several hundred miles during training walks, varying between 10 and 25 miles in distance. I'm fortunate to live in an area where there is a wide selection of walks nearby, including the River Thames towpath, Windsor Great Park, various cycle paths and a range of footpaths which run close to lakes, rivers, railways and moors. For a typical training walk, I would head out of the front door without any particular route or destination in mind and walk on the spur of the moment, determining my route and destination as I walked. My family found this concept very difficult to comprehend, but I enjoyed the flexibility it offered. On the real walk, of course, I had to revert to following a pre-planned route to a pre-determined destination.

My training had started in January, so the early walks were undertaken in thick woollies, warm coats and gloves. Refreshment stops were short and the cold temperatures had turned my Snickers snacks into solid bars of chocolate, caramel and nougat. With most wildlife in hibernation and trees bearing no leaves, there was little to observe in the way of nature. As the harsh winter slowly gave way to spring, the temperatures gradually began to increase, so the gloves were discarded and the heavy coat gave way to a lighter fleece. In the weeks prior to the walk, I was down to a tee-shirt and shorts, but the reduction in clothing was counter-balanced by an increase in liquid intake. Towards the end of my training programme, when temperatures had risen to the levels associated with summer, outdoor refreshment stops at conveniently located pubs became a regular feature of my afternoons.

It was fascinating to observe the impact of the changing seasons on my regular training routes. Warmer temperatures brought an increase in wildlife, but also an increase in human activity. Diehard joggers and walkers were gradually joined by their fair weather colleagues. Some footpaths were transformed as nature took hold – one narrow path which ran parallel to a railway line was quite innocuous in early spring, but a month later was completely shrouded in tall nettles, which soon left their evidence on my bare legs, while another footpath was a muddy quagmire in February, but by May the mud had dried out to form a solid track.

My favourite training walk involved joining the scenic Thames footpath a few miles from home, then following it through the centre of Windsor and as far as Eton Dorney. It was here in the London 2012 Olympics that the rowing events took place, with Team GB winning nine medals, their most successful rowing haul ever. My destination, just beyond Eton Dorney, was The Pineapple, a fifteenth century roadside inn, which serves real ales and over one thousand variations of award winning sandwiches. The pub is named after the first pineapple grown in Britain in 1661, which occurred a few hundred yards away at Dorney Court. The walking distance from my home to The Pineapple is exactly ten miles, so a round trip enabled me to satisfyingly tick off a twenty mile walk.

One of the drawbacks of the Thames Valley is that there are no meaningful hills, so I needed to find a way of replicating some of the mountainous terrain I would encounter during a significant part of my JOGLE walk. To address this, I spent a few days walking in Snowdonia in North Wales, which provided steep mountain tracks, windswept moors, undulating hills and even sand dunes. The sand dunes proved to be the toughest terrain of all – ascending them required immense effort, as the underlying sand naturally forced the boots back downhill, resulting in sluggish progress.

I had been fortunate in being able to fit in two holidays after finishing work, but before starting my journey. Despite my good intentions, neither had really helped me from a training perspective. The first was a week's skiing in France which, in theory, should have been beneficial for my fitness. However, apart from being extremely cautious and not wanting to risk a late injury prior to my walk, I discovered that skiing uses completely different leg muscles to those used for walking, so having developed my walking muscles, skiing was a great strain on my calf muscles.

The second break was a relaxing beach holiday in Turkey, just a week before my walk was due to commence. I was conscious that this would be my last opportunity to relax for several months, but had planned to take a couple of long walks there, just to keep my legs supple for the journey ahead. However, I had barely walked half a mile when a pack of dogs appeared from nowhere and followed me menacingly. I quickly discovered that large, intimidating dogs patrolled most of the local roads so, for my own security, I abandoned the idea and returned to the relative safety of my sun lounger.

I felt in good physical shape at the end of my training programme and, when it was time for me start the walk for real, I was raring to go. I'd started to become jaded with the same familiar training walks and was desperate for the virgin paths and scenery that the real walk would offer. In addition, I wanted each mile walked to be meaningful, bringing me closer to my ultimate destination, rather than just being accumulated fruitlessly as part of my training regime.

Land's End was now starting to become very slightly closer, but I was beginning to experience for the first time the loneliness of the long distance walker. During six hours on the road, I only spoke to six people – four passing cyclists and a middle-aged couple at a roadside house who kindly refilled my water bottle. Part of me felt that I should enjoy this tranquillity while it lasted, as I would perhaps pine for it when accompanied by friends and family on future stages of my journey!

I progressed through the tiny villages of Thrumster, Ulbster, Occumster, Lybster, Lobster and Hamster (well, I made up the last two!). Lybster was once a big herring fishing port, but had declined in recent years. It now hosts the World Championships of Knotty, a variant of the game of shinty, which is widely played in the Scottish Highlands. Knotty was once very popular, but it ceased to be played around the end of the 19th century until 1993, when it was revived by local enthusiasts. It involves a stick (the 'knotty'), which can be almost any form of wooden implement, and a cork fishing float as ball. Local history books suggest that knotty was invented by the fishing wives of Lybster to help keep their men sober when they were ashore!

At Latheron, the A99 joined the main A9 road, which would accompany me for a large stretch of my journey to Inverness over the next few days.

I reached Dunbeath, my destination for the day. The village's welcome sign made reference to it being Neil Gunn's birthplace. I must confess that he had escaped my attention until now, but I learned later that he was a prolific novelist, critic, and dramatist in the 1920s and 1930s. With over twenty novels to his credit, he was regarded as one of the most influential Scottish fiction writers of the first half of the 20th century.

It was a relief to be able to have a proper conversation with the owner of my B&B in Dunbeath. My spirits were raised when she commented that my rucksack was more sensibly sized than those carried by many of the JOGLE walkers she had accommodated previously!

After my first day's walk carrying a full load, I appreciated a hot shower and a short late afternoon nap. I inspected my feet and noticed that a couple of small blisters had appeared, so I made my first foray into my sizeable first aid kit and employed some cushion pads and plasters.

I strolled a short distance down the road to the aptly named

Bay View restaurant, which did indeed offer magnificent views across the bay. I savoured the coastal scenery and enjoyed my fresh Scrabster haddock and chips.

Day 3 – Dunbeath to Loth
Distance: 19.4 miles
Cumulative distance: 57.2 miles
Weather: Cloudy

A quiet, uneventful, lonely Sunday in northern Scotland

After leaving Dunbeath, it was a hard slog down the A9, but the scenery was pleasant, consisting of sea views, gorse covered moorland and a single red deer. It was, however, not a day for interaction with *homo sapiens* and my only conversations (if exchanging 'Hi' classes as such) were with three cyclists and two dog walkers.

The toughest part of the route was at Berriedale Braes, where the road drops steeply into a gully via a series of hairpin bends to cross a river, then climbs steeply for a longer distance. Even the cyclists struggled! This section of road was evidently not a favourite with the drivers of heavy goods vehicles, with one dedicated website highlighting that "a year does not pass when an HGV / LGV does not have a serious accident, brake failure, and even running out of the emergency sand pit run off road near the bottom". The writer went on to warn "If you ever take that first trip to the far north, please take that extra care, remember someone loves you".

Nearby was the site of a remarkable unresolved wartime mystery. On 25th August 1942, Prince George, who was Duke of Kent and the youngest brother of the reigning monarch King George VI, died along with fourteen others on board an RAF flying boat, which crashed while en route from Invergordon to Iceland. The flight had been expected to follow the coastline of Sutherland and Caithness, but for some reason the aircraft turned inland and crashed on Eagle Rock, above the village of Berriedale. One crew member survived the accident, but was immediately forced to sign the Official Secrets Act. The official enquiry into the crash concluded that a "serious mistake in airmanship" was to blame.

The official version of events was that the Duke was on a visit to RAF personnel stationed in Iceland, but the case is fraught with mystery, rumour and conspiracy theory. A memorial stands on the remote hillside at Eagle's Rock, bearing the names of those who died while on a 'special mission'. What was this 'special mission'? Why was an attaché case containing one hundred Kroner notes handcuffed to the Duke's wrist, when the notes were worthless in Iceland at the time and only of value in Sweden? Why did the plane divert from its coastal route? Why was it reported that the plane crashed in heavy mist and rain, when locals had stated that weather conditions were favourable? Why did important documents go missing?

Conspiracy theories about the crash have evolved over the years. One claims that Rudolph Hess, Hitler's deputy, who had flown to Scotland in 1941 to negotiate peace, was on board. Another suggests that enemy infiltrators had tampered with the flight before it took off. Colourful stories exist about Prince George's private life, but it is known that he had met a series of international leaders and, for several years, had been involved in discussions to bring about peace. Perhaps the true facts will never emerge, but in their absence, only speculation remains.

I'd been warned that the A9 would be busy and even dangerous, but it was remarkably quiet on this Sunday in June and at times you would never have guessed that it was an 'A' road at all.

I had an unplanned deviation from the route not far from Helmsdale when I joined a welcoming pedestrian and cycle track, only to find that it did not re-join the A9 immediately, but sent me instead on a very scenic detour which added half a mile to my already challenging distance! I vowed to be more cautious in future.

My B&B in Loth was very comfortable – Culgower House is a beautifully restored Victorian farmhouse nestling in the hills and overlooking the sea. It was a pleasure to soak my feet in a hot bath for the first time – to avoid any doubt, I'd been restricted to showers until now! My host, Catriona, served a delicious three course home cooked meal and even included a complimentary glass of wine, as an apology for being a few minutes late for my arrival.

Culgower House had been the product of careful accommodation planning, which I'd undertaken during the winter months. I'd set myself some guidelines:

Firstly, I wasn't going to camp. Although camping in theory gives much greater flexibility, especially in areas where accommodation is limited, I'd read numerous tales about other End to Enders who had set out intending to camp, but had discarded their tents and sleeping bags after a few days due to the excessive weight being carried. The prospect of erecting a tent in the rain after a full day's walking didn't really appeal to me – a comfortable bed, en suite facilities, the provision of a nearby hot meal and somewhere to update my blog and provide any medical attention to my feet certainly did entice me! Perhaps I was becoming less hardy in my advancing years, but my mind was firmly set!

Secondly, I would book all of my accommodation in advance. June and July would be the high season for many areas on my route and I didn't want to risk walking all day, then reaching my intended destination only to discover that the nearest available bed was another five miles distant. Peace of mind was important, but booking early would in theory also give me a better choice of suitable and convenient accommodation and, hopefully, cheaper rates. The latter was an important factor, given that I would have to finance accommodation and meals throughout my two month journey. However, booking early was also a double-edged sword – it would be inflexible, especially if I was to experience injury, illness or other delays. To counter this to an extent, my planned rest days and the option of reducing daily mileage on certain days by deploying more direct (but less scenic) routes, would offer a degree of flexibility.

Thirdly, I wanted to stay in a variety of different accommodation. I would cover the full spectrum from youth hostels (I wasn't too old for them, apparently!), B&Bs and guest houses to inns, budget chain hotels and higher quality hotels, the latter being earned as occasional 'treats' for completing sections of the route. With a few nights to be spent with family or friends who lived close to my route, this would leave me with around fifty nights' accommodation to secure.

I'd been faced with similar but smaller accommodation challenges on two previous occasions. The first was way back in the Eighties, when I was organising a youth hostelling trip for fellow students. After consulting my YHA guide, I posted scribbled booking requests and enclosed stamped self-addressed envelopes, to receive in return over subsequent days a collection of flimsy handwritten confirmation slips. Some years later, I needed to find accommodation for a motoring trip around Scotland. This time, armed with glossy tourist board brochures and a Rough Guide, the bookings were completed painlessly by telephone.

With so many nights to be secured for my latest journey, I opted to fully embrace the 21st century by booking on-line. This was not particularly driven by a desire to avoid all human interaction, but more that it offered an efficient solution to a time-consuming process, most of which would be undertaken late at night.

With the ground rules in place, on a chilly evening in the depths of January I sat at my laptop, opened multiple screens on my browser, populated them with maps, long distance trail guides, local and national accommodation websites and review sites, and set out to book nearly fifty beds. This turned out to be an arduous and frustrating process.

Although I'd targeted to walk around 18 miles each day, it soon became apparent that this guideline would have to be adapted, especially in northern Scotland, where 16-20 miles walking would have taken me to uninhabited areas of the route. I soon became an expert in tracking down any accommodation, using local websites, national booking websites (e.g. *booking.com* and *laterooms.com*) and scouring Google maps for the infamous bed symbol. I deployed *tripadvisor.co.uk* extensively to review any available customer feedback and became quite demanding in my requirements, before selecting my final accommodation preferences.

After my initial setback of failing to secure accommodation in John O' Groats, I had a sequence of successes booking bed & breakfasts and guest houses. Most of this type of accommodation provides its own website, but the content varies enormously, from the very basic provision of tariffs to a vast library of information about the accommodation itself and the surrounding area. Some offer the facility to book direct on-line, whereas others provide a "contact owner" email link. The latter proved to be a source of immense frustration and, several months later, a few still had not replied to my original enquiries! I couldn't ascertain whether they had closed down as a result of the dire economic situation, simply didn't monitor their emails or, in contrast, were reaping last year's profits with an extended winter break in the sun, but I didn't have time to await the official explanation and quickly had to find alternatives. To my delight, official and independent youth hostel sites all catered well for on-line bookings – a far cry from my experiences in the last century!

As a solo traveller, exorbitant single supplements were another source of frustration which sometimes, counter-intuitively, resulted in a hotel room being cheaper than a B&B. Their loss was my gain.

There were additional obstacles further into the route. A sudden steep rise in hotel rates which coincided with my arrival in Glasgow turned out to be due instead to Robbie Williams, who was scheduled to perform in the city for a couple of nights. I had to adjust my plans, not necessarily to avoid him, rather to secure a more reasonable overnight rate. I encountered another challenge in North Wales, when my enquiry elicited a rapid response, pointing out that my planned visit clashed with the International Eisteddfod and that all rooms in the area had been booked months ago. An adjustment to my route (i.e. walking another 5 miles!) enabled me to locate a room further south.

Booking on-line also brought several dilemmas – if the website didn't make special reference to being 'walker friendly', how would the owners respond to having muddy boots and the powerful aroma of a day's walking invading their pristine home? How do you select between a budget chain hotel (universal standard, but sometimes rather antiseptic) and a 'character' private hotel (distinctive, but perhaps dated and in need of refurbishment)? Such decisions were taken based on limited criteria, but in reality the outcomes of my selections would not be revealed until I arrived during the walk.

Sometimes it became necessary to revise the original route to incorporate suitable accommodation. At times the process became obsessive, as I searched in vain for the perfect combination of walking (scenic, interesting and close to my daily mileage target) and accommodation (comfortable, hospitable and good value, with an evening meal available in the vicinity). Gradually and painstakingly, I pieced together each day's walking with an overnight stay, linking such diverse places as Drumnadrochit, Crianlarich, Ecclefechan, Penyffordd, Llanymynech, Sampford Peverell and Mousehole until my chain from John O' Groats to Land's End was complete.

Booking a wide range of accommodation over a lengthy period generally transpired to be an efficient and straightforward on-line process. I managed to secure a bed for each night and, by booking early, I benefited from wider choice and more favourable rates. However, the downside was that the automated efficiency of on-line usually resulted in a detached, impersonal experience in which my name was transformed into a mere booking reference number. What a delight when true customer service emerged when, miraculously, a few thoughtful owners gate-crashed the automated process by sending a personal email (Thank you for booking with us... we look forward to meeting you... you'll need tea and cakes after all that walking... we can pick you up from town if you wish... just to warn you that mobile reception is intermittent here...). I was most grateful to those bed & breakfast owners who made the effort to add such a personal touch!

Whatever the trials and tribulations I encountered in booking the accommodation, I was in no doubt whatsoever that undertaking the walk itself would be much more demanding, frustrating and time-consuming. But at least I knew I could now look forward to a bed at the end of each day, somewhere to dine, and, in at least a few places, a warm welcome!

Back at the very welcoming Culgower House, my host Catriona informed me that another End to End walker had stayed there with his parents during the previous week, having just successfully completed the walk to John O' Groats. Coincidentally, this was Matt, a student I'd been in contact with, having heard about his walk from a cousin in North Yorkshire, who knew his aunt. I emailed him to send my congratulations and suggested that he must have had a few tales to tell about his adventures. He replied that he envied me for just beginning my walk and wished that he was still walking. One of his tales had involved getting caught in a blizzard on top of the Lairig Ghru mountain pass in Scotland. With my right boot starting to become more uncomfortable, I couldn't imagine how somebody could possibly miss walking, but at least in June, I was unlikely to be caught in a blizzard (although in June 1975, more than 10 centimetres of fresh snow fell over the highlands of Scotland!).

With 3 days' walking now completed, I'd walked further than I'd ever walked before on consecutive days. From now on I would be in new territory! Most of my body felt in remarkably good physical condition, but my right foot was beginning to cause me concern. Specifically, my right baby toe had become swollen and tender. My diagnosis was that it was being compressed too much inside the boot and the cushion pad I'd fitted to protect it had only compounded the problem. Although I'd worn the same boots during around 250 miles of training walks, I simply could not have replicated the wear and tear of walking on consecutive days. I concluded that I would need to have the right boot stretched to provide more space for my baby toe. I'd read about this procedure on the website of an outdoor equipment supplier, but I wouldn't be able to test out my proposed solution practically until I reached the relative civilisation of Inverness, which was a further three days' walk away.

Day 4 – Loth to Dornoch
Distance: 23.8 miles
Cumulative distance: 81.0 miles
Weather: Sunny

A long, but rewarding day, with a couple of 'incidents' towards the end of the walk

After a delightful and filling breakfast courtesy of Catriona, I set out in the knowledge that this would be a long day, but unaware that it would also be an eventful one. I headed along the main road for a few miles and, according to my map, was due to join a footpath across the golf course. Unfortunately the path didn't materialise (it was probably overgrown), but as I didn't want to waste further time hunting for a potentially non-existent path, I opted for the longer route along the road to the coastal village of Brora. Then it finally happened – an extensive en route conversation! I spoke to an Australian couple who were touring Britain in a motor home and had stopped in a lay-by. They were charmed by the Scottish scenery, but also observed that Britain was very clean!

The next part of the walk was idyllic. I finally escaped the A9 for a period and followed a well-defined footpath along the coast from Brora to Golspie. I walked along deserted golden sands for a few miles and came face to face with two groups of seals basking in the sun at the water's edge. Although I was only a few yards away, they barely reacted to my presence and didn't flinch when I photographed them.

The footpath ran parallel to the impressive Dunrobin Castle, the largest house in the northern Highlands, and ancestral home of the Earls and Dukes of Sutherland, some of whom were notorious for their role in the Highland Clearances. Most of the castle was built in Victorian times by Charles Barry, who also designed the Houses of Parliament. My Bradshaw's Guide described it as "a magnificent pile of buildings." The castle even has its own private railway station, where trains stop during the tourist season.

The first Duke of Sutherland was George Granville Leveson-Gower, who acquired the title shortly before his death in 1833. However, it was as the Marquess of Stafford that he and his wife, Elizabeth Sutherland, 19th Countess of Sutherland, rose to prominence. He is considered to have been the wealthiest man of the 19th-century, owning land and property in Staffordshire, Shropshire and Yorkshire, while his wife owned most of the county of Sutherland. He also inherited a major art collection and the Bridgewater Canal from his uncle, the 3rd Duke of Bridgewater. To give a flavour of his substantial wealth, two works by Titian, a small part of the art collection, were recently sold by the current 7th Duke for £95 million.

Highland estates were gradually switching from arable and mixed farming, which supported a large tenant population, to the more profitable sheep-farming. Surplus tenants were 'cleared' off the estates from about 1780 and many emigrated to the Americas and Australia to seek new lives, with the first mass emigration in 1792, known as the 'Year of the Sheep'. The wealthy landowners sought to resist emigration, since it deprived them of a source of cheap labour. Over nearly 70 years, many thousands of tenants were forcibly evicted out of their homes.

The first Duke of Sutherland and his wife were controversial figures for their role in the Highland Clearances. Initially, they relocated their tenants to coastal villages, where they were expected to take up fishing, but such evictions were met with opposition, which was then ruthlessly repressed. Patrick Sellar, who was employed by the Sutherlands to manage the evictions, personally threw people out if they showed any reluctance to leave and burned down their crofts to ensure that they never returned. The Sutherlands were responsible for brutal clearances between 1811 and 1820, and the forced eviction of two thousand families in one day was not uncommon. Many starved and froze to death where their homes had once been. Condemnation was widespread and the Highlanders' grievances were heard in the British House of Commons. However, little was done in practice to prevent the forced emptying of the glens. It wasn't until 1886 that the Crofters' Holdings (Scotland) Act granted real security of tenure of existing crofts and established the first Crofters Commission.

The Duke of Sutherland's one hundred foot tall statue stands on top of Ben Bhraggie and dominates the skyline above the village of Golspie and surrounding area. Known locally as 'The Mannie', some local people believe the statue should remain as a reminder to what happened in Sutherland during the clearances, but others have campaigned for the statue to be removed. An attempt was made to dynamite the monument in 1994 and graffiti, including the word "monster", has been sprayed across the plinth.

The footpath I was following bisected the castle and the shore, passing through delightful woodland which was carpeted with bluebells. At nearby Golspie, I took a short break at a deserted pub and refreshed my thirst with two glasses of iced Coke. Shortly after re-joining the road, a JOGLE cyclist waved me over and passed on good wishes from Alan and Lynne at the Wick B&B – he had stayed there the previous night and they had asked him to look out for me! It was quite fortuitous that he'd spotted me here, as my route from Brora along the beach and coastal footpaths was unsuitable for cyclists.

I had my first mishap of the trip when I stopped next to a stone bridge to fetch my sun hat out of my rucksack. A gust of wind blew my map holder over the edge of the bridge and it landed ten feet down in a bank of nettles. By a stroke of luck, there was a perfectly situated outlet pipe, which I was able to use to support me as I gingerly climbed down the side of the bridge to recover the map holder. A near miss and no nettle stings!

I reached The Mound, an embankment which carries the A9 across the River Fleet, and concluded from the nearby road signs (CAUTION! Otters for 1 ¾ miles) that I was in otter country. Otters have large territories and regularly travel within them, but when rivers are fast flowing following wet weather, they are reluctant to pass through existing culverts or under bridges. Instead, they have no option but to cross the road, which results in a relatively high risk of being killed by passing vehicles. However, around The Mound, a number of measures had been put in place to protect the otters, including underground passages, roadside reflectors and warning signs.

I made good progress towards Dornoch and was heading along the A9 in open countryside, when I was suddenly disturbed from behind by a screeching sound. A large car braked sharply and pulled over on to the opposite roadside, parallel to me. I immediately crossed over to investigate and quickly ascertained that they were a party of six stylishly dressed Italian tourists, but they had just suffered a puncture in their hire car. Although they might conceivably have been in the area to visit a branch of the local Sutherland Mafia, the evidence appeared to suggest otherwise! Unfortunately, they didn't speak a single word of English between them and, with my Italian limited to *pizza quattro stagioni, gelato al limone* and *Chianti Classico*, I gestured to them that I would telephone the car hire company on their behalf. I had an initial conversation with the hire car helpline, in which I explained the predicament of my Italian travellers, then I was transferred to the RAC roadside recovery helpline. After repeating the story, a challenge compounded by a blustery wind, which made the mobile phone conversations crackly and difficult to follow, the RAC eventually arranged for a local garage to attend. This episode had by now added a lengthy delay to my walk and I could not afford any more time to await the arrival of the recovery vehicle, but the Italians seemed very appreciative nevertheless. Their senior driver spotted my Cancer Research UK tee-shirt and gave me some quizzical looks, so using sign language, I tried to explain my mission. Our spontaneous game of roadside Charades was obviously a success, as the Italians immediately organised a collection amongst their group and donated fifty euros to my cause! My first foreign currency donation!

Five minutes after bidding *arrivederci* and just a few miles from my destination of Dornoch, I had an embarrassing fall. I somehow managed to stumble clumsily over my own feet at the roadside, lost my balance and the weight of my rucksack then propelled me towards the gravel. I landed awkwardly on my right hand, piercing the tips of two of my fingers and grazing my arm badly. The back of my right hand swelled up and blood dribbled onto the road. Fortunately, nobody was around to see the incident, so my pride was unharmed. For a few galling seconds, I feared that my entire walk would be finished on Day 4 and briefly considered how I would explain my self-inflicted failure to friends and supporters, but then I quickly determined that I definitely would be able to continue, even if I ended up with one arm in plaster! After all, long distance walking mainly involves legs and feet!

Less than an hour later I arrived at my B&B in Dornoch with my hand covered in blood, looking totally dishevelled! Thankfully, my hosts were most sympathetic and welcomed the recently arrived tramp into their spotless home. I just hoped that there would be no lasting damage.

Despite my fragile physical condition, I managed to clean myself up and made extensive use of my first aid kit. I ventured into town in search of a meal, but my run of bad luck continued as the restaurant recommended by my hosts was closed for the evening. However, the local hostelry provided a more than adequate meal and a welcome couple of pints.

At dusk, I had a very brief wander around Dornoch (or The Royal Burgh of Dornoch, to be precise), which is an historic small town on the edge of the Dornoch Firth and a designated National Scenic Area in the Highlands of Scotland. Its championship golf course helps it to attract numerous visitors and (to quote The Royal Burgh's own website), the town is "small in population, but large in hospitality".

Day 5 – Dornoch to Alness
Distance: 19.9 miles
Cumulative distance: 100.9 miles
Weather: Cloudy with sunny spells

A tough physical day, mostly along deserted country lanes

Perhaps I'd better start with a medical update. Two fingers on my right hand were slightly swollen, but I could now manoeuvre them more than I could last night, so I was confident that they were not fractured and would recover in due course. The rest of the injuries to my arm and hand were superficial and would, hopefully, heal quickly. The blister on my baby toe, however, had not improved and I realised that it was now causing me to walk with a slight limp.

After another full Scottish breakfast, I left my B&B, which formerly had operated as a high street bank, and set off down a quiet country lane which meandered towards the bridge which crosses the Dornoch Firth. From the outset, I'd been keen to utilise any paths which would help to reduce my daily mileage and keep me away from main roads, so I was delighted that a short cut I'd researched using Google's Street View service materialised successfully. The photographic evidence online had appeared to indicate a footpath and viable access onto the causeway, but it was always a relief to turn a theoretical route into practice.

Before the Dornoch Firth Bridge was constructed, the Meikle Ferry was the only way to reach Tain to the south without a considerable overland journey. In August 1809, this busy ferry route became the scene of a tragic disaster, when over one hundred people boarded the ferry at the Dornoch end for the half mile crossing, most of whom were en route to visit the popular Tain Lammas Fair. The conditions were calm, but the overcrowded boat was dangerously low in the water and, as the boat turned broadside to the tide, it became swamped and suddenly capsized into the cold waters, resulting in the loss of 99 lives and only 12 survivors. It was later alleged that the ferryman was under the influence and had allowed too many people and animals to board the boat.

I crossed the bridge and, just after passing the Glenmorangie Distillery and before reaching Tain, I left the A9 and joined a long country lane (Scotsburn Road) which would lead me all the way to Alness, my destination for the day.

I passed by many substantial houses on considerably sized plots, but I failed to spot any occupants, either through the windows or in the copiously stocked gardens. Was everybody out at work, did the residents never venture outdoors, or were these second homes? With no shops or pubs en route, my diminishing water supplies would have to wait a little longer to be refilled. My thirst could manage, but my right foot was becoming more of a hindrance. My swollen, blistered baby toe continued to cause problems and I had, by now, noticeably adapted my walking step to try to minimise the discomfort. The effect of this was to slow me down considerably as I could no longer walk with a spring in my step, but at least I was still making steady progress towards a remedy in Inverness.

The houses gradually became sparser and the landscape more forested. During the Second World War, this area had been populated by members of the Canadian Forestry Corps, who had crossed the Atlantic to support the war effort by helping to cut down trees. The Scottish conditions proved to be quite challenging for them, with perpetual rain and boggy ground creating an environment which was quite different to that in Canada, where thick, frozen snow was the norm. Back home, the Canadians worked mainly in the winter, so they were not used to working throughout the year, which the demands of the war now required. The Canadians, however, brought with them the latest logging techniques and modern machinery, which fascinated the locals, most of whom had never seen before the type of tractors and winches now being used to pull the trees out of the ground.

Surprisingly, the Canadians were the subject of German propaganda on the radio:

"The Canadians arriving in your midst will not be much help in your war effort. Lock up your daughters and stay off the roads. Give these men a motorcycle and a bottle of whisky and they will kill themselves."

Of course, there was no truth in this. The local community warmly welcomed the arrival of the Canadians and it was reported that they provided the locals with shows, entertainment, free wood and tools. It is also documented that they provided husbands for the local girls, with frequent weddings taking place in the Highlands during this period!

I felt rather fatigued at lunchtime, so I found a perfect spot to lie down for a rest – two inspection covers located on the verge at a quiet road junction. The space was just large enough to accommodate my prone body and I slept blissfully for an hour or so, disturbed only by the noise of an occasional passing tractor. I felt much refreshed afterwards, but after any prolonged stop now, it took a few minutes for my swollen toe to readjust to walking again and I was visibly limping for a few hundred yards until I regained my normal stride.

For the first time on my walk to date, I turned on my portable DAB radio and tuned into some soothing music on Radio 3, not my usual choice of listening. A symphony from the early 20th century English composer Ernest Moeran (who I'd not been acquainted with previously) seemed to fit the mood. Bizarrely, although I'd regularly listened to music during my practice walks, this was the first time I'd listened during the actual walk itself and would subsequently prove to be the only occasion on the entire journey. I reasoned that as most of my practice walks were undertaken on familiar routes, so the music and radio offered a form of escapism. On the real walk, the surroundings were new, so not only was it appropriate to observe and enjoy the scenery, but I also needed to concentrate more to check maps and to pay attention to passing traffic.

With the exception of the long distance footpaths, for which I had purchased dedicated guide maps, my daily routes had been sourced from Ordnance Survey Getamap, an online version of 1:25,000 scale mapping (about 2.5 inches to one mile for those from an older generation). I'd copied each day's route onto A4 sheets, with each day covering between six and eight sheets, and had used a yellow highlighter pen to ensure that the route was clearly visible. The day's sheets then fitted neatly inside my transparent map holder. It had taken me many hours to align and print my entire set of A4 sheets, but the effort was certainly rewarded as it avoided the need to purchase and carry multiple copies of the original map.

I took great pleasure in completing each sheet's route and

replacing it with the next page, mentally ticking off another completed section of the journey. On difficult days like today, I would track progress across each square on the map and set a target to reach a specific square by a given time, checking off landmarks such as buildings and road junctions along the way. This way, I progressed square by square and sheet by sheet, until I reached my accommodation destination.

Shortly before reaching Alness, I'd identified another likely short cut around a disused quarry, courtesy of a satellite photograph on Google maps. In my fragile state, I didn't want to waste unnecessary steps on a fruitless diversion, but fortune accompanied me as the track fully resembled its satellite image and led me to the outskirts of Alness.

I had a slight doubt about my accommodation in Alness. Although I'd arranged all of my accommodation some months earlier, this B&B did not initially provide confirmation of my booking, despite several email reminders. A few weeks before I set off, I telephoned the B&B to seek confirmation. Worryingly, the owner had no record of my booking, but she then went on to inform me that her son managed the email bookings and confessed that he wasn't "very reliable". She said she was fully booked for several months with wind farm contractors, but then noticed in her diary that one of them was on holiday for a few days at the time of my arrival, so to my relief, she was able to accommodate me after all.

The B&B turned out to be comfortable enough, although it was clearly targeted to cater for young, male contractors who worked on long term wind farm construction projects in the area. With my expanding blister, my light canvas shoes were rather uncomfortable, as I hobbled down the high street to seek out my evening meal.

Over the last forty or so years, the Highland town of

Alness had become a boom town, due largely to the employment opportunities generated by the construction of an aluminium smelter and oil-related projects around the Cromarty Firth. The town's population quickly doubled in size and the pace of change that local people experienced was unique, compared to other areas of Scotland and the United Kingdom. The smelter closed in 1981 and unemployment in the town rose by twenty per cent, but a vibrant voluntary sector, which had developed with the expansion of the town, managed to help maintain a resilient community spirit. In 1997, Alness first entered the Scotland in Bloom Competition and achieved notable successes in subsequent years, culminating in the award of the Royal Horticultural Society's Gold Medal as Champion of Champions, Britain in Bloom Winners in 2006, when they triumphed over rivals Harrogate and Garstang. The floral achievements had a positive impact on the town, resulting in increased numbers of shoppers and tourists.

The floral passion was in evidence as I dined at the local Indian restaurant, which inconveniently was situated as far from my accommodation as was possible. The summer plant displays were being delivered to the high street that evening and a dozen or so volunteers, whose ages ranged from eight to eighty, were delicately unloading them and planting them into brightly coloured containers, which were neatly positioned along the pavement on each side of the road. Although I was the only customer in the restaurant, the food was decent and the window seat had provided me with the opportunity to observe the local community in action!

Day 6 – Alness to Inverness

Distance: 19.8 miles
Cumulative distance: 120.7 miles
Weather: Sunny intervals, rain showers later

Steady progress towards a rest day and soaked by the first rain

My single objective for the day was to reach Inverness, where I was confident that my foot problems could be resolved during my first rest day. After taking a minor road from Alness, I joined the A9 for the last time on my journey, following the scenic Cromarty Firth for several miles. I crossed the Cromarty Firth Bridge, which was built in 1979 to cut twelve miles from the previously circuitous journey, and plodded on towards Inverness.

After five days on the road, I was beginning to conclude that my rucksack felt heavier than it needed to be, which was probably compounding my foot problem. I remembered that in the build up to the walk a few people had asked how my kit would be transported from one location to the next and some enquired about my 'support' vehicle. Sir Ian Botham might have benefited from such luxuries when he twice completed his charity walk from Land's End to John O' Groats, but the simple truth was that in my case there was no support vehicle and the transportation solution was me. A few were astounded when I broke this news to them, but it would be a question I would encounter on numerous occasions during my journey!

As everything I needed for the journey would be carried on my back, I had set out to minimise the weight. The importance of this was re-iterated to me in a booking confirmation from the owner of the Dunbeath bed & breakfast, who warned "Be ruthless with what you think you need – remember you're not going to Outer Mongolia". She went on to state that she sends a lot of big parcels home for walkers! I was broadly aware of this early de-cluttering process from various blogs I'd read, with some walkers ditching more than half of their original load within the first week!

Although I had tried very hard to be ruthless, it was difficult not to be cautious when setting off on such an expedition for the first time. To compound matters, I had been showered with a plethora of walking-related gifts by family, friends and colleagues, but I simply didn't have the capacity to accommodate all of these items in my rucksack. So the foot massage gel, the safety light sticks, the insect bite relief, an array of flavoured lip balms and a kilogram of emergency rations would be forced to stay at home to await another adventure, whether my own or somebody else's.

The secret formula to lightening my load would be to reduce the number of items carried and to minimise the weight of each item, supplemented by a few carefully planned drop-off and collection points en route, allowing me to discard a few used items (maps and clothes) in exchange for new ones (maps and clothes). I consulted the equipment lists of numerous other long distance walkers, then made a few revisions to reflect my personal requirements. For my single luxury item, I decided to include a Cancer Research UK collecting jar. But alas, to devotees of *Desert Island Discs*, I didn't have space to carry a copy of the Bible or the *Complete Works of Shakespeare*!

My final kit consisted of the following groups of items, each carried in a separate sack within my rucksack:

- Walking kit (walking boots, adjustable walking trousers, 4 x tee-shirts, 4 x walking socks, 4 x underwear, waterproof jacket and trousers, fleece, hat, gloves, gaiters, spare laces)
- Casual clothes (2 x polo shirts, a pair of chinos, swimming trunks and light canvas shoes for evenings and rest days)
- Toiletries (toothbrush, toothpaste, shower gel, flannel, comb, deodorant, travel towel, shaver, travel wash)
- Medical items (first aid kit, scissors, blister pads, sun cream, lip balm)
- Other items (maps, phone, camera, radio, chargers, compass, torch, Swiss army knife, collecting jar, hi-visibility top)
- Food & drink (3 x water bottles, energy bars, chocolate, raisins and apples)

On the sixth day of my walk, I now appreciated that I needed to be even more ruthless! I determined that I would try to lighten my load in Inverness and considered two possible ways of achieving this. The first involved posting a package of unwanted items back home, but the preferred option was to meet up with a former work colleague who was holidaying in northern Scotland over the next few days.

I took great pleasure in mentally listing all the items that I would cast aside from my pack and repeated this throughout the morning's walk, each time attempting to be more ruthless in my choices. The prospect of shedding a few pounds of baggage really motivated me and I noticeably increased my pace.

My journey so far had offered very few opportunities to sit down en route, which resulted in snack breaks being taken whilst standing. Occasionally, a stone wall would provide a seat, but this was the exception. However, today's lunch venue was luxurious by comparison – a bus shelter, which offered a comfortable seat and a shield from the busy traffic – although the drivers of several passing buses seemed genuinely disappointed that I would not be joining them on their road trip to Inverness.

The traffic became more intense as we neared Inverness. A sign in a roadside field advertised the nearby Black Isle Brewery (the UK's premier organic brewery, no less) and a herd of cows had gathered next to it, as if forming a queue for the next brewery tour. I wished that I had time to join them, but I needed to press on.

As I approached Kessock Bridge, to the north of Inverness, lane closures on the bridge resulted in slow moving traffic. Before long, the traffic speed had reduced down to my walking pace and I was conscious that this was the first time I had been accompanied on my walk since leaving John O' Groats. Drivers and passengers shouted words of support, waved, and raised their thumbs. Some even clapped and a few took photographs. I had become an object of interest and amusement!

Then, it finally happened. After nearly 6 days and 120 miles, the heavens opened and rain fell like bullets from the sky. I was close to the bridge and, with nowhere to shelter, I was completely exposed to the elements. I rashly decided that as I was only about two miles from Inverness, I would resist putting on my waterproofs. Within minutes I was completely soaked, my hat providing the only protection from the rain. A lorry driver took pity, wished me some words of encouragement and tossed a fresh meat pie towards me!

The Kessock Bridge carries the A9 trunk road south from the Black Isle to Inverness across the Beauly Firth, an inlet of the Moray Firth. Before it opened in 1982, drivers faced either a ferry crossing or a much longer journey via Beauly. The bridge has proved to be a key factor in the economic growth of the city of Inverness.

The first landmark I reached on the Inverness side of the bridge was the Caledonian Stadium, home to Inverness Caledonian Thistle football club, which currently plays in the Scottish Premier League. Following the merger of two lower league clubs, Inverness Thistle and Caledonian, the new stadium was completed in 1996. There were initial concerns from the local Harbour Trust that the stadium floodlights would interfere with marine traffic in the Moray Firth, but these issues were subsequently resolved and the new team flourished.

At the end of my day's walk, there was still time to introduce another Street View short cut, which allowed me to climb down the grassy bank of the dual carriageway and join the road to my hotel, saving a valuable two thirds of a mile of walking. I arrived at the Premier Inn somewhat bedraggled and soaked to the skin, but they welcomed me regardless.

My check-in was more straightforward than on a previous occasion at a Premier Inn, where I was staying with my daughter for the evening. We'd been allocated a family room, but the new on-line check-in system was experiencing some teething problems and would not allow me to enter just two guest names. The receptionist advised that I needed to enter four names and duly suggested that I should simply invent two additional names. I don't recall what we christened the new family members, but it struck me later that, during any incident, the emergency services might have been searching in vain for them had they relied on the hotel's guest list.

It was a relief to flee from the Inverness rain and, minutes later, I soaked in a hot bath and then curled up under the duvet for an hour's sleep before dinner.

I reflected on my progress so far and concluded that tomorrow would be a critical day. I was placing heavy reliance on using my rest day to resolve my foot problems and to reduce the weight of my rucksack. Without adjusted boots or, at worst, new boots, I seriously doubted whether I would be able to continue my journey and I briefly contemplated how I would confront such failure.

Day 7 – Inverness
Distance: 1.1 miles
Cumulative distance: 121.8 miles
Weather: Sunny intervals

Boot repairs, a reduced load, shopping and a night out in company

A new day with no serious walking. After a pleasantly relaxing 'eat-as-much-as-you-like' breakfast, I received an email from Lynda, a former work colleague, informing me that she would be in Inverness tonight and would like to meet. Apart from having company and catching up, this would be my solution for offloading my excess kit.

I moved into ruthless mode and eagerly extracted the following items from my rucksack:

- Used maps (50 x A4 sheets)
- Spare tee-shirt
- Polo shirt (one casual top would have to suffice until Carlisle)
- Spare pair of socks
- Travel wash (I would have to use soap to wash my clothes in future)
- Various toiletries

- Travel towel (towels had been provided most nights and I would manage without if necessary)
- Leather belt
- Swiss army knife (I hadn't used it so far)
- Passport (I had needed this for identity purposes at Heathrow, not to gain access to Scotland!)

I placed all the items into a large plastic carrier bag and then took immense pleasure in lifting it up and feeling its weight. I estimated that it would tip the scales at around five pounds, but psychologically it felt like much more.

I walked down the hill into the town centre and located Craigdon Mountain Sports shop, which I had found on the internet and which, I hoped and prayed, would come to my rescue. I explained my boot predicament to Calum, the very helpful boot specialist. He listened intently and nodded in the direction of the boot stretching machine. He kindly agreed to have my right boot stretched overnight, but also recommended a padded insole support for the boot – he advised that this would allow my foot to sit further back in the boot. I arranged to collect the newly stretched boot early next morning and walked out of the shop in a state of elation, sensing that although my boot hadn't yet been fixed, I now had the support of a knowledgeable and obliging expert who would enable my journey to continue.

I had a couple of hours to kill before I could re-locate to a more central Premier Inn (last night's had been more convenient for yesterday's route), so I stocked up on plasters and foot padding in the local Boots store. I had become increasingly acquainted with their range of foot care products and probably could have advised on them more readily than the staff working there.

I stopped for a light lunch at a wonderful pub called Hootananny. It was predominantly a music venue, but inside the décor oozed character and the staff were genuinely hospitable. The Red Kite bitter from the local Black Isle Brewery went down well with the homemade pea and watercress soup, served with a salmon and cream cheese bloomer.

I checked into my second Premier Inn in 24 hours, with a fine view of the city and the river from my bedroom. A free afternoon gave me the chance to wash some clothes. The washing itself was straightforward, but I had to construct makeshift coat hangers and then used the room's hairdryer to accelerate and complete the drying process! It was then time to explore Inverness.

Inverness is situated at the mouth of the River Ness (which flows from nearby Loch Ness) and is at the southwestern extremity of the Moray Firth. The city lies at the end of the Great Glen with Loch Ness, Loch Ashie and Loch Duntelchaig to the west. The Caledonian Canal runs through the Great Glen connecting Loch Ness, Loch Oich, and Loch Lochy, all of which would become more familiar to me during the next few days.

The city is the administrative centre for the Highlands area and is regarded as its capital. It is also the northernmost city in the United Kingdom and one of Europe's fastest growing cities, with a third of the Highland population living in or around the city. The city is high on quality of life, being ranked fifth out of 189 British cities, the highest of any Scottish city.

One of the city's claims to fame is that in September 1921, the first British Cabinet meeting to be held outside London took place in the Town House, when David Lloyd George, on holiday in Gairloch, called an emergency meeting to discuss the situation in Ireland.

Inverness Castle sits on a cliff overlooking the River Ness and dominates the city. There have been a succession of castles on the site since 1057, but the current red sandstone structure was built in 1836. Today, it houses the Inverness Sheriff Court, but is not open to the public.

I met Lynda at the Castle Tavern, which advertised "the tantalising aroma of freshly prepared hot food" and "the sound of friendly banter emanating from the terraced beer garden". It was gratifying to have company for the evening and to be able to exchange travel stories over a relaxing meal and a few beers. Lynda was touring Scotland by car in a unique figure-of-eight shape, but seemed to have experienced more rain than me. She hoped to be able to join me for part of my walk along the Great Glen Way later in the week. At the end of the evening, I walked down the hill and returned to the hotel, just as Cinderella's coach was about to depart – my latest night so far.

CHAPTER TWO

The Great Glen Way and West Highland Way to Glasgow

Day 8 – Inverness to Drumnadrochit

Distance: 15.6 miles

Cumulative distance: 137.4 miles

Weather: Sunny

A new lease of life, a route change and an introduction to Loch Ness

I'd chosen to use my walk to raise funds for Cancer Research UK. Sadly, all of us have been impacted by family, friends and colleagues who have been diagnosed with cancer. Cancer Research UK has made significant progress in understanding and treating cancer; their work has helped to save millions of lives through funding research projects, yet one in three of us will still get cancer at some point in our lives. Their research is funded entirely by public donations; without this, the work they do to diagnose cancer earlier, make treatments kinder, and ultimately save more lives would simply not be possible.

One of the most frequent questions I was asked during my preparation for the walk and especially throughout the walk itself was why had I chosen Cancer Research UK? The question was not being posed in any negative sense, but at this point, most people expected me to launch into a tear-jerking story about how I had been impacted by cancer personally. My answer, which must have disappointed many, is much less dramatic and more pragmatic. Given the geography of my walk, I wanted to raise funds for a charity which had national appeal. I'd supported Cancer Research UK when I had taken part in a few marathon runs (so long ago that it seemed like in a previous life!) and, more recently, I was really impressed by the positive impact of their ongoing research on cancer survival rates, so I chose them as my charity on that basis.

I was a somewhat reluctant fundraiser – I've never been one to 'shout from the rooftops' and it felt out of character to contact hundreds of friends and colleagues to inform them about my adventure and to politely ask for sponsorship.

I'd set myself a fundraising target of £10,000 when l kicked off my project, which I considered to be a significant sum. However, thanks to the generosity of family, friends and colleagues, news reached me over breakfast in Inverness that I'd now reached this target. In truth, I knew that I was close to this goal, so I'd mentioned it in my blog on the previous day and set a challenge to see whose donation would bring me to my target. This did the trick, as several people vied for the honour, but it was a former work colleague who generously propelled me over the line. Rather than settle for this sum, I decided to increase my target to £15,000 and duly informed my supporters. My daughter Hannah immediately advised me that my new target was far too ambitious, so we agreed that if I ever achieved it, she would cook me a three course meal (I can't recall what my forfeit would have to be!).

Breakfast entertainment at the Premier Inn was provided by a two year old Chinese girl, who managed to pour an entire pot of fruit yogurt all over her head and then proceeded to run about the restaurant in front of the bemused onlookers!

Fully breakfasted, I crossed the River Ness by the footbridge to collect my boots from Craigdon Mountain Sports. This was the moment of truth. I cautiously pushed my right foot into its newly extended boot, carefully fastened the laces and took a few tentative steps across the shop. It immediately felt more comfortable and my baby toe now had room to manoeuvre. I gasped with relief – my epic journey could continue towards Land's End. I couldn't thank the staff at Craigdon Mountain Sports enough – they had understood my predicament and resolved my problem quickly and courteously.

I returned to the Premier Inn in buoyant spirits and checked out, ready to continue my journey in comfort, my adjusted boot and lighter load effectively providing me with a new lease of life. The two girls at reception kindly made a donation to my cause when I explained what I was doing. The Premier Inn had been perfect for a long distance walker seeking rest and recovery. The spacious rooms, hot baths, comfortable beds, eat-as-much-as-you-like breakfast, early check in / late checkout, and friendly staff ticked every box. It was just a shame that Premier Inn Head Office hadn't replied to either of my earlier invitations to make a donation – I'd written on the basis that I had personally funded a handful of nights' accommodation in their hotels throughout my journey. I recognise that they are probably inundated with charity requests and that they raise significant sums for Great Ormond Street Hospital, but a simple email courteously declining my request would have been appreciated.

Due to my late start and to give my newly 'adjusted' boot a gentler introduction to my walk, I shortened today's route slightly. Rather than joining the start of the Great Glen Way in Inverness, I decided to take the low level canal towpath and road route to Drumnadrochit. The first few miles, along the gorse-lined towpath of the Caledonian Canal, were idyllic and reminiscent in many ways of my training walks along the River Thames towpath back home.

The Caledonian Canal runs along the steep sided spine of the Great Glen, a large geological fault line which cuts the Highlands into two. The canal runs from Inverness to Fort William, a distance of almost sixty miles, but is in fact several canal sections which link a series of lochs, including Loch Ness. It was built by Thomas Telford to enable sailing ships to avoid the treacherous west coast waters, but was also conceived as a means of providing employment following the Highland Clearances, which resulted in many people losing homes and jobs. The project was fraught with challenges, including having to deal with variable ground ranging from solid rock to mud, constructing the largest lochs ever built, and managing a frequently absent labour force. When it finally opened in 1822, it was twelve years late and significantly overspent. Unfortunately, many of the sailing ships for which it was intended had by now been converted to steam, so were able to negotiate the sea routes more safely. To make matters worse, the depth of the canal had been reduced to save costs, so the latest iron-hulled steam ships were too large to use the canal. As a consequence, the canal never really paid for itself.

Following extensive restoration work which was completed in 2005, the canal is now a popular tourist attraction, but despite it being mid-June and the weather very favourable, there were remarkably few boats on the canal as I progressed along the towpath.

The canal towpath ended near the picturesque village of Dochgarroch as the canal prepared to enter Loch Ness. I had little option but to join the narrow, but busy, A82 road which skirted the banks of Loch Ness. At one of several viewpoints on the road, I clambered down to the loch itself and enjoyed my picnic lunch, perched precariously on a rock at the water's edge.

Further down the road, a car pulled up alongside me and offered me a lift. The driver, a local man in his sixties, was concerned that I was walking along a busy road without a pedestrian walkway. I told him about my walking challenge and explained that I was not permitted to accept a lift. I did manage to find a short section of footpath which followed a scenic woodland track, but this re-joined the main road after a mile.

I arrived early in Drumnadrochit, so popped into a local bakery shop to buy a cool drink. Taking pity on me, the lady gave me a home cooked sausage roll, which I consumed on a bench in the memorial garden.

Drumnadrochit is home to the Loch Ness Centre and Exhibition Experience, which explores the mysteries and discovers the history of the world famous loch and its resident monster. The earliest report of a monster associated with the vicinity of Loch Ness relates to St Columba in the 6th century, but the beast's existence was first brought to the world's attention in 1933, when George Spicer and his wife saw "a most extraordinary form of animal" cross the road in front of their car. They described the creature as having "a large body (about 4 feet high and 25 feet long), and a long, narrow neck, slightly thicker than an elephant's trunk". Numerous 'sightings' have been reported subsequently, but much of the evidence is anecdotal. The scientific community regards the Loch Ness Monster as a modern-day myth, and explains sightings as a mixture of misidentifications, outright hoaxes, and sheer fantasy.

I had trouble finding my bed and breakfast, due to its location being incorrectly positioned on Google maps, but my host was very welcoming when I eventually arrived at her front door. In the comfort of my room, I reflected on my day. My newly extended right boot had been very comfortable and, having discarded a few pounds in kit, my rucksack had felt so much lighter. My blisters would probably take a few days to heal, but at least my baby toe was no longer being compressed against the end of my boot. The outlook was promising!

Dinner at Fiddlers restaurant in the village was a truly international affair. In a small room in a quiet Highland village, I dined amongst Australians, Americans, Canadians, Russians and Germans. My Scottish fayre was excellent – Orkney herring, followed by venison casserole, washed down with Nessie Monster Mash bitter and Cromarty coffee-infused stout.

Day 9 – Drumnadrochit to Invermoriston
Distance: 15.3 miles
Cumulative distance: 152.7 miles
Weather: Mostly sunny

A pleasant walk through woodland tracks high above Loch Ness

I checked out of my very hospitable B&B a little later than planned as my host was rather talkative and wanted to know more about my proposed route. The weather forecast indicated rain, so I packed my waterproofs at the top of my rucksack to ensure that they would be readily accessible.

Drumnadrochit village was surprisingly lively for early on a Saturday morning. As I walked through the village, I noticed a number of passing vehicles with black and red scarves and banners draped from their windows, then I spotted some people gathered in the doorway of a social club sporting similar colours. This was the day of the Mactavish Cup Final which, as somebody somewhere will appreciate, is a major fixture in the shinty calendar. Shinty, which is an integral part of the Highlands and Islands, is a team game played with sticks and a ball. It is similar to hockey, but in shinty a player is allowed to play the ball in the air and is permitted to use both sides of the stick (called a *caman*), which is wooden and slanted on both sides. The stick may also be used to block and to tackle.

Today's final, played at Bught Park, Inverness was a local derby, being contested by Glen Urquhart (based in Drumnadrochit) and Lovat (based in Kiltarlity, 12 miles west of Inverness). In front of BBC Scotland television cameras, a tense game ended 1-1 after extra time, but sadly for the locals, the youthful Lovat team won after a penalty shoot-out, capturing their first trophy since 1953.

Just beyond the village I took a right turn and joined the Great Glen Way for the first time.

The Great Glen Way is a long distance footpath which opened in 2002. It loosely follows the route of the Caledonian Canal, but frequently diverts onto steeper forest tracks and woodland paths, resulting in a longer route of 73 miles. It is popular with walkers and mountain bikers, attracting interest from different parts of the world.

I followed an energy sapping woodland track which climbed for several miles. The promised rain didn't materialise and the clouds dissipated, so I was privy to breath-taking views of Loch Ness and the mountains beyond. After passing through a wooden gate, I stumbled across a young deer a couple of metres away, but I wasn't nimble enough to pull out my camera before it disappeared to safety into the woods. I also exchanged greetings with a few walkers who had travelled over from Denmark and Germany, but nobody appeared to be heading in my direction.

I'd been pleasantly surprised by the quality of the mobile phone and data signals which I was experiencing on my walk to date. I'd not expected to be in communication range for large tracts of northern Scotland, so it was pleasing to be able to receive emails and text messages, but also to make the occasional mobile phone call to family and friends as I walked.

High above Ruskich Wood, there were fine views across the water to Foyers and the nearby hydro-power station. Water from lochs in the hills above Loch Ness is forced down through pipes to generate electricity, and when demand for power reduces at night, the water is pumped back up ready for the next day. The old aluminium smelting works could also be seen – this was one of only a few local places to be bombed during the Second World War as the metal from the factory was used to make fighter planes. The track later descended to a bridge at Alltsigh, where a sign indicated that the last she-wolf in Scotland was killed here in the nineteenth century.

I arrived in Invermoriston, but couldn't immediately identify my B&B. The village shop had a sign stating "back at 2.30" but by 2.50 I gave up waiting and went into the village pub to enquire. The B&B, as it turned out, was just up the road and I was made very welcome by the host, a friendly lady from Bridlington, who had moved up here with her husband.

As it was Saturday night and I hadn't reserved a table, I wandered down the road to eat early at the village pub, The Glenmoriston Arms. The original hotel dated back to 1740, 6 years before the battle of Culloden, when the building was a drover's inn, a stop-over point for farmers taking their cattle to and from market. Surprisingly, some of this original structure remains in place today, forming the Moriston bar and the reception area with granite walls three or four feet thick. The hotel was also a favourite haunt for Charlie Chaplin in the 1930s when actors and actresses of the time wanted a little peace and relaxation in the Highlands.

My meal was pleasant, but I only wished that the boisterous group who were stood shouting animatedly at the bar had adopted the silent movie approach, for the benefit of the other diners. On reflection, maybe they were supporters of the Glen Urquhart shinty team and were drowning their sorrows after the team's cup final defeat earlier in the day.

Day 10 – Invermoriston to South Laggan
Distance: 18.1 miles
Cumulative distance: 170.8 miles
Weather: Cloudy

Forest tracks, canal paths and company en route!

After breakfast, my host provided me with a sizeable packed lunch, the contents of which would probably keep me going for two or three days. Taking a cautious approach, I had accumulated a wide selection of sustenance since the beginning of the walk and, coupled with the supplies I had transported from home, this now resulted in my food bag being the heaviest item in my rucksack. I had since made a conscious decision to try to increase my en route consumption and, in doing so, to reduce the weight of my rucksack. However, this was easier said than done as I generally did not feel the need to consume much during walking hours.

The short cut from the village centre of Invermoriston to re-join the Great Glen Way had disappeared since my route map was published, resulting in a one mile detour in the wrong direction and a mile returning on a slightly more elevated path. I was having none of that, though! Instead, I left the village, passing by the old Telford's Bridge which crosses the River Moriston falls and was celebrating its bicentenary, then followed the A82 along the banks of Loch Ness for a short distance, before scrambling up a steep minor track and using my GPS to relocate the Great Glen Way.

This elevated track ran parallel to Loch Ness before eventually descending to the village of Fort Augustus, whose residents appeared to be rising late on this sleepy Sunday morning. The footpath re-joined the Caledonian Canal in the village and, as I reached the towpath, a coach load of tourists was just being deposited next to the bank of locks. Shortly afterwards, my mobile phone rang, so I rested on a convenient bench situated on the towpath. It was Lynda, who was parked a few miles further down the path, so we arranged to meet en route an hour or so later.

As soon as I'd ended the call, I spotted a couple heading along the towpath in my direction – this was a rare occurrence on my journey so far, so I took the opportunity to engage in conversation. Jeff and Christine from Preston had taken up long distance walking in their retirement and had since covered an impressive number of footpaths across the UK. We wandered along this particular footpath together for a few miles – they were fascinated to hear about my 'ultra' long distance walk. It was really refreshing to see their enthusiasm for walking and a pleasure to have my first company en route in ten days. Before they left me for a refreshment break, they kindly made a donation to my charity jar.

Soon afterwards, I had my second company of the day (and of the walk to date!) when Lynda appeared with her dog Megan. Since we'd met in Inverness, Lynda had continued her driving and camping tour of Scotland, but had not shared my good fortune with the weather. Megan was very protective of her as we strolled for a few miles along a dismantled railway, which had now become part of the Great Glen Way.

In 1896, despite much local opposition, the Invergarry & Fort Augustus Railway received permission to build a 24 mile section of line along the Great Glen from Spean Bridge to Fort Augustus. After costly construction the line was completed in 1901, but initially there was no money left to buy any rolling stock. Services eventually started in July 1903, but were not economically viable. The company advertised the disposal of the line for scrap, but in spite of the fact that the local people hardly used the railway, there was a public outcry. A campaign was mounted to save the line and the fate of the railway become a major local issue in the 1912 General Election. Eventually, Inverness County Council agreed to subsidise the line and it was reopened in August 1913. During the two years the line was shut the railway company had been better off financially than when it was open, as there were fewer employees to pay, empty staff houses could be let and local tradesmen rented the station buildings. Passenger services were withdrawn in December 1933 and the line closed completely in 1947. It is remarkable that, in this remote and unpopulated part of the Highlands, the line was built at all.

Today, some of the line has been built over by roads and holiday parks, but much of the track bed, bridges and a tunnel have survived. A restoration project is under way at Invergarry Station, the last remaining station that is largely intact. Much of the vegetation has been cleared, with repairs and renovation planned to the platform and underpass. The Invergarry Station Preservation Society has plans to create a static museum, with a short length of track and several freight wagons.

We stopped for lunch by Loch Oich, but didn't hang around for more than a few minutes as the infamous Scottish midges (*Culicoides impunctatus*) made their first appearance of my journey. I hastily extracted a bag from my rucksack and produced a small container of Avon Skin So Soft, which the Army apparently uses to deter the wee beasties. I duly smeared the cream over my arms and face as we strode on to keep the midges at bay. Whether it was the instant effect of the Avon product, our brisk military pace, or a combination of the two, we were no longer troubled by the midges.

As we arrived at my youth hostel accommodation at Laggan, Lynda and Megan returned to her car in search of a slightly more up market bed. I hadn't stayed in a youth hostel for over thirty years, so approached with a little trepidation. I need not have worried as the warden was very welcoming and I soon settled in. My dormitory companions were a group of senior cyclists from Lancashire, so I was far from being the oldest hosteller that night.

I booked a table for dinner at the Eagle Barge Inn, a Dutch barge moored at nearby Laggan Locks. I'd discovered this when researching the route online and it struck me as a being a little different from the standard pub dining and worthy of a visit.

During the day I had developed a slight pain in my right leg, which was causing me to walk uncomfortably. On closer inspection, my lower shin was swollen and tender. I wasn't sure what had caused this, but it certainly slowed me down as I walked the mile or so to the inn, and was a slight cause for concern.

The meal on the Eagle Barge Inn was a memorable experience. The venue was a converted Dutch Barge dating back to 1921, which started life as a sugar beet carrier in Holland and was taken over as a troop carrier by the German Army during the Second World War. At the end of the war, she again was used as a cargo carrier until bought in 2001 and converted into a fully licensed floating pub and restaurant which specialises in seafood.

The restaurant is run by an older couple, Paul and Jill from London, and seats about 14. I'd been required to order my main course when I'd booked the table earlier, as all the food is cooked from scratch. After my wonderfully fresh sea bass and an immense cheese board (I forwarded my leftovers to my neighbouring diners!), I climbed a few short steps into the lounge bar and shared some local beers (Orkney Dark Island and Isle of Skye Red Cuillin) with Carleen and Debbie, both HR professionals from Calgary in Canada, and Ike and Max, both students from Dortmund in Germany. They were all walking the Great Glen Way, but naturally, in the opposite direction to me! We exchanged stories of our hiking experiences, while the chef-cum-magician Will entertained us with a selection of tricks, before kindly driving us back to our respective accommodation. It was a strange experience to be travelling in a car and, after ten days at 3 or 4 miles per hour, it seemed that we were being transported at racing speeds.

Day 11 – South Laggan to Fort William
Distance: 24.7 miles
Cumulative distance: 195.5 miles
Weather: Sunny

A long stroll in the sun to end the Great Glen Way and a brief encounter with a fellow End to Ender

I arose early after a poor night's sleep. Although the window in my dormitory was open, it was warm and stuffy and the mattress was uncomfortable. Without my accustomed full Scottish breakfast, I decided to eat on the move. I left at 7.30am, by far my earliest start, but I was concerned that this 25 mile walk to Fort William was to be the longest walk of my entire journey and, with a swollen lower shin, my normal walking pace would be reduced.

In glorious sunshine, I followed forest tracks which traced a route around Loch Lochy, although the tall pines concealed the loch for most of the way – this was one of the frustrations of the Great Glen Way. A deer bounded across the path just in front of me, but had disappeared by the time I'd removed my camera from my pocket – this was becoming a habit! I passed through a few remote communities in the area around Loch Arkaig and noticed several recently constructed executive country homes.

The path eventually led to the hamlet of Gairlochy, where I re-joined the Caledonian Canal at the locks. Along the canal path I met my first fellow End to End walker of the trip. Nobby had left Land's End in April and was hoping to reach John O' Groats in 12 days' time. He told me that the strangest experience of his journey had been encountering a wallaby in Cornwall (it had escaped from a nearby wildlife park apparently!). Part of me was envious that Nobby's journey was nearing its end, whereas I had completed only a fifth of my own.

Despite the extended mileage to be covered during the day and nagging doubts about my latest injury, I was making swift progress towards Fort William. The final highlight of my walk along the Caledonian Canal was Neptune's Staircase, the longest staircase lock in Britain. Its eight locks manage a change in the water level of 64 feet and it takes about 90 minutes for a boat to pass through the system.

I reached Fort William just as the steam train on the West Highland line to Mallaig was departing. This is regularly described as the most spectacular rail journey in Britain, starting near the highest mountain in the Britain Isles (Ben Nevis), passing close by the deepest freshwater loch in Britain (Loch Morar) and the shortest river in Britain (River Morar), crossing the 21-arched Glenfinnan viaduct (made famous for its appearance in the Harry Potter films) and offering fine views of deserted silvery beaches (Morar) and distant isles (Rum, Eigg, Muck and Canna), before finally arriving at the deepest seawater loch in Europe (Loch Nevis).

I walked down the high street, which was thronged with tourists and locals, and noted that I'd reached civilisation for the first time since Inverness. My arrival in Fort William marked my completion of the Great Glen Way, although for most walkers this is the start of the journey. The Way perhaps included too many forest roads for my liking, but I wouldn't forget the wonderful vistas of lochs, mountains, woodland, rivers and wildlife.

Fort William is a major tourist hub with Glen Coe to the south, Aonach Mòr to the north and Glenfinnan to the west. It is an important centre for hillwalking and climbing, due to its proximity to Ben Nevis and many other three thousand feet plus 'Munro' mountains. In addition to being the start or finish point for both the Great Glen Way and the West Highland Way footpaths, it is also a major mountain biking centre, regularly hosting World Cup events at the nearby downhill track.

I was booked in to the Travelodge at the end of the high street, a brand new hotel with fine views across the loch. I took delight in noticing that the current room rate was £81, which compared most pleasingly with the £25 I'd paid when I booked in January. Maybe I should have invested in a few rooms!

I ate at Cobb's, a bistro bar attached to a sports shop at the station end of the high street. Given its undistinguished location, it was surprisingly an excellent, good value meal – venison and stilton pie, new potatoes and four servings of fresh vegetables, accompanied by a couple of pints of Otter ale from the Isle of Skye brewery. After a full day's walking, the prospect of my evening meal was becoming a daily incentive to complete my allotted miles.

After dinner, I went for a stroll by the loch and came across a striking 14 feet tall sculpture made of recycled mountain bike parts. *Ben Mhor*, or 'Big Ben' for those of us not familiar with the Gaelic mother tongue, sits on the Old Town Pier looking up to the peaks that inspired it, and helps to promote the Fort William Mountain Festival.

Day 12 – Fort William to Kinlochleven
Distance: 15.5 miles
Cumulative distance: 211.0 miles
Weather: Cloudy

Starting the West Highland Way and managing to miss the rain

As the Travelodge only offered an unappealing continental breakfast in a box, I'd visited the nearby Tesco Metro shop to buy my own assortment of breakfast and lunch items for the next couple of days. These were more enticing and much better value than the Travelodge version, so I was able to enjoy a croissant, a banana, fresh fruit salad and a cereal bar, all washed down with a fruit smoothie drink.

The West Highland Way starts (or technically, finishes) from right outside the Travelodge and, from my bedroom window, I could see the plaque and the sculpture of a weary male walker sat on a bench, otherwise known as "Sore Feet". The West Highland Way is a 97 mile path which links Glasgow (or Milngavie to the north of the city, to be precise) with Fort William. Until a few years ago, the route ended at an undistinguished roundabout in Fort William, but the finish is now more welcoming and inspiring.

My introduction to the West Highland Way was less inspiring as it weaved its way out of town, through a residential area and into countryside along the banks of the River Nevis, in the shadow of Ben Nevis. Eventually the path climbed steeply up a track through the Nevis Forest, where the tall trees created a dark canopy through woodland. After a few miles the trees disappeared and the path transitioned into a narrow stony track through a deserted glen which was flanked by the one thousand metre mountain peaks of Stob Ban, Sgurr a' Mhaim and Am Bhodach. This was real mountain country, a remote and desolate landscape populated only by sheep. I'd left civilisation behind once more and I had the entire upland to myself. It was cloudy throughout the day and the air felt damp, but somehow it didn't actually rain. I stopped for lunch behind a stone wall and passed by the old ruins at Tigh-na-sleubhaich, a rare man-made feature on the landscape.

I was beginning to establish myself into the routine of daily walking by now. I started to treat my journey as if it were my job, my sole objective each day being to transport myself and my weighty rucksack safely on foot from my departure accommodation to my destination accommodation, within a maximum timeframe of nine hours. Stripped down to its basics, it became a more straightforward and manageable task.

Nevertheless, each day was a physical and mental test, which brought with it a variety of challenges which I had to overcome. Whilst I was aware in advance of some of these challenges, such as difficult walking terrain, steep hills or sections requiring more extensive navigational skills, most of the challenges would emerge indiscriminately as the day evolved. These unplanned obstacles could include dealing with more extreme weather conditions, coping with injuries such as blisters, managing a diversion from the route or temporarily getting lost, sourcing food and liquid refreshments en route, or simply triumphing over a multiplicity of minor dramas which would inevitably confront me along my journey. These challenges kept me constantly alert and added spice and diversity to my daily walk, which might otherwise have become humdrum and monotonous.

After lunch, I passed about fifty hikers and ten mountain bikers making the journey in the opposite direction. The rocky, mountainous terrain was particularly challenging for the mountain bikers and a few looked close to exhaustion and even closer to tears. I eventually caught up with a couple who were walking in my direction – they were returning to their car, but mentioned to me that it had rained earlier in the day. My good fortune with the weather had continued for another day. The path then descended steeply into Kinlochleven, a small tourist destination which is surrounded on three sides by mountains.

Kinlochleven was best known for its aluminium smelter, which was powered by a hydroelectric scheme situated in the mountains above. This made Kinlochleven the first village in the world to have every house connected to electricity, coining the phrase the "Electric Village". The aluminium plant closed in 1996, a major blow to the local economy, having employed more than 700 people at its peak. Today, Kinlochleven is home to the National Ice Climbing Centre and a micro-brewery.

I checked into my second youth hostel of the trip and found myself in a four bed dormitory with en suite facilities. I met Ross, one of my roommates, who was from Glasgow and was helping to construct a *Via Ferrata* ("iron way", in Italian) zip wire walk nearby in a spectacular setting beside the third biggest waterfall in Scotland, the 90 metre high Grey Mare's Tail. This would allow participants to access a stunning and exhilarating setting by means of fixed cables, staples, ladders and bridges, without the risks associated with unprotected scrambling and climbing. By all accounts, the construction work was very demanding physically and Ross had multiple cuts and bruises to prove it.

I walked a few hundred yards into the centre of the village to dine at the local pub, where I enjoyed my staple diet of lasagne and chips. On the noticeboard in the tourist office, I was amused to see that the daily weather forecast was accompanied by a Scottish midge forecast – high levels were anticipated! Back at the hostel, the midge count was already high as I stood in the doorway in conversation with the hostel warden, but admitted defeat when the wee beasties became overbearing.

Outside the youth hostel stood a row of large wooden cylinders, lying horizontally on the ground. They were microlodge hobbits, well insulated pods which were designed to provide an upmarket alternative to camping. They came in both two and four bedded form and were equipped with TV, microwave, kettle, small fridge and an electric heater. It beats camping!

While I rested in my dormitory, I took stock of my journey to date. I had now completed 211 miles, which is exactly the distance from my home to Liverpool, a journey which I drive regularly. This perspective undoubtedly made it feel like a very long way on foot. My philosophy of taking each day at a time was paying off so far and it was satisfying to celebrate landmarks being achieved, but I wouldn't allow myself to contemplate the much greater proportion of the journey remaining. On the medical front, the swelling on my lower shin had eased considerably and the blister on my baby toe had reduced significantly, so I remained hopeful that I would be able to complete the West Highland Way, probably the most challenging part of my entire journey.

Day 13 – Kinlochleven to Inveroran

Distance: 18.4 miles
Cumulative distance: 229.4 miles
Weather: Sunny

A long and lonely day in the mountains

For the second time in a youth hostel, I had an uncomfortable night's rest. The mattress was too hard, the bed too narrow and, being in the top bunk (which was not very accessible for someone of my advancing years), I had an irrational fear of falling out and ending my journey in drama. I arose early, ate a hasty breakfast from my rucksack (fruit smoothie, instant porridge in a pot and a croissant) and set off at 7.45am, long before anyone else had arisen.

The path out of Kinlochleven involved a long and gradual climb out of the village, which transported me back into tough, uncompromising mountain terrain again. The track consisted of small, sharp rocks, so it was difficult to walk quickly, even where the path was not uphill. Progress was unsurprisingly slow and it took me two and a quarter hours to cover the first five miles, during which time I didn't meet another soul.

The path continued to climb and, eventually, the serpent-like Blackwater Reservoir came into view. Constructed by hand by a large team of navvies and measuring over 13 kilometres in length, this is the longest dam in the Highlands and was built to provide the electricity needed to operate the aluminium smelters at Kinlochleven. The navvies lived in a basic camp on the bleak moor and a number of them perished in serious weather conditions while returning there from the nearest pub at King's House.

Two cairns marked the summit, offering stunning views of the Glencoe mountain range. The descent to the valley was marked on my map as the 'Devil's Staircase', which sounded ominous. I pictured a steep, slippery, narrow stairway with a sheer drop on both sides. In fact, it was little more than a scree path which zigzagged gently down the mountain – what a disappointment! Here, I met three Cornishmen, who were walking the West Highland Way to raise funds for Motor Neurone disease. I naively remarked to one of them that it was a long way to drive from Cornwall to the Scottish Highlands, but he responded instantaneously, pointing at the sign on my rucksack, and highlighting that I was planning to cover an even greater distance and that it was much easier by road than on foot! I also met four Scousers, who wished me well with expected good humour.

The route then skirted the lower slopes of the magnificent Buachaille Etive Mor, a towering, photogenic pyramid of a mountain, which I'd climbed as a student in Glasgow exactly twenty years earlier. After a few miles I reached the King's House, believed to be one of Scotland's oldest licensed inns. Built in the 17th century, the building was used after the Battle of Culloden (1746) as a barracks for the troops of George III, hence the name King's House. It was their task to keep the

Highlanders under subjection and to capture the elusive Bonnie Prince Charlie.

The inn's history is colourful and varied. Dorothy Wordsworth, sister of William, wrote in 1803: "Never did I see such a miserable, such wretched place, – long rooms with ranges of beds, no other furniture except benches, or perhaps one or two crazy chairs, the floors far dirtier than an ordinary house could be if it were never washed. With length of time the fire was kindled and after another hour of waiting, supper came, a shoulder of mutton so hard that it was impossible to chew the little flesh that might have been scraped off the bones."

Although not influenced by Dorothy, I sought only liquid refreshment and enjoyed a thirst quenching pint of Coke before re-joining the path, which soon crossed the A82 road close to the Glencoe Outdoor Activities Centre and plotted a route across Rannoch Moor. My guide notes had described this as one of the most inhospitable places in Britain, especially in adverse weather conditions. Today, however, the sun gods were with me again and I was rewarded with impressive views of forbidding mountains circling the vast wasteland. I passed over fifty hikers but, as is now a familiar story, only a couple were following my route.

At the side of a stone bridge, I spotted a small plaque hidden in the nettles. It stated that the bridge had been repaired through funding from the Caledonian Challenge, a team event in which participants complete 54 miles in 24 hours along part of the West Highland Way. This was more than twice my daily mileage, 2 marathons back to back, with a vertical elevation equivalent to climbing Ben Nevis twice. I felt humbled in admiration of those who complete this demanding endurance event.

I finally arrived at my accommodation, the Inveroran Hotel,

situated on a minor road in the middle of nowhere. I'd been dreaming for some days of soaking in a hot bath at the end of a day's strenuous walk, but I was again to be disappointed and would have to make do with an invigorating shower instead.

I must have cut a lonely figure seated at my table for one at dinner. I'd already ordered my meal when two jolly ladies invited me to join them at their table (which completely confused the waiting staff when they delivered my food!). Jill and Trish were walking the West Highland Way in a more relaxed manner, with their luggage transported from one location to the next, leisurely start times and tea shops to be sampled (this is known as "spa walking" apparently!). They were good fun and showed much interest in my walk – they even offered me the use of their en suite bath! Jill told me that her son had recently been diagnosed and treated for a rare cancer, melanoma of the iris, but fortunately the treatment appeared to have been a success.

The hotel manager informed me that a number of deer come to feed at the hotel during the evening, rubbing their noses against the door to attract attention, so I asked her to call me if they appeared that night. An hour later, she apparently knocked on my bedroom door, but I was outside at the time and missed the evening's deer antics.

Day 14 – Inveroran to Crianlarich
Distance: 17.8 miles
Cumulative distance: 227.2 miles
Weather: Cloudy and damp
A low level valley walk, rain threatening, and an extension

The Inveroran Hotel has welcomed many famous guests over

the years, including Charles Dickens, Charles Darwin, Samuel Taylor Coleridge and Dorothy Wordsworth. Dorothy, who had been most critical of her accommodation and meal at the King's House, was clearly a difficult lady to please, as her comments confirm: "breakfast was brought and… it proved a disappointment: the butter not eatable, the barley cakes fusty, the oat bread so hard that I could not chew it, and there were only four eggs in the house, which they had boiled as hard as stone". Fortunately, I could not find any fault with my own breakfast, which would equip me well for another day's walking, but I concluded that Dorothy would probably fare well as a restaurant critic, were she alive today.

I checked out of the hotel, but the receptionist called me back. I wondered whether they had undercharged me for my dinner, but in fact the owners kindly wanted to make a donation to my cause. The hotel may be in the middle of nowhere, but it was extremely cosy and the staff very friendly.

The footpath climbed up over the hill and then descended into Bridge of Orchy, a tiny village which boasts a hotel, church and railway station, before following the valley down to Tyndrum, sandwiched between the road and the railway. Tyndrum is a small Highland settlement which boasts two railway stations. Even more bizarrely, you can catch a direct sleeper train from here to London!

I regularly spotted unusual birds on my walk and this day was no exception. I wished that one of my 'twitcher' friends had been here to help me identify them, as I've never been particularly adept at differentiating one species from another. I'd also read that red squirrels and even a golden eagle were frequent visitors to the area, but I'd spotted neither.

Beyond Tyndrum I came across a party of three people taking a short rest at the side of the path. They were from

Cambridge and Birmingham, but originally from South Africa, and were really interested in the journey I was undertaking. They kindly made a donation and also insisted on taking my photo before I left them behind.

Throughout the day the air felt damp and, occasionally, a few drops of rain appeared on my waterproof map cover, but nothing merited removing my waterproofs from the rucksack pocket they had been secured in for two weeks by now!

Near to the end of my scheduled daily route, I made a momentous decision to extend the day's walk. This was not madness – I had my reasons. Firstly, it was mid-afternoon and I still felt reasonably fresh. Secondly, my destination of Crianlarich was not directly on the West Highland Way, so heading down into the village now would result in an uphill reverse trip to re-join the path next day. Thirdly, and most significantly, I'd been advised that parts of the next day's walk would be quite tricky, involving clambering over slippery rocks near to the banks of Loch Lomond. So I figured that walking a few extra miles now would help to make tomorrow's walk easier. I eventually walked three additional miles and left the footpath close to the A82, so that I could hitch a lift back to Crianlarich. Although I hadn't thumbed a ride since I was a student in the Eighties, the magic thumb still worked, as within two minutes a car pulled over. The driver was heading to catch the ferry back home to South Uist, after going to see Bruce Springsteen play a concert in Glasgow. He deposited me right at the front door of the Crianlarich Hotel, my base for the evening.

My comfortable room overlooked the main road and the railway, with lofty mountains in the distance. The only disappointment was that, yet again, I had to manage with a shower, rather than a bath. The shower turned out to be an even bigger let down. It resembled a large plastic unit which had been slotted into an alcove in the bathroom, but suffered from three fundamental faults. The shower head could not be attached to the wall of the unit, but in any case it produced only a tiny trickle of water. To compound matters further, the water would not drain out of the shower base unit. I reluctantly admitted defeat and resorted to giving myself as thorough a wash as I could manage in the wash basin.

Dinner at the Crianlarich Hotel was a mainly Scottish and distinctly fishy selection – Cullen Skink (a rich creamy soup of smoked haddock and potato), haddock and chips, and an impressive cheeseboard selection (Blue Monday, Mull Cheddar and Morangie Brie) with oatcakes and quince, washed down with Colonsay bitter. I had convinced myself that this fine dining was an important way of returning the calories that I had been burning so aggressively during my walking day.

I had become accustomed to taking a short wander around the local area after my meal each evening, as this was often the only opportunity I had of being a tourist for a few minutes and it gave me a brief chance to explore my destination. I really wanted to avoid spending a night in an interesting village or town, only to have to admit later that the only landmark I'd seen or visited was the accommodation itself. As I returned from my leisurely amble down the short main street in Crianlarich at around 9pm, three middle-aged women carrying weighty backpacks appeared from a side road and asked for directions to the hotel. They had been walking all day from Rowardennan and looked completely exhausted. This would be my destination for the following day, but fortunately the additional mileage I'd covered today had at least reduced the original distance by three miles.

From my bedroom window, I watched the night sleeper train glide gracefully into Crianlarich station, collect a handful of passengers, and head off London-bound into the fading light minutes later. Did part of me wish that I too was speeding south through the night, to wake in the big city in the morning? No way!

Day 15 – Crianlarich to Rowardennan
Distance: 16.8 miles
Cumulative distance: 264.0 miles
Weather: Sunny

Slow progress along a challenging path, then arrival in paradise

I checked out of the hotel, which was excellent apart from the dodgy shower, somewhat out of keeping with the rest of the facilities. Now I had to find a means of being transported some 3 miles further south to re-join the West Highland Way. The Glasgow-bound bus immediately arrived at the stop right opposite the hotel entrance, but the "jobsworth" driver explained that he wasn't allowed to drop me off before the next scheduled stop, which was at least 6 miles away. Temporarily defeated, I set off walking in the right direction and waited for a lift. Crianlarich certainly wasn't going to trouble the road traffic reporters during the 8.30am rush hour – in fact it was so quiet that a family of hedgehogs could have safely crossed the road and returned without being flattened. Fortunately, after about ten minutes, a delivery van driver responded to my outstretched arm and drove southwards. En route, we skirted the new Crianlarich bypass, which was being constructed to tackle the delays experienced by road users during the busy tourist season – it was due to be completed within a year. My chauffeur kindly dropped me off right at the spot where I had left the route the previous day.

The footpath followed the river, where there were several small waterfalls. A little further on, once the path had climbed away from the river, the impressive Falls of Falloch could just be glimpsed through the birches ahead and soon afterwards the route passed a narrow section of river where the water had worn great circles into the rocks.

Close to the Drover's Inn, the path turned away from the river and climbed gently to Dubh Lochan and I soon had my first view of Loch Lomond. For the next five miles, the narrow rocky path clung precariously to the wooded hillside just metres from the loch itself. Ancient trees with gnarled roots consumed the pathway and hefty boulders frequently blocked the direct route. Progress was really laboured as it was necessary to use hands to clamber over the rocks and roots, and I had to concentrate on every step to ensure that I didn't lose my balance. This part of the route was every bit as slow and hazardous as I'd been advised, but at least it was dry, so the rocks weren't slippery.

I stopped for a snack from my bag of provisions at a beautiful secluded beach at the edge of the loch, one of the most scenic pit stops I had experienced during my journey. This was a momentary reward for conquering the challenges of the loch-side path.

There was time to chat to a few approaching walkers along the way. A lady from Inverness recalled the long hot summer of 1976 and two men from Seattle waxed lyrical about the magnificent scenery. I also engaged in conversation with two oil rig workers from Edinburgh and Essex, who were walking the West Highland Way to raise funds for the Alzheimer's Society.

I stopped for a refreshing pint of iced Coke at the Inversnaid Hotel, located on Loch Lomond and with its own jetty and harbour. This was another hotel which was seemingly inaccessible by road, but in fact there is a minor road which links it to Aberfoyle, some 15 miles distant. As I sat outside on a bench admiring the view of the loch and the hills beyond, a fellow walker hobbled towards the neighbouring table and duly removed her boots and socks, revealing a painful collection of blisters.

The path continued along a densely forested area below the slopes of Ben Lomond, the most southerly of the Scottish Munros. Its spectacular views and close proximity to Glasgow make it one of the most climbed hills in Scotland.

I finally arrived at my next accommodation, an impressive country house, positioned in substantial tree-lined gardens on the banks of Loch Lomond. My room was spacious, so I was able to carefully empty out the entire contents of my rucksack. After a refreshing hot shower, I basked in the early evening sunshine next to the loch, before heading to the restaurant. Dinner was corn, coconut and red pepper soup, spinach and ricotta cannelloni, and tiramisu ice cream cake. Afterwards, I relaxed on a comfortable sofa in the library and savoured a pint of Bonnie N' Bitter from Loch Lomond brewery, whilst enjoying the stunning vista across the loch.

Remarkably, this was not an upmarket country house hotel. Amazingly, this was another youth hostel. But this was no ordinary youth hostel, this was Rowardennan, this was paradise!

Throughout my journey so far, I had maintained contact with my family at home through a daily phone call, except on the rare occasions when no signal had been available. This was often in the form of a Skype video call, which enabled my family to gather around a computer screen, while I would be located in or around my accommodation. At first, the call focused on where I had been walking that day and news from the family, but my children inevitably became less interested in my daily updates and more occupied in seeing the layout of my bedroom or the views from the window. My video call from Rowardennan undoubtedly provided some of the best views to date.

In addition to the daily phone call, my daughter Hannah had instructed me to send her a daily text, to be received on weekdays by the time she left school each afternoon. This seemingly simple task was more challenging to deliver than I had imagined, as it firstly relied on me remembering to send the text at the right time each day and, secondly, it required a signal to be available at the critical moment. Fortunately, I had just about managed to keep the texts going.

Day 16 – Rowardennan to Drymen
Distance: 15.1 miles
Cumulative distance: 279.1 miles
Weather: Rain showers, sunny later

RAIN, a steep hill and an early arrival

My waterproof jacket and trousers may have been waiting for sixteen days to make their debuts, but when called into action, they were ready to serve. The showers had been forecasted for a few days, so it was no surprise when the heavens opened late on Friday night.

I checked out of Paradise Hostel and followed a path along the shores of Loch Lomond. The rain was light and it was not too unpleasant walking in it. My waterproof rucksack cover was also being employed for the first time, but this brought with it an added inconvenience – I couldn't reach for my water bottle without stopping to remove the cover.

Approaching Balmaha, I spotted a newly born Highland calf with its mother. Neither seemed to object to having their photo taken. Highlands are known as a hardy breed due to the rugged nature of their native Scottish Highlands, with high rainfall and very strong winds. Their hair gives protection during the cold winters and their skill in looking for food allows them to survive in steep mountainous areas. An elderly couple on the footpath dutifully informed me that a group of Highland cattle is known as a fold, rather than a herd.

Balmaha sits on the eastern shores of Loch Lomond and is a popular tourist destination for day trippers from Glasgow, as well as walkers on the West Highland Way. There were regular boat trips from the jetty to the villages of Balloch and Luss on the opposite shore, as well as to nearby Inchcailloch Island, a "magical island steeped in history and a haven for wildlife" according to the notice I spotted.

After an iced Coke at the local pub, I had a difficult decision to make. The West Highland Way route offers an alternative here – to climb up Conic Hill or to continue along the road. It was wet, there was low cloud around and a shorter low level route seemed attractive, but masochistically I opted instead to climb the hill. Conic Hill is on the Highland geological fault line which separates the mountains of Northern Scotland from the lowlands of the South. The climb was steep, but the views across Loch Lomond, its many islands, and beyond in all directions were splendid. A further reward was that the rain ceased.

The path continued through forest plantations on my map, but through a felled wasteland in reality. This dramatic change in the landscape made navigation a challenge, especially with official signposts at a premium. I decided to take a detour from the route to go directly to my B&B, before heading into Drymen village centre for food later.

The Green Shadows B&B was stunningly situated amid the peaceful and beautifully forested surroundings of the estate of Buchanan Castle, overlooking the golf club, just over a mile from the village of Drymen. Due to the lack of a Wi-Fi signal, I hadn't checked the opening time for the B&B, so when I arrived on the doorstep at 3.10pm I wasn't sure what to expect. It transpired that the official opening time was 4 o'clock but Gail, the owner, kindly welcomed me in and showed me to my room. After the rain, it was a delight to have a hot shower and to dry out my damp clothes.

The Clachan Inn, the oldest registered licensed pub in Scotland (1734) was recommended for my evening meal. I set off to walk there, but I couldn't find the footpath across the fields, which had been indicated when I had stopped to ask for directions at a stables en route. I soon became lost and had to resort to walking across a stream, climbing up a steep bank and tiptoeing through deep mud. It was quite a relief when I finally reached the pub and, although the restaurant was full, they managed to find me a small table in the bar. The food (king prawn, salmon and monkfish kebabs) from the daily specials board and drink (Sheepshaggers Gold Ale from Cairngorm Brewery) were well worth the adventure. Gail kindly came to chauffeur me back from the village to the B&B.

Day 17 – Drymen to Glasgow
Distance: 20.7 miles
Cumulative distance: 299.8 miles
Weather: Cloudy

End of the West Highland Way and a warm welcome to Glasgow

I breakfasted with a young Spanish couple from Valencia. David and Maria had come to the UK to seek better employment prospects, but were touring in Scotland for a couple of days. They kindly offered to drive me to the village to re-join my route. I checked out of the delightful B&B and Gail (otherwise known as Lisa) made a generous donation to the cause.

Drymen, which means 'on the ridge', is located about twenty miles to the north west of Glasgow. Despite the growth in the numbers of villagers commuting to Glasgow for work, there remains a strong agricultural tradition in the area, culminating in the annual Drymen Show. Unfortunately, the previous year's show had to be cancelled just days before the event, due to a failure to remove livestock from the show field within the recommended period of four weeks beforehand. The show planned for May this year had also been cancelled because the show field was too wet after months of persistent rain, but the event was now being re-scheduled to another venue in August.

The final 12 miles of the West Highland Way passed along country lanes and a disused railway line. The highlight was an "honesty shop" outside a house in a small hamlet, which offered cold cans of drink, chocolate bars and ice creams, housed in a small display refrigerator. All items were £1 and the cash box was situated on one of the shelves. It was most heartening to see such a trusting approach to commerce.

For the last few miles the route was busy, with a parade of walkers passing me from the familiar opposite direction. One man even asked me why I was walking in the wrong direction! The people varied from rucksack-laden long distance walkers who had just started their West Highland journey, to large numbers of Sunday morning walkers of all ages, ranging from lone hikers, couples, families and organised groups. Many were revelling in their weekly chance to escape the rat race by heading for the hills, but some appeared to be reluctant participants, dragged out of their homes to join the rest of the family for a dose of unwanted fresh air.

The West Highland Way ended suddenly in the centre of Milngavie (pronounced 'mul-guy'), a town situated about 8 miles north of Glasgow. A small monument, a couple of ornate benches and some decorative lettering marked the start of the route, or my finish. There were no flags, no welcome party, but just a few Sunday morning shoppers carrying their well-stocked Iceland bags. I managed to persuade a suited elderly gentleman to take my photograph standing next to the official obelisk, but it was evident that he was not familiar with the workings of a smartphone camera and almost succeeded in missing me from the photo entirely!

I had really enjoyed walking the West Highland Way and would recommend it to anybody considering undertaking a varied and challenging long distance walk for a week. The route covers a rich tapestry of topography, from country lanes to wooded glens, from forest tracks to loch shores, and from barren moorland to mountain footpaths. I was delighted that I had included it in my JOGLE itinerary, despite the additional physical efforts involved and I mentally ticked a large box to mark its completion.

My route into Glasgow initially followed the A81 road through the suburbs of Hillfoot and Acre. After days in the mountains and glens it took me a while to adjust to the constant stream of traffic, the endless rows of houses and the unattractive appearance of small estates of light industry. At Maryhill I was able to escape the clutches of the city access roads, joining instead a delightful footpath alongside the River Kelvin. Here was an oasis of calm in a busy city, lush and green, a hidden gem. On the summer Sunday afternoon of my arrival, the paths and parkland areas were alive with families, students, joggers, dog walkers, and cyclists. The paths were remarkably well signposted, with directions to local stations and city streets, clearly part of a wider strategy to integrate the walkways with transport links and to encourage walking and cycling.

A mile or so across the nearby River Clyde stood Ibrox Stadium, the home of Rangers Football Club. The club shares an intense rivalry with Glasgow neighbours Celtic, but Rangers have won more league titles than any other club in the world. However, in 2012 the parent company became insolvent and entered administration, resulting in liquidation. The business was purchased by a new company, but the Rangers football team was forced to re-join the league from the lowest division.

The Ibrox Stadium was the scene of tragedy on three separate occasions. In 1902, during a match between Scotland and England, the rear of one of the stands collapsed after heavy rainfall, resulting in 25 deaths and 517 injuries. In September 1961, two supporters were killed when a barrier collapsed on one of the stairways, but the worst disaster took place in January 1971, near to the end of the traditional New Year match between Rangers and Celtic, watched by a crowd of 80,000 spectators. As fans were starting to exit from the steep terracing, some stumbled on the steps and their momentum caused a tidal wave of supporters to descend and the steel barriers to crumple under the impact.

In total, 66 people were crushed to death and more than 200 were injured. The Government ordered a detailed review of safety at all British football grounds and the subsequent recommendations were enshrined in the Safety of Sports Grounds Act of 1975. Ten years after the disaster, Ibrox was transformed into a safe and modern stadium, but with a much reduced capacity of 44,000.

The crowds were lining the streets and clapping as I walked into Glasgow city centre, which was most uplifting. Sadly it wasn't for me, but instead for the participants in the British National Road Race Championship cycle race, which was taking place around the city streets. It was fascinating to witness the speeds the riders achieved, even on the uphill sections of the route. The cyclists sped past in a blur, much too fast to be identified, but I discovered later that the race had included the GB Olympic heroes Mark Cavendish, Laura Trott and Lizzie Armitstead (who would go on to win the road race gold medal at the Commonwealth Games in Glasgow a year later).

Having lived in Glasgow for a year, some twenty years ago, this was like a homecoming for me. The welcoming crowds reminded me of a previous arrival during that era at Glasgow Airport. My flight from London had landed and I headed innocuously towards the arrivals lounge, only to be greeted by hundreds of screaming girls. It transpired that I was walking alongside the members of boy band Take That, who were performing in the city as part of their first concert tour!

My weary legs ambled up the hilly city streets and I finally located the Buchanan Galleries Premier Inn, my city centre base for the next two days. My room was located on the 18th floor, with impressive views over the city and beyond. But what I appreciated most of all was something that I'd dreamed about since Inverness – a hot bath!

Glasgow is Scotland's largest city and is renowned for its culture. Described as vibrant, energetic and stylish, the city has regularly attracted high-profile exhibitions and cutting-edge productions and, supported by its strong architectural heritage, was crowned as European City of Culture in 1990. It was recently named as the number one UK destination "on the rise" by the travel website, Trip Advisor.

Glasgow developed from a small settlement on the River Clyde to become one of the largest seaports in the world. From the eighteenth century, the city was one of Britain's main hubs of transatlantic trade with North America and the West Indies. During the Industrial Revolution, the population and economy of Glasgow expanded rapidly due to chemicals, textiles and engineering. The city was renowned for its shipbuilding and marine engineering industry and, in places such as Bowling Harbour, Denny's Shipyard in Dumbarton, John Brown's Shipyard at Clydebank and Govan Graving Docks, shipbuilding became a major source of commerce for Glasgow. George Bradshaw commented on the city's industry in 1866 and concluded that "the commercial activity and restlessness of its inhabitants have caused the immense impulse its trade has received in the last fifty years."

The city had become yet more cosmopolitan since my time as a resident back in the Nineties. Even at four o'clock on Sunday afternoon, the streets were bustling with shoppers and tourists from all corners of the globe. There were also more bars and restaurants than I recalled and everybody seemed intent on enjoying themselves.

After dining at a Pizza Express restaurant in the elegant Princes Square shopping centre, I ambled through the pedestrianised streets and headed back to the 18th floor.

CHAPTER THREE
Crossing the border to Carlisle

Day 18 – Glasgow to Hamilton
Distance: 11.0 miles
Cumulative distance: 310.8 miles
Weather: Sunny

A leisurely morning, a short walk through suburbia and a train back to Glasgow

I enjoyed a later start and a leisurely breakfast, then left my 18th floor apartment to go shopping for a few essentials in neighbouring Sauchiehall Street, one of the most famous streets in Glasgow and rich in history.

The Glasgow Empire Theatre was once located here, notorious within show business circles as "The English comic's grave". Bob Monkhouse, Tommy Cooper, and Morecambe and Wise all suffered here, while Des O'Connor apparently pretended to faint when the Glasgow audience started to jeer his act and was promptly dragged off stage. On the other hand, top American performers were welcomed heartily, including Frank Sinatra, Bob Hope, Tony Bennett, Judy Garland, Laurel and Hardy, Eartha Kitt, Danny Kaye and Jack Benny. After its heyday, variety theatre's popularity gradually declined, as television entertainment at home developed and rock 'n' roll took a stranglehold of the music scene. This eventually took its toll on the theatre and the Empire closed in 1963.

In 1849, at the nearby Theatre Royal in Dunlop Street, a false fire alarm caused a disastrous panic in the audience, resulting in the death of 65 people in the ensuing crush. Shortly after the Saturday evening performance had commenced, an alarm was given that a fire had broken out in the upper gallery. The theatre manager quickly realised that the fire had been caused by an explosion of gas, and it was quickly extinguished. However, the arrival of the fire brigade had the effect of increasing the fears of the audience, leading to a general rush towards the exit doors. A contemporary report noted that "without scarcely a single exception the sufferers belong to the lower class of society, and are for the most part lads between 14 and 17 years old".

I needed to purchase some glue to repair the protective toe cap lining on one of my boots, so I ventured into the Poundland store just around the corner from my hotel. Four pots of super glue for £1 was a bargain, even if I ended up carrying them all the way to Carlisle, where my next exchange of kit was scheduled to take place. I tried without success to locate a light elasticated belt for my walking trousers. With my pockets laden with wallet, camera, and mobile phone and, having undoubtedly shed a few pounds in weight during 400 miles of walking, I'd found that my trousers were constantly slipping down during the day! In the end, Poundland came to the rescue again, although it was more of a standard belt. Unfortunately, even the tightest notch on the small size belt was too loose to make a difference, so some careful scissor work back in my hotel room was required to make the belt effective.

By this time, I had decided to bring forward part of the next day's walk, thereby earning myself yet another leisurely morning. This approach had worked well for me in Crianlarich, so I was happy to repeat it. I set off mid-morning along the River Clyde walkway in fine sunshine and found myself being overtaken by small groups of joggers at regular intervals. I followed the river for several miles, then exited at Dalmarnock and joined the A724 road which led me through the Glasgow suburbs of Cambuslang and Cairns, towards Hamilton.

At Blantyre (birthplace of David Livingstone exactly 200 years ago), a car pulled up alongside me. Eight year old Carragh had spotted me after her mum had collected her from school and she really kindly decided to donate her pocket money to Cancer Research UK. That was a grand gesture!

The Blantyre mining disaster, which happened in October 1877, remains Scotland's worst mining accident. An explosion in two pits at William Dixon's Blantyre Colliery killed 207 miners, the youngest being a boy of 11. It was known that firedamp was present in the pit and it is probable that this was ignited by a naked flame. At the time, rescue provisions were inadequate and previous complaints about the working conditions had been ignored. In fact, a year earlier, Blantyre miners had been so fearful for their safety in the mines, that they went on strike when Dixon's refused them a compensatory wage rise. The miners were immediately sacked.

Unfortunately, safety lessons were not learnt after the disaster and, just months later, six men were killed when the cage they were in overturned, throwing them to the bottom of the 900 feet pit. Then, the following year, there was a second explosion at one of the pits, with the loss of 28 lives.

A few miles further into my day's route, Scotland's second worst coal mining disaster took place at Udston Colliery in 1887. 73 miners died in a massive firedamp explosion, which was thought to have been caused by unauthorised shot firing.

At Hamilton West, after walking for 11 miles, I caught the train back into Glasgow. It felt strange playing the role of commuter in the big city after nearly three weeks in the Scottish outback, but I was conscious that this would only be a temporary release from my rural existence.

I wandered up the hill to re-visit the University, where I had studied for my MBA some twenty years earlier. The Business School had been relocated to a palatial new building and I could find no evidence of the original building, so I concluded that it must have been demolished, along with a number of neighbouring buildings which also appeared to be missing. Or perhaps my memory was just playing tricks many years afterwards!

After eating at another Pizza Express restaurant, I briefly visited The Counting House, the flagship JD Wetherspoon pub in Scotland. As the name implies, it was once a bank, owned by the Bank of Scotland. The building was designed for the bank in the 1860s in the Italian Renaissance style, which set the tone for the west end of neighbouring George Square. Inside the building there is an impressive ornate ceiling decoration and an equally impressive range of cask beers, which numbered eighteen at the time of my visit. For the beer aficionados, I had a pint of Flying Scotsman from the Caledonian brewery.

I just had time to pay my respects to George Square, one of my favourite locations in the city centre. The elegant square, named after George III, is dominated by Glasgow City

Chambers and contains twelve statues (eleven men and one woman), including Queen Victoria, Prince Albert, Sir Walter Scott (who is perched on top of an eighty foot column above the Cenotaph), Robbie Burns and James Watt. When I visited, the square was being refurbished in readiness for the 2014 Commonwealth Games, which would be held in the city. However, George Square had been the subject of major controversy a few months earlier.

The City Council had announced a competition to redevelop the square in preparation for the Commonwealth Games, while also encouraging a design that could be used as public space. Six entrants were short-listed to develop designs to present to the jury. The competition prompt called for a removal of all but one of the statues and a design that included seating, greenery, water installations and pop-up cafes. As part of the review process, the public was consulted to review the six submissions, but they were strongly opposed to the water installations and preferred more green space. The jury reviewed the submissions and the winning design was announced, but within minutes, the leader of the Glasgow City Council, Gordon Matheson, announced that his administration would not proceed with the redesign after all, and the square would be given a "facelift" instead. His press release declared: "The people of Glasgow have made it clear that they do not want a radical redesign – I am proud that I am listening to them." Another councillor commented "It's like Carry On Council sometimes. You couldn't make it up."

I strolled across the square as the sun was setting and returned to my base on the 18th floor.

Day 19 – Hamilton to Larkhall

Distance: 6.6 miles
Cumulative distance: 317.4 miles
Weather: Cloudy, sunny intervals

Another leisurely morning, another train ride and another short walk

After another relaxing morning (I was beginning to get used to them!), I checked out of my 18th floor apartment at the Premier Inn and strolled down the hill to Glasgow Central station.

I had enough time to explore the station and its impressive concourse, which I'd commuted to on a daily basis during my year in Glasgow, before I boarded my local train back to Hamilton from the low level platform.

Having covered most of the original distance during my rest day, today's journey had been reduced to a short afternoon stroll and I almost felt guilty for undertaking such a condensed walk. I left the bustle of Hamilton behind and entered a pleasant, rural area close to Chatelherault Country Park. Before long I had arrived at Larkhall, a commuter town and terminus on the railway line. The main road was lined with shops, but it didn't portray itself as a prosperous town.

For some years, Scotland, and Glasgow in particular, have been tagged the "sick man of Europe" as a result of the unhealthy physical condition of its citizens relative to most of their European counterparts. Mortality rates in the working age population are comparatively high and, for circulatory diseases and many cancer related diseases, are higher than in most other Western European countries. Scottish deaths from chronic liver disease are among the highest in Europe, with only Hungary having a worse record, and mortality rates are almost 70% higher than the average across the UK.

A range of recent reports provided data which highlighted some of the underlying issues, for example:

- A quarter of men and almost one fifth of women in Scotland drank at levels considered "hazardous".
- 22.2 % of adults smoke in Scotland, compared to 19.5% in England.
- According to a BBC survey, Scotland is second only to the US in the obesity league table, with two-thirds of adults overweight or obese.
- According to new government research, Scottish people consume more fizzy drinks and sweets, and eat less fruit and vegetables when compared to the UK average.
- More than half of Scots rely on ready meals or takeaways at least three times a week.

To many, the symbol of all that is wrong with the high-fat, high-sugar Scottish diet is the deep-fried Mars bar. The snack is said to have originated about twenty years ago in a fish and chip shop in Stonehaven, Aberdeenshire, but is now widely available in Scottish chip shops. As one reporter commented, "The deep fried Mars bar might as well be a deep fried nuclear bomb."

Here in Larkhall, I witnessed at closer quarters some of the behaviours and consequences which had been identified in the reports. It was lunchtime and there were lengthy queues outside most of the chip shops and takeaway cafes. On the streets, I observed an unusually high proportion of smokers amongst the shoppers. But, try as I did, I couldn't find anybody consuming a deep-fried Mars bar.

I eventually located a bench seat on the pavement just outside of the town and settled down to consume my lunch (a healthy ploughman's on wholemeal bread, followed by a cereal bar and fresh fruit!). Free entertainment was provided by two workmen, who were trying to remove the bunting from the streetlights using a hydraulic lift. It was comical – they were completely uncoordinated and, judging by their industrial language, clearly didn't have any respect for each other. The bunting frequently fell into the road and on one occasion became attached to a passing vehicle, as the younger worker chatted on his mobile phone, oblivious to the danger he was causing. A health and safety officer would have had a field day.

After lunch I caught up on my emails, texts and blog messages. Various friends and colleagues had regularly sent me a few brief words of support throughout my walk to date and probably didn't realise how much I valued their kindness. These messages helped to reconnect me to the world I'd left behind temporarily. I'd especially appreciated the messages I'd received during the first few lonely days in Scotland and the difficult days when I was troubled by my blister, and found them to be really inspiring – they undoubtedly helped to keep my spirits high.

I arrived an hour early at my B&B, an old school building, which was situated very conveniently for the neighbouring M74 motorway junction. Fortunately it was already open for guests, so I didn't need to wait outside. While I was enjoying a refreshing drink in the reception coffee bar, I observed a regular flow of vehicles pulling into the car park. One passenger would then spring out of the car and hurry towards reception. It soon became apparent what they were up to. They were fans of Robbie Williams, on their way to the Hampden Park concert venue, but desperately searching for a bed for after the performance. The receptionist politely and consistently informed each of them that the B&B was fully booked and that there was no other accommodation in the vicinity. Recalling back in January, when I'd discovered that Robbie's visit to Glasgow coincided with my arrival in the city, I was grateful that I'd booked my accommodation well in advance.

I was soon installed in my spacious room, which offered a free view and live sound effects of the very closely situated M74 motorway. As the B&B offered no evening meal, the only dining option involved a half mile walk to a local hotel and restaurant, which had changed hands recently and been extensively refurbished. The feedback reviews I'd read were favourable, but a few referred to the poor quality of food and service under the previous management. Fortunately my meal was enjoyable and I was well attended to by an oversupply of waitresses.

My call to home brought good news on the athletics front. My son Daniel and daughter Hannah had won their 100m and 600m races respectively at the School Sports' Day. Future long distance walking material, clearly!

Day 20 – Larkhall to Abington
Distance: 20.7 miles
Cumulative distance: 338.1 miles
Weather: Sunny

A brisk walk along deserted roads, surrounded by wind turbines

After yet another night at welcoming, clean and well equipped accommodation, I set out early in bright sunshine into the Lanarkshire countryside.

I was immediately alerted to the number of wind turbines within my line of sight, from single ones within a gust of wind from the B&B, to entire farms of them on the near horizon. Today wasn't particularly windy, but no doubt there are many more days when it blows strongly.

A recent report had highlighted that Scotland's onshore wind generating capacity was 84 per cent higher than the total for England, Wales and Northern Ireland combined. Scotland had been advancing wind farm development at a rapid pace and, at the time of my walk, had over two thousand operational turbines onshore, with a further four hundred under construction and consent granted for a further one thousand.

One of my bugbears on the walk was the amount of debris which littered the roadside, especially on the main roads. I'd noticed it on some of my training walks back home, particularly around Heathrow Airport, but it was more conspicuous south of Glasgow than on other roads I'd encountered. The litter included drinks cans, plastic drinks bottles, cigarette packets, fast food containers, sandwich packages, crisp packets and, more bizarrely, protective gloves. Where did it all originate from? Who was responsible for it? Why did they do it? I was not the only person to be concerned. A campaign group call Zero Waste Scotland had undertaken a study and reported that an average of seven bottles and cans can be found along every 100 metres of major roads. They were planning a Litter Week of Action in August, raising awareness of the problem with the snappy slogan "Flingin's Mingin' – Drive Your Carbage Home".

One of the items I had regularly identified at the roadside was an empty plastic Coke bottle bearing somebody's first name. A few months previously, Coca Cola had launched their summer marketing campaign by swapping the iconic logo on their bottles with 250 of the most popular first names in Britain (a similar campaign in South Africa used 600 names, apparently). During my walk, I had started to develop a practice of drinking iced Coke, in part because it was a refreshing drink, but also because it provided a brief 'sugar fix' to replace the calories I was burning. On the increasing number of occasions when I was walking along a road and in desperate need of a drink, I would dream of my own personalised bottle of iced Coke waiting for me at the roadside. Sadly, my first name didn't feature in the initial list of 150 British names, but it did appear in the subsequent list of 100 names which were added. Despite this, I hadn't yet spotted one bearing the name 'Russell', so my dream was destined to remain a dream.

After a few miles, the road ahead was closed to traffic due to resurfacing work (or maybe it was really to clear the intrusive roadside litter). The car's pain was my gain and for two miles I had the entire road to myself, as the tarmac gangs had not yet started for the day. This solitude was, however, only a taster for the rest of the day's walk. Most of the 'B' road I was journeying on was previously the main route between Glasgow and Carlisle, until the motorway was later constructed less than a mile away. The dual carriageway main road was then downgraded to become a 'B' road, with one carriageway used by the occasional farm vehicle or local motorist and the other dedicated as a cycle path. As a consequence, I had my own personal road on what must surely be the quietest dual carriageway in Britain.

I had planned to stop for a drink at one of the only refreshment opportunities on the route, but unfortunately the bar/ restaurant was closed on my arrival and wouldn't be open for another three hours. I had no option but to continue stoically towards my destination.

At the roundabout junction where the 'B' road crossed over the motorway, I was bemused to see a large traffic sign which commanded 'Drive on the left', with the same message translated below into German, Italian, French and Spanish, alongside their respective flags. The sign appeared to be completely superfluous in this remote area of Scotland and I struggled to rationalise its existence. However, it does remind me of the news reported by The Guardian newspaper, that the Scottish National Party was planning to switch to driving on the right hand side of the road if the country voted in favour of independence. The giveaway was that the article was published on 1st April!

With perfect walking conditions on deserted roads and only a five minute snack break, I arrived at the village of Abington much earlier than anticipated. In addition to the motorway services and a general stores, it was home to the Abington Hotel, my base for the night. After another early check-in courtesy of welcoming hotel staff, within minutes I'd finished my iced Coke and was soaking in a hot, refreshing bath again.

The hotel boasted a chair that supposedly had been sat on by Prince Louis Napoleon, French Emperor to be, when he spent the night at the Abington Coaching Inn in 1839, having travelled by stage coach on the hazardous Carlisle to Glasgow route, after a wet and tiring day of grouse shooting on the nearby moors. No sitting rock was available for him, so he took supper beside the kitchen fire before retiring to bed. He left on foot early next morning on his way to the Eglington Tournament in Edinburgh.

Unlike Napoleon, I was fortunate enough to be seated in a comfortable dining chair at my dinner table in the hotel restaurant, but grouse wasn't on the menu.

Day 21 – Abington to Beattock
Distance: 20.1 miles
Cumulative distance: 358.2 miles
Weather: Rain

RAIN! Waterproofs on, head down, feet forward. A day of endurance.

I checked out of another friendly hotel and the management kindly made a donation to the cause.

I hoped that I would escape lightly with the promised rain, but after a mile it soon became apparent that this would not be the case. Out came my waterproofs for their second appearance in three weeks, but this would prove to be more challenging for them as the rain was sustained.

After a few miles on the road, I noticed that my maps were becoming soggy and, on closer inspection, discovered that my plastic map cover had split, allowing the rain to penetrate. Fortunately, today's routing was quite straightforward and didn't really require much cartographic assistance, but I would need to invest in a replacement cover before too long.

I knew from my route planning that this was not a particularly inspiring day's walking, so I could let my mind drift and keep stepping closer to my destination, trying to be oblivious to the rain. For the entire day's walk, my companions on the quiet 'B' road were the A74 (M) motorway, the Glasgow to Carlisle West Coast railway line, and the fledgling River Clyde, with occasional exchanges of position as we progressed along the heavily forested and wind turbine lined Clyde Valley.

The valley twisted and turned serpent-like as it plotted a route around the surrounding hills, a relentless series of gentle peaks which furtively sidled closer to the valley's ascending arteries, as if attempting to strangle the valley itself. Each peak bore a name which hinted at a secret past but, as they lined up in procession up the valley, they were more reminiscent of the starting field for the Grand National – Castle Hill, Craig Dod, Kirkton Rig, Ellershie Hill, Coupland Hill, Wellshot Hill, Harryburn Brae, Bodsberry Hill, Watchman Hill, Cow Hill, Fall Kneesend, Hill End, Ring Hill, Nap Hill, Williemont Hass, Bidhouse Knowe, Horse Pow Hill, Tinny Bank, Whiteside Hill, Urchin Knowe, Wee Dod, Greenhill Dod, Campland Hill, Archie's Hill, Mosshope Bank, Bught Knowe, Blacklaw Hill, Coats Hill, and finally Beattock Hill.

By now, I had entered Dumfries and Galloway, which formerly consisted of three counties, Dumfriesshire, Kirkcudbrightshire and Wigtownshire. This would be my final Scottish county or region, before crossing over the border into Cumbria in England.

Having experienced the mighty River Clyde in Glasgow, I was now close to its very source. The river originates from two streams, Potrail Water and Daer Water, which join forces at the unimaginatively named Watermeetings. From here the Clyde deviates in a north-easterly direction towards Biggar, before taking a sharp turn towards the west on its frustratingly circuitous 106 mile journey towards Glasgow, where it eventually flows into the Firth of Clyde near to the town of Helensburgh.

A mile or so before my bed and breakfast destination, I reached the small village of Beattock, my first sight of civilisation during the entire day. For no particular reason, I'd expected Beattock to be a sizeable town, where I could seek shelter from the drizzly rain at a selection of coffee bars. Unfortunately, it was what you might describe as a "one horse town", but it did at least offer the Old Stables Inn and Restaurant, where I sought refuge in the bar. With a couple of hours to kill, I laid out my rain-sodden waterproofs and multiple sheets of damp mapping across the table and neighbouring chairs, then ordered a toasted ham sandwich and several pots of coffee. In another corner of the bar, frustratingly just beyond my field of vision, a large television screen provided live coverage of tennis from Wimbledon, which the landlady watched avidly. They were evidently enjoying more favourable weather in the SW19 district of London. My maps were still damp when it was time to leave, but at least I was somewhat drier.

As I walked up the tree-lined driveway of my B&B, a delightful country house set in five acres of gardens and woodlands, Sally the owner and her young daughter Samantha came walking towards me. Sally announced that they had just locked themselves out of their house and were heading to a neighbour's to collect the spare key. Ten minutes later they returned without the key – the neighbour was unexpectedly out. There was no alternative but to fetch the ladders and, as I supported the base at ground level, Sally climbed upstairs and squeezed in through my open bedroom window. I couldn't have made it up!

After the drama, Sally kindly provided tea and homemade biscuits, and apologised profusely for locking me out. I was soon ensconced in my bedroom, where it was gratifying to soak in another hot bath, but even more rewarding to be able to turn on the two radiators and the heated towel rail (despite it being June!) and dry out my damp clothes and maps.

I decided not to venture back into Beattock for an evening meal, mainly due to the continued driving rain, but in part as it provided an opportunity to lighten my load by consuming some snacks from my bulging bag of provisions. So I dined on a banana, a packet of ginger biscuits, a heavily crushed bag of ready salted crisps and a somewhat brutalised Snickers bar. Not necessarily a balanced diet, but it did at least help my rucksack to lose some weight!

Day 22 – Beattock to Ecclefechan
Distance: 19.0 miles
Cumulative distance: 377.2 miles
Weather: Rain, clearing later

Groundhog Day. More rain, similar route.

After the best night's sleep to date, largely due to a very comfortable king size bed and total silence, I had a leisurely breakfast and chatted to some fellow guests from Ross on Wye. I checked out of the B&B and Sally kindly made a donation to CRUK.

The rain had arrived on schedule, but was expected to clear by midday. Most of my route followed a safe cycle track on the verge of the 'B' road, with my close colleagues the A74 (M) and the railway ever present again. In many ways it felt like a repeat of yesterday's walk, but with a little more civilisation sprinkled in. The other noticeable difference was that, while yesterday's hills hovered between four and five hundred metres in height, today's barely reached two hundred metres. The sense of déjà vu filtered through to my photography – I took fewer pictures than on any other day of my walk.

I skirted the town of Lockerbie, where in December 1988 Pan Am flight 103 bound for New York and Detroit was destroyed by an explosive device and crashed to the ground, destroying 5 houses and killing all 259 on board and 11 local residents. It remains Britain's deadliest aircraft incident and deadliest act of terrorism.

The wing section of the plane hit Sherwood Crescent at more than 500 mph and exploded, creating a crater 47 metres in length. Another 21 houses were damaged so badly that they had to be demolished. The fireball rose above the houses and moved toward the nearby Glasgow–Carlisle A74 dual carriageway, scorching cars in the southbound lanes and leading motorists and local residents to believe that there had been a meltdown at the nearby Chapelcross nuclear power station. The British Geological Survey at nearby Eskdalemuir registered a seismic event measuring 1.6 on the Richter scale, which was attributed to the impact. All around, the smell of aircraft fuel lingered and wreckage was scattered across an area of 845 square miles, with the cockpit located 3 miles away.

It is difficult to grasp the impact that the disaster must have had on the local community of this peaceful town, especially just a few days before Christmas. Whilst the physical impacts of the disaster would gradually fade away, the mental scars would remain for many years.

Just to the west of Lockerbie, lies the town of Dumfries, where a major cholera epidemic occurred during the autumn of 1832. The disease had arrived in the north east of England from Europe a year earlier and quickly spread to Scotland. The town had been given advanced notice to prepare for the disease and undertook some sanitary improvements, but most of its water supply was delivered in dirty wheeled barrels from just below the main sewerage outlet in the River Nith. The disease arrived in Dumfries on 15th September and, by 27th November when the town was declared clear, a total of 837 cases and 421 deaths were reported and in the neighbouring burgh of Maxwelltown (now a suburb of Dumfries), 237 cases and 127 deaths. These were the official figures, but an even higher figure of nearly 700 deaths was calculated by counting the number of coffins made during the attack.

In 1848 cholera struck the town again, this time with a combined total of 814 cases and 431 deaths. The lessons of the decontaminated water supply were finally learnt, which led to clean gravitation water from Lochrutton Loch being introduced to the town.

It was difficult to reconcile the tragic events at Lockerbie and Dumfries with the peaceful, rural scene through which I was travelling. It seemed inconceivable that such carnage, destruction and significant loss of life could have occurred within this innocuous, agricultural landscape, which bore no indication of the turmoil and heartbreak it had once suffered.

A few miles later I arrived in Ecclefechan, my destination for the day. George Bradshaw observed that the town was "remarkable for nothing but its frequent and well-attended markets and fairs". With neither being held there today, my observation was that it was a remarkably quiet place.

Ecclefechan was the birthplace of Thomas Carlyle, the writer and social historian. He left home aged thirteen and walked eighty four miles to go to university in Edinburgh. His Calvinist parents wanted him to enter the Church after graduating, but he became a maths teacher instead, having suffered a 'crisis of faith' at university. He began writing and developed an interest in German literature and philosophy, translating German writers such as Goethe and Schiller. These books, together with his essays and letters, highly influenced 19th-century British political and social thought.

In 1826 he married Jane Welsh, an educated woman, and in 1834 they moved to London. They soon became a literary society couple, socialising with the likes of Charles Dickens, William Makepeace Thackeray, Robert Browning, and Alfred Lord Tennyson.

Carlyle was such an influential figure that when he died in 1881, he was due to be buried at Westminster Abbey. However, he had remained true to his roots, having requested to be buried in Ecclefechan churchyard, next to his parents. His house in the centre of the town is now managed by the National Trust for Scotland and is open to the public. The interior is modest, with just three small, sparsely furnished rooms, which makes an interesting comparison with his infinitely grander residence in Chelsea.

I checked into the Ecclefechan Hotel and engaged in conversation with the owner. He was originally from Salford, near Manchester, had bought the hotel with his parents and was gradually refurbishing it throughout. Like most building projects, the work had taken much longer than originally planned and the budget had suffered as a consequence. My room, with another welcome bath, was certainly spacious and very comfortable.

Dinner was remarkably good value – macaroni cheese with chips, salad and garlic bread, Ecclefechan tart (raisins and nuts in pastry!) with custard, washed down with a couple of pints of Greene King Bohemian ale. I'd never tasted Ecclefechan tart before, but it gained national prominence in 2007, when the supermarket Sainsbury's promoted it as an alternative to mince pies at Christmas, and the tarts subsequently proved to be very popular!

This would be my last evening in Scotland, with a significant component of my JOGLE journey nearly completed. Most people from outside of Scotland grossly underestimate the scale of the country, but I would never make that mistake again. I had walked 377 miles along its length and had another ten or so miles still left before I reached the border, which is only about five miles shorter than the distance from London to Edinburgh.

With Scotland almost ticked off on my itinerary, I was now just left with England and Wales, followed by another stretch of England to complete my journey!

Day 23 – Ecclefechan to Carlisle
Distance: 23.0 miles
Cumulative distance: 400.2 miles
Weather: Cloudy

Company en route, England, a navigational error, 400 miles, and almost two stranded vehicles

I checked out of the hotel and set off in the direction of Gretna, still following a cycle path on the minor 'B' road which runs parallel to the A74 (M) motorway and the railway line.

Not only would I be crossing the border into England today, but I would also be meeting up with some of my extended family. I had arranged a rendezvous with my mother and step father, my brother Howard and my young nephew Henry.

After 10 quick step miles, much of which had been along a minor road just a few yards from the northbound carriageway of the motorway, I passed by Gretna motorway services, close to Quintinshill, the site of the worst rail crash in Britain in terms of loss of life.

The disaster, which occurred in May 1915, killed an estimated 230 passengers and injured a further 246. The horrific accident happened early in the morning near to Quintinshill signal box, where the night signalman was finishing his shift and handing over to his colleague on the early day shift. A critical failure by the signalmen to follow documented procedures resulted in five trains (a troop train, a local train, an express, a goods train and some empty coal wagons) being involved in two collisions at speed. The casualty toll was made much worse by fire, caused by the ash pans of two of the locomotives and several gas cylinders on the carriages being ruptured – the use of obsolete rolling stock with wooden frames on the troop train, due to a wartime shortage of carriages, merely compounded the situation. Those killed were mainly Territorial soldiers from the Royal Scots heading for Gallipoli – it was later recorded that 42 per cent of the casualties suffered by the battalion during the war were due to the crash.

The Board of Trade inquiry into the Quintinshill disaster and the Coroner's Court hearing both found the two signalmen to blame for the entire accident, owing to poor working practices on their part. Both men were tried for involuntary manslaughter and were subsequently convicted. Somewhat unusually, on their release, both were re-employed by the Caledonian Railway.

However, theories abound that the cause of the disaster was less straightforward than negligence on the part of the signalmen. In the recently published *The Quintinshill Conspiracy* by Richards and Searle, the authors challenge the independence of the inquiry (even the archived report was produced on Caledonian Railway notepaper!) and argue that the criminal trial was biased, failing to adequately address some potentially important aspects of the disaster, including the impact of the significantly increased wartime rail traffic on the signalmen's workload. It was also suggested that the day shift signalman suffered from epilepsy, but this line of enquiry was not pursued in the inquiry. The authors also point out that most of the evidence in the trial was provided by managers and employees of the Caledonian Railway company (no independent experts were called upon) and that cross-examination of these witnesses was ineffective. In short, they claim that there was a cover up, intended to protect a wartime government in crisis, but which also benefited the mighty railway company. The signalmen were easy targets but, whilst they had clearly flouted the rules, the Caledonian Railway had not been challenged regarding significant shortcomings in its supervisory procedures.

I continued my journey and arrived in Gretna Green, joining the coachloads of tourists who were enjoying a pilgrimage to the village on this summer Saturday.

Gretna Green is one of the world's most popular wedding venues. Being the first village in Scotland, it was conveniently situated to take advantage of the more relaxed age of consent north of the border, where it was possible for boys to marry at the age of fourteen and girls at the age of twelve with or without parental consent. Since 1929, both parties in Scotland have had to be at least sixteen years old, but they still may marry without parental consent, whereas In England and Wales, the age for marriage is now sixteen with parental consent and eighteen without.

I had anticipated Gretna Green being a tacky tourist centre, so was pleasantly surprised to find some historic buildings, including the famous Old Blacksmith's Shop, built in 1712. Within a few minutes I arrived at Gretna itself, where a designer outlet village was situated.

The town of Gretna was built during the First World War to provide homes for the mainly female employees of a cordite munitions factory that was the biggest in the world – 9 miles in length and 2 miles wide. With the tide of the First World War turning in Germany's favour and Britain and her allies suffering from a shortage of artillery shells, it was clear that much more ammunition would be required, so the factory was constructed in 1915 with the aid of 10,000 navvies. The output of the HM Factory Gretna was more than all other munitions factories in Britain combined and played a key role in the

Allies' victory. The factory was known locally as "The Devil's Porridge", after the nickname given to the explosives made there. However, the labourers and workers had such a reputation for drunkenness, seen as such a threat to the national interest, that in 1916 the Government brought all the pubs and breweries within a wide area under tight state control, known as the 'State Management Scheme'.

I met my family members at the Gretna Inn. My mother didn't recognise me initially, although she explained later that this was because I was wearing a wide brimmed hat. They ate a light lunch (I had already eaten), then my brother Howard and Walter the dog joined me for the remainder of the walk to Carlisle.

Within minutes, we successfully crossed the border into England, leaving Scotland behind after 22.5 days and 388 miles. Howard took a few photographs of me by the border signpost as evidence.

Minutes into England, I made the first navigational error of my journey to date. It wasn't a case of misreading the map, more a case of being too busy talking to my brother to have time to look at the map. After a while I noticed a lake to the west of the road, so checked the map sheet to determine our location. I couldn't see the lake on the map and, for a moment, wondered whether it had been created after the map had been published. I quickly ruled out this scenario and considered instead whether we might have taken a wrong turn.

The bottom line is that we had missed the turning for the minor road we should have taken shortly after reaching England. My error resulted in a 3.5 mile detour, poor Walter the dog ended up walking almost half marathon distance, and Howard had walked much further than he'd expected. There was a small silver lining, however, as the detour did result in the total distance for my journey breaking through the 400 mile barrier.

It's probably fair to say that this was the least scenic and least walker-friendly (or dog-friendly) road on the journey to date and, quite probably, of my entire journey. There was no panorama to speak of, the terrain was flat, and the busy A7 road we were following had no pedestrian path for most of the route. However, Howard had really wanted to join me on the walk and, due to a forthcoming family holiday, this was the only day he could make.

We finally arrived in Carlisle and I checked into another Travelodge. We had a table booked for an early dinner at a restaurant in the town centre, so there was only time for a rapid shower and change of clothes. As I waited for the hotel lift, I accidently dialled a contact on my phone, but stopped the call before it rang for long. Seconds later, my phone rang – it was Di, a friend and former work colleague. She had taken a great interest in my walk, but had displayed a motherly concern about my welfare during the more remote and mountainous sections of the route, in case I had an accident and needed urgent medical attention. When she saw my number appear on her phone on a Saturday evening, she had naturally assumed that I was in trouble! Immediately, I was able to reassure her that the call was an accident and that I was safe and well. Nevertheless, it was enjoyable to be able to talk to a real person and to provide a live, spoken update on my progress, rather than relying entirely on my written blog. After this unplanned diversion, I headed out immediately to the waiting car to join the family for dinner.

After a delicious Italian meal, Howard, Henry and Walter the dog had to dash to Carlisle station to catch the train back to Warrington. Howard drove us from the restaurant in my parents' car, but the one way system and lack of signposting in the city centre proved to be a navigational challenge. With three minutes to spare before the train was due to depart, he stopped the car in the main shopping street, as close to the station as we could reasonably find, then he and his two fellow travellers jumped out of the car and ran towards the station.

Seconds after they had disappeared out of sight, we realised that Howard had left his own car keys behind and had taken in error the keys for the car we were sat in. I hastily climbed out of the rear seat and, despite wearing my flat canvas travel shoes and having walked an extended 23 miles earlier in the day, I managed to sprint about 300 metres to the station platform. That I was able to sprint this distance for the first time in a few years was due entirely to the level of fitness I had developed during three weeks on the road. Luckily, I managed to locate my prey on the station platform just as their train was arriving. Howard was quite oblivious to his mistake, but we hurriedly exchanged keys and parted for the second time in a few minutes! Had I arrived seconds later, the train would have departed and I would have missed him, leaving two cars stranded 100 miles apart, one in Carlisle and the other in Warrington.

Re-united with the correct set of car keys, I jogged back to the stranded car and, by now, we were able to see the funny side of the drama which had just unfolded!

CHAPTER FOUR

Around the Lake District and along the canals to Liverpool

Day 24 – Carlisle to Burthwaite
Distance: 4.8 miles
Cumulative distance: 405.0 miles
Weather: Cloudy

A short walk, Sunday lunch and becoming a tourist

After breakfast, I wandered into Carlisle's pleasant main shopping street to purchase a plastic map cover, to replace my previous one which had developed a split, preventing it from providing waterproof protection for my maps.

Carlisle was originally a Roman settlement, established to serve the forts on Hadrian's Wall. During the Middle Ages, the city became an important military stronghold, due to its proximity to the Kingdom of Scotland. By the time of the Norman Conquest of England in 1066, Carlisle was part of Scotland, but in 1092, William Rufus invaded the area and Cumberland became part of England, with construction of Carlisle Castle commencing in the following year. Carlisle became an industrial city in the nineteenth century with many textile mills and engineering works, but the city also became a major railway centre, serving seven different rail companies at one time.

My Bradshaw's Guide made reference to a visit to Carr and Co., manufacturers of fancy biscuits in the city. "If curiosity should induce the tourist to make a visit to the manufactory of this noted firm, we do not hesitate to say that it would be found highly interesting. If any prejudice exists against the free use of fancy biscuits, it will at once be removed on an inspection of the works and the process of production, even from the minds of the most fastidious, – the most scrupulous cleanliness being observable throughout the whole works."

Known as the Border City, Carlisle has a compact historic centre with the castle, museum, cathedral, and reasonably intact city walls all within easy walking distance. Today, the city serves as the main cultural, commercial and industrial centre for north Cumbria.

I returned to my hotel room to organise my rucksack, offloaded clothes in need of a wash, used maps and a few ruthlessly pruned items, then replaced them with clean clothes and new maps, which my mother had delivered. It would feel strange no longer wearing the same evening attire that I'd worn for the last three weeks, but nobody had complained so far!

Although this would officially be a rest day, following a now familiar pattern, I had decided to bring forward nearly five miles of the walk to today. This was partly to take advantage of favourable weather conditions, but more to do with reducing a marathon distance to Kendal in a few days' time.

I walked lightweight through the residential suburbs of Carlisle, then without any notice, as if the housing development budget had been suspended at a stroke, the scene suddenly became rural. The road transformed into a narrow country lane surrounded by farmland on both sides. A few farmhouses were rivalled by a handful of modern executive houses, but fields of crops dominated the landscape.

After walking for an hour and a half, my parents picked me up at the agreed junction on a quiet country lane in Burthwaite and we drove one mile to the conveniently located country pub at Wreay, where I'd booked a table for Sunday lunch. The homemade soup and roast beef dinner were both excellent, accompanied by some Corby ale from Cumberland Breweries in Carlisle.

In the afternoon I became a complete tourist, when we visited the walled gardens of Hutton-in-the-Forest House, the family home of Lord Inglewood. Most of the drive there, on a long, ramrod straight Roman country road, would be part of my next day's walk, so I had the new experience of previewing the route.

After 400 miles on the road, it was time to take stock of my general condition. The blisters of the first week had more or less disappeared completely and the troublesome baby toe now resembled the size and shape of a baby toe once again. The swelling above my right ankle had vanished too, leaving my feet and legs in remarkably good shape. The swelling on my right hand and grazing on my arm, both sustained during my roadside fall near to Dornoch, had also fully recovered. I had shed a few pounds and felt fitter than I'd been for many years, to the point where walking twenty miles in a day for consecutive days was no longer daunting. Mentally, I felt very strong, with the only minor negative impact being the loneliness of the initial days in northern Scotland. With a clean bill of health, I could now look forward to the prospect of having company for the majority of my remaining days on the walk.

Day 25 – Burthwaite to Penrith
Distance: 18.2 miles
Cumulative distance: 423.2 miles
Weather: Cloudy and breezy, sunny later

The Lake District, a closed pub, a closed restaurant, and a lift in a van

My parents collected me by car from outside the Travelodge and ten minutes later deposited me where I'd finished my short walk on the previous day. In the time it took me to walk the length of the flat, die-straight road to the next motorway junction, they were most likely relaxing with a pot of tea back in the comfort of their Cheshire home.

Soon after the motorway junction, I was delighted that a planned short cut materialised. During my planning for the walk, I'd used Google Street View to try to circumnavigate a road which was blocked off as a result of a newer road which cut across it. On the image, I spotted that there was a hole in the fence next to the new road and a short scramble through some nettles on the other side of the road. I celebrated successfully avoiding a half mile detour and the short cut paid further dividends as the driver of a Range Rover stopped to enquire about my walk and kindly made a donation.

I arrived in Penrith, gateway to the Lake District, and received another donation from a cyclist undertaking the Coast to Coast route. The sun came out and I caught a glimpse of the Lakeland fells in the distance. Although I was staying overnight in Penrith, I'd decided to walk a few miles further south so that I could reduce the following day's distance.

Just south of Penrith I reached King Arthur's Round Table, which is a prehistoric circular earthwork. Misleadingly, the site has nothing whatsoever to do with King Arthur himself, predating him by at least 2,500 years!

I adjourned for a short lunch on a wooden bench in a children's playground in Clifton, where the last battle on English soil took place in 1745 between the English army under the Duke of Cumberland, and the retreating Jacobites of Bonnie Prince Charlie. Apparently, there are at least three other contenders for the site of the last battle, with some historians claiming that Clifton Moor was merely a "skirmish". Despite this, 12 Jacobites and 10 Government soldiers were killed.

I walked as far as the village of Hackthorpe and had planned to pop into the local pub for a convenience stop and a refreshing drink until the bus, which would return me to Penrith, was due. The plan failed miserably, as the pub closed at 2pm and wouldn't re-open until 6pm.

With a couple of hours to kill, I sat on the village bench (kindly provided for the Queen's Diamond Jubilee) and caught up on some emails. Some builders, who had just finished working at the village primary school opposite, saw me and kindly offered me a lift to Penrith, depositing me right at the door of my B&B. Penrith had already made its mark as a welcoming town.

Penrith is a market town in the county of Cumbria and lies just outside of the Lake District National Park. Known as the "old red town" because of its sandstone buildings, it was once famous for the number of pubs in the town and at one time had five working breweries. In keeping with the national trend, many pubs had closed subsequently, but I still managed to lose count of how many remained.

After the customary checking in and hot shower, I wandered into the town centre and visited the castle ruins. I had planned to eat at the Chinese restaurant we'd been to for my daughter Hannah's birthday, when we had stayed in the Lake District during the previous October, but unfortunately my visit coincided with the only day of the week the restaurant was closed. Instead, I dined at a pub near the station and had a filling lasagne and chips, washed down with Sneck Lifter and High Spy bitters, both from the Jennings brewery. The brewery produced a regular seasonal ale and I noted with amusement the names of some of the recent and forthcoming products – Cross Buttock, Cocky Blond, Lakeland Stunner and World's Biggest Liar. What a shame I couldn't stay for longer!

Day 26 – Penrith to Kendal
Distance: 21.3 miles
Cumulative distance: 444.5 miles
Weather: Cloudy and windy, rain showers later

A bleak, windswept walk over Shap, and a long-awaited reunion

At breakfast, I was joined by a young couple, who were cycling the Coast to Coast route, from Whitehaven on the West coast to Sunderland on the North East coast. The previous day's ride had obviously been a tough physical challenge for the girl, and her boyfriend was clearly trying to play down the steep gradients of the hills they were due to face today. He looked knowingly across to my table as if to say "please don't tell her how steep the roads really are!" A thoughtfully located laptop in the breakfast room indicated heavy rain for later in the day.

I checked out of yet another welcoming and comfortable B&B, and strolled down the road to Penrith's tiny bus station to catch the bus to Hackthorpe, where I'd finished yesterday.

The bus trip was an interesting insight into life in Cumbria. I was one of just two passengers on the single decker, the other being a widowed grandmother who made a donation to my cause and briefed me on the regular bus journeys she made with her free bus pass. She explained that as her journey to Kendal started before the permitted time for using her pass, she paid the standard fare to the next village, by which time her bus pass was valid for the rest of the day. Surprisingly, the bus driver also joined in our conversations while we travelled and enquired with interest about my walk – he was keen to understand the mechanics of the JustGiving website, as he was contemplating taking part in a sponsored running event himself. A couple of hours later, when I had progressed half a dozen miles down the road and he was on his return trip, he spotted me, slowed down the bus and waved – his passengers seemed to join in too, as if under instructions!

Much of my walk was along the undisturbed A6 as it gradually climbed up over Shap Fell. It is a remote, windswept area but, prior to the opening of the M6 motorway in 1971, this was the principal route to Scotland from the western side of England. Drivers heading to Scotland were forced to negotiate the treacherous climbs of the A6 over Shap Fell, where they could experience all types of adverse weather conditions. According to reports, in winter many vehicles didn't make it, with some wrecked in the valley below.

A red traffic sign at the roadside warned approaching drivers that winter conditions could be dangerous, but I was more interested in a stone plaque, which was situated near to the summit:

"This memorial pays tribute to the drivers and crews of vehicles that made possible the social and commercial links between North and South on this old and difficult route over Shap Fell before the opening of the M6 motorway. Remembered too are those who built and maintained the road and the generations of local people who gave freely of food and shelter to stranded travellers in bad weather."

I negotiated the climb in a strong headwind, but I was fortunate that the rain held off. At Kids Howe, I detoured via a bridleway to avoid the main road and encountered Greg, a long distance walker from Lancaster, who was piecing together a string of walks that may one day form his own John O' Groats to Land's End journey.

At Garth Row, I deviated from the main highway and joined a quiet narrow road, its steep sides being reminiscent of a Cornish lane. When I reached a quaint rural hamlet, I had a choice of two un-signposted footpaths to take. I consulted my map, which showed only a single path, so I took a gamble on the right hand track. This led me through open countryside before re-joining another minor road, which happened, conveniently, to be the one marked on my map.

In the back lanes of Kendal the ever present rain clouds finally decided to shed their load, so I was more than a little wet when I finally met up with Chris, a friend from university days who I'd not seen for more than twenty years. We clearly had some catching up to do! We'd arranged to meet at a car park near to the river, but there seemed to be several to choose from, so I called him on his mobile and it transpired that he was just a few yards away around the next corner. Despite the passage of time, he was instantly recognisable, just a little older, greyer and stockier. I loaded my rucksack into his car and, in ever more persistent rain, Chris drove us to the Lake District lodge that his family had bought the previous year. It was set in the heart of a remote, tranquil woodland amphitheatre, with nature visible from every aspect. Unfortunately, the incessant rain prevented me from exploring the large plot more closely, but I was able to identify a varied range of birds, which were attracted by generous supplies of feed on the veranda.

I'd first met Chris during my initial weeks at Liverpool University, where he was staying a few doors away in the same student hall of residence. With a couple of other friends, we subsequently shared a house for a few years, before he became a tenant in my own house for a year. My career took me to the South East, while he had remained in the North West, so we had gradually lost contact, apart from the annual exchange of Christmas cards. When I'd contacted him about my JOGLE walk, he and his wife Alison had kindly offered to accommodate me for a few days and to chauffeur me to my various start and finish locations, in part, he explained, to "pay me back" for the many lifts I had given to him in the past.

Chris cooked a tasty pasta meal and then drove us in driving rain to the Eagle and Child pub in Staveley, where we sampled Windermere ale from Hawkshead brewery and Pennine Pale, whilst embarking on the start of a lengthy catching up process.

Day 27 – Kendal to Carnforth
Distance: 19.3 miles
Cumulative distance: 463.8 miles
Weather: Cloudy with sunny intervals

Variety on the Lancaster Canal and a brief encounter with Carnforth

I was awoken by nature's sounds – the crowing of pheasants

in the garden. Being in the lodge was analogous to sitting in a bird hide, watching a constant theatre of feeding activity. Chris cooked a delicious full English breakfast, but minus the eggs which had accidentally remained on his shopping list.

For the first time on my journey, I'd been unable to charge my smartphone overnight, due to the electricity at the lodge being provided by an on-site generator. I would now have to manage for most of the day on a minimal charge.

We set off in the car for Kendal, but a procession of cows being led down the road by a local farmer delayed our arrival. Chris performed an overtaking manoeuvre that Lewis Hamilton would have been proud of to leave the cattle behind and, thirty minutes later, he deposited me back in the town's car park next to the river.

Kendal is a pleasant market town, probably best known for its Kendal Mint Cake, a glucose-based confectionery bar made from sugar, glucose, water, and peppermint oil. Kendal Mint Cake has been used on many expeditions around the world as a source of energy, including for Sir Edmund Hillary and his team's first successful ascent of Mount Everest in 1953. This supply was achieved thanks, in part, to the staff at the manufacturers who, due to the short notice given, willingly gave up their post-War sweet ration coupons to comply with the laws in force at the time. Hillary commented "We sat on the snow and looked at the country far below us… we nibbled Kendal Mint Cake." Kendal Mint Cake had also been provided to Sir Ernest Shackleton's Imperial Trans-Antarctic Expedition of 1914–1917 and, in the depths of my own rucksack, I too was carrying a couple of bars on my own expedition to Land's End.

For the next few days, my route would follow the Lancaster canal from Kendal to Preston. The main section of the canal was completed in 1819, after construction work which lasted for twenty five years. The canal's principal purpose was to transport coal north from the Lancashire coalfields, and limestone south from Cumbria. The Glasson branch, which opened slightly later, enabled the transfer of cargo from ships that could not navigate the shallow Lune Estuary into Lancaster.

The footpath started inauspiciously at Canal Head on the edge of Kendal, sandwiched awkwardly between the council household waste recycling centre and the waste management recycling centre in an industrial part of the town.

It was an interesting walk in that, during the course of a single day, it highlighted the differences in the navigational status of the three stages of the canal. The first section of six miles from Canal Head to the Hincaster Tunnel was dry, largely in-filled or overgrown after being closed in 1944. The footpath here was mainly narrow and muddy and I became rather wet battling through what appeared to be a plantation of nettles. In some parts, it was even difficult to recognise the existence of the canal. Oddly, many of the original bridges across the canal still remain intact, but they fulfil no practical purpose, apart from serving as curious memorials to a bygone age.

The next section resembled a normal water-filled canal, but wasn't fully navigable due to being severed in several places by a number of man-made features, including the M6 motorway and an 'A' road. I managed to miss a signpost hidden in a hedgerow and ended up walking to where the towpath ended abruptly next to the motorway and had to retrace my steps to follow the diverted path. At Tewitfield, a flight of eight locks remains (the only ones on the canal), but they are no longer in use.

For over fifty years, there have been ambitious long term plans to restore, and re-open to navigation, the 14 mile section of the canal from Tewitfield to Canal Head in Kendal. In the

1990s, what is now the Lancaster Canal Regeneration Partnership was formed, including South Lakeland District Council, Cumbria County Council, Kendal Town Council, Canal & River Trust, Lancaster Canal Trust, The Inland Waterways Association, Lancashire County Council, Lancaster City Council and other interested groups. The partnership has faced a plethora of planning and funding issues over the years, but some progress has been made and they remain optimistic that their goal will be achieved one day.

The final section, from the Tewitfield terminus about 4 miles north of Carnforth, is navigable for 41 miles to Preston, where the Millennium Ribble Link provides a connection to the rest of the UK canal network. At Tewitfield the canal immediately sprang to life and the colourful canal boats, which had been discernibly absent from the severed sections of my walk until now, lined the banks in abundance.

It was fascinating to look for the names painted on the side of the canal boats. Some were clearly named after wives and girlfriends (Sally, Emma Jane, Pippa, Dolly Daydream and Waterwitch – perhaps not the last one, on second thoughts), others after birds (Kestrel, Kingfisher and Heron), but many seemed to hint at escapism (Nirvana, Carpe Diem, Life of Brian – always look on the bright side of life, Stealaway, The Good Life, Happy Days and Vin Rouge).

I arrived in Carnforth and departed from the towpath in the town centre to await my chauffeur.

In 1945, the romantic classic "Brief Encounter" starring Celia Johnson and Trevor Howard was filmed at Carnforth station. The location was chosen by the Ministry of War Transport as it was so remote and likely to receive sufficient warning of an air-raid attack, that there would be time to turn out the filming lights to comply with wartime blackout

My kit

John O'Groats

Seals, Brora beach

Loch Ness

In the mountains, Kinlochleven

Rocky path, Loch Lomond

The old 'A' road, near Abington

Railway, motorway, windfarm

Former canal bridge, near Kendal

With John Lennon, Liverpool

Pontcysyllte Aqueduct

View towards Welshpool, Offa's Dyke

Llanthony Priory

Severn Bridge footpath

Finger signpost

Blocked path, Somerset

Black Dog Inn, near Crediton

With the family, Land's End

Completed route

A well-earned pint, Land's End

restrictions. Filming took place at night between 10pm and 6am to avoid interference with daytime train operations. The station clock was repeatedly shown in the film and became a powerful icon and Noël Coward made the station announcements.

Carnforth Station still retains many of the period features present at the time of filming and remains a place of pilgrimage for fans of the film. There is now a visitor centre and a "Brief Encounter" Refreshment Room, although the film version was actually a studio re-creation.

Chris collected me from the main road and drove me this time to his home, situated between Preston and Blackpool. Chris and his wife Alison, who I'd also not seen for over twenty years, cooked an excellent dinner of pork chops, followed by home grown strawberries and a single raspberry from the garden. We continued the catching up process and reminisced about our university days.

Day 28 – Carnforth to Garstang
Distance: 21.0 miles
Cumulative distance: 484.8 miles
Weather: Cloudy, sunny later

HALF WAY, a pleasant canal walk and some surprise visitors

Chris cooked a fine breakfast (still no eggs!) and then we retraced our route as he drove me the 34 miles back to Carnforth, while he returned to the Lake District lodge to clear some more of the items from a lengthy list of maintenance jobs.

By the time I started walking the early morning rain had abated. It was an easy walk along the towpath – flat and comfortable underfoot. At Hest Bank, the canal briefly ran adjacent to the coast, close to the Morecambe Bay Nature Reserve. This was the first time I'd seen the sea since leaving the north east coast of Scotland, but it would be a long time before I would be re-acquainted with it in Cornwall.

Morecambe Bay is notorious for its fast running tides, moving channels and dangerous areas of quicksand, which can quickly cut people off from the shore. It was here in 2004 that 23 Chinese cockle pickers lost their lives. Cockles can only be picked when the tide is out and the sands are uncovered, so the cocklers headed out towards the water's edge, which in Morecambe Bay can be several miles offshore, picked the cockles and planned to return to dry land before the tide came back in. However, with high tides and poor weather conditions, they became stranded as the tide rushed in, and they later drowned. The criminal trial uncovered a complex web of illegal immigration, gang masters and unscrupulous businessmen, and three people were subsequently convicted.

As the canal advanced nearer to Lancaster, I noticed that debris became more conspicuous, both in the water and around the canal banks. Within a short timespan I spotted numerous empty bottles, disposable nappies, a child's bicycle frame, a rusty supermarket trolley and a car tyre. Perhaps this was just evidence that I was approaching civilisation again.

There were fine views from the Lune Aqueduct, completed in 1797 to carry the canal over the River Lune. It cost about £48,000 to build, far exceeding its original budget of £18,000. This massive overspend had major ramifications – there wasn't enough money for the planned aqueduct over the River Ribble at the southern end of the canal, which prevented the Lancaster canal from being connected to the main canal network. As I walked across, the aqueduct was just undergoing the final stages of a £2.3million facelift, after a three year project to equip it for the 21st century. It had sprung several leaks, so had to be drained, before new concrete liners were installed and some of the missing and cracked masonry replaced.

Close to Lancaster, I officially reached the halfway point of my entire walk. It felt worthy of a small celebration, so I fished out a battered (weather-beaten, rather than coated in batter and deep-fried the Scottish way!) Snickers bar from my rucksack. I was aware that a few people were plotting my route towards Land's End. My daughter Hannah had been tracking my journey on a map of the British Isles and placed a coloured pin at each day's completed destination. Each week she texted me an updated photo – it now looked like visible progress since John O' Groats, but there were still many challenging miles ahead, evidenced by the lack of pins in the lower half of the map.

I successfully negotiated the Glasson Dock junction on the canal, ensuring that I was still heading in a southerly direction, despite the fact that the signpost to Preston was disconcertingly (and incorrectly) pointing to the west.

A few miles to the east of the Glasson junction lies the village of Abbeystead, where in May 1984, a methane gas explosion destroyed the valve house of the waterworks. The purpose of the pumping station, which had been officially opened by Her Majesty the Queen four years earlier, was to pump water from the River Lune to the River Wyre, from where it could then be pumped out for domestic usage. On the fateful evening, forty-four visitors were inside the underground building to attend a public presentation on the operation of the station. The explosion caused the concrete roof to collapse on to the group, destroying the steel mesh floor and throwing some of the victims into the water chambers below, which rapidly filled with water. Eight people were killed instantly by the explosion and a further eight subsequently died of their injuries.

The official inquiry into the disaster concluded that the methane had seeped from coal deposits nearly four thousand feet below ground and had accumulated in an empty pipeline. The sudden pressure of water as the pumps were switched on had caused the gas to be ejected into the valve house. The cause of ignition was never determined, but the building's designers were ultimately found to be fully liable in negligence for failing to exercise "reasonable care" in assessing the risk of methane.

There were picture postcard scenes at numerous places on the canal and an abundance of wildlife to be observed, including herons, moorhens, coot, ducklings and cygnet swans. I was desperate to see a kingfisher, but this was a bird that would elude me along rivers, streams and canals throughout my journey.

As predicted, the clouds gradually disappeared and a warm sun took control – would this be the start of summer? The weather forecast for the next few days certainly looked promising.

With about five miles to go to Garstang, I noticed a couple of people waving in my direction from the top of a canal bridge. At first, I thought they were gesturing to me to stop, so that they could photograph a heron, which was stood on the towpath a short distance ahead of me, but they continued to wave after the heron had departed. On closer inspection, I realised that it was Jeff and Christine, the long distance walking couple I'd met on the Caledonian Canal on Day 10.

The couple had been following my blog avidly and had decided to meet me en route as they lived nearby! They had determined correctly that I would be following the canal towpath for my entire day's walk, so it was unlikely that they would miss me, but my later start did mean that they'd waited several hours for me to arrive and were about to give up, when I finally appeared in the distance. It was a lovely surprise to see them and I enjoyed recounting all of my experiences since Day 10, as we walked the final few miles in glorious sunshine. Christine seemed to have memorised every detail of my blog, so it was quite surreal when she enquired about some of the people I'd met en route, mentioning each of them by name. By coincidence, they had parked in the same pub car park from which Chris was due to collect me and, on cue, Chris arrived at the same time, fresh from his day's work at the lodge. Jeff and Christine insisted on buying us a drink, so I enjoyed a pint of Radical from the Kirkby Lonsdale brewery.

Minutes later, I received a text with the news that my nephew Callum had just been informed that he'd achieved a first class honours degree, so it had turned into quite a day of celebrations.

Chris and Alison cooked a tasty coq au vin dinner, then we drove to a pub in nearby Lytham St Annes, where I had a pint of Knobber from the Ramsbury brewery and a pint of Freshly Squeezed from the Blakemore brewery (I assure any doubting Thomases that these names are not invented!).

Day 29 – Garstang to Preston
Distance: 19.5 miles
Cumulative distance: 504.3 miles
Weather: Warm and sunny

A leisurely stroll in the sun, a pub lunch and a few extra miles

The breakfast eggs were now available, but just to be awkward, I opted for a bowl of Shredded Wheat instead. Chris and

Alison had agreed to join me for a more leisurely walk today, which had the added incentive of a pub lunch. This would be my last day for a while of being able to leave most of the contents of my rucksack behind and walking 'light', so I was determined to make the most of it.

Before walking could commence, we had to position the cars at either end of the route. This entailed driving two cars to Preston, leaving one car there, then driving back in the second car to Garstang, where I had finished yesterday. Consequently, it was after 10 o'clock when our boots finally touched the towpath.

At a Public Town Meeting on Thursday 27th April 2000, the people of Garstang voted unanimously for the town to become the world's first Fairtrade Town and, in the following year, the Fair Trade Town campaign was first launched by the local Oxfam Group. The initiative, which aimed to promote Fair Trade certified goods in the town, was highly successful and soon influenced many other towns and cities around the UK to work towards the same goal. The town now boasts the FIG Tree, the world's first international Fair Trade Visitor Centre, which is located centrally.

Summer had certainly arrived and the weather forecast for the next few days promised sunshine and warmth. This was the weather I had dared to dream about back in the depths of January when I had planned the route, but the unpredictable British summer climate ensured that it was not something that could be guaranteed.

We followed the towpath for seven miles, entertained by the many mallard ducklings and young moorhens seeking parental security as we approached, then we left the canal for the final time. After some initial hesitation regarding which footpath to follow, we crossed several fields and headed through a farmyard, before finally reaching our chosen pub, The Plough at Eaves. We had a relaxed lunch, ably supported by a couple of pints of well-kept cask ales (Wainwrights and Lancaster Bomber, both from Thwaites brewery).

In the sun's warm glow, we followed country lanes towards Preston, and watched as the rural scene slowly transformed into residential communities. I was beginning to feel guilty that I was pushing my generous hosts towards half marathon distance and their less practised feet were starting to suffer. They quietly mentioned blisters and, as the pace slowed, it was evident that the final couple of miles to the car park would be a struggle. As Chris and Alison both had evening appointments and I was still feeling energetic, I opted to continue walking, thereby reducing the following day's mileage.

My Bradshaw's Guide informed me that Preston was noted for the gentility of its inhabitants and was "an elegant and economical town, the resort of well-born, but ill-proportioned and ill-endowed old maids and widows". Preston came to prominence in the Industrial Revolution, experiencing rapid economic growth from the industrialisation and expansion of textile manufacturing. The town became "Coketown" in Charles Dickens' novel *Hard Times*.

The town was by-passed by Britain's very first motorway which opened in 1958 and is now part of the M6. Following the decline of the textile industry, new industries such as electrical goods manufacturing and engineering took over, until further economic decline took place in the 1970s. In 2002, Preston was granted city status, becoming England's 50th city in the 50th year of Queen Elizabeth II's reign.

I skirted the city's docklands, ever vigilant for "well-born, but ill-proportioned and ill-endowed old maids and widows", but none of the women I encountered in the vicinity appeared to match that description, then I joined the elevated main road as it crossed the River Ribble. Logically, I chose to follow the pavement at the side of the south bound lane, but discovered, when it was too late, that the direct cycle and pedestrian path was situated on the north bound side. This resulted in an extended walk in a complete circle around the exit slipway, before I could re-join the A59 to continue my journey.

On the bank of the River Ribble, a few miles to the west of Preston, lies the village of Freckleton. During World War II, the nearby Warton Aerodrome was operating as an air depot of the United States Army Air Forces (USAAF), from which thousands of aircraft were processed on their way to active service. In August 1944, a heavy bomber on a test flight aborted its landing during a violent storm, but tragically crashed into the centre of the village, colliding into a primary school and demolishing three houses and a snack bar. In total, 61 people were killed, including 38 school children.

The official report into the crash concluded that the exact cause was unknown, but suggested that the pilot had under-estimated the violence of the storm. It recommended that U.S. pilots based in England should be warned about the dangers of British thunderstorms, as many considered British storms to be little more than showers, compared to those encountered back home.

In the tranquil surroundings of Penwortham, and over the last couple of days, I'd noticed a squeaking sound which appeared to be emanating from my left walking boot. On closer inspection, I swiftly ruled out the existence of a mouse, but did identify that a small crack had appeared around the heel of the boot. The boot was still comfortable and roadworthy, but I envisaged that it would gradually deteriorate and the heel would eventually collapse. The boots had covered a distance of about 750 miles in total, on training walks and then from John O' Groats until now, so although they were advertised as lasting for up to one thousand miles, with the rough terrain I'd encountered and the additional pressure from the weight of my rucksack, I couldn't really complain.

I reached the conclusion that I would have to invest in a replacement pair of boots, but how long would the damaged boot last and where would I purchase new boots? After assessing my planned route for the weeks ahead, it became evident that I would not be walking close to too many towns that were likely to sell good quality walking boots. I didn't want to imagine the boot treading its final step on a remote section of Offa's Dyke path, leaving me stranded and defeated. After considering the evidence, I decided that I would acquire new boots in Liverpool, the last major shopping venue that I would visit on my entire journey. I stopped in a secluded cul-de-sac to escape the noise of the traffic and telephoned the Liverpool branch of Cotswold Outdoor, who helpfully agreed to put a pair of size ten-and-a-half boots aside, for me to collect a couple of days later.

After a further five miles of walking in the warmest conditions of my trip to date, I located a convenient roundabout from which Chris could collect me after his appointment. Feeling thirsty, I popped into a nearby hostelry, the Longton Arms, and drank a refreshing iced Coke. The bar staff enquired about my journey and kindly made a donation. They had automatically assumed that I was cycling and suggested that I brought my bike indoors, where it would be more secure. They were flabbergasted when I explained that I was on foot, and immediately offered another drink and further donations!

Chris picked me up on schedule and drove me back to the house, where we watched Andy Murray battle his way into the Wimbledon final.

Day 30 – Preston to Aughton
Distance: 16.4 miles
Cumulative distance: 520.7 miles
Weather: Warm and sunny

A perfect summer's day, good company, canal-side pubs, a birthday barbeque (and some walking!)

Chris cooked another fine breakfast, including eggs (finally!), and then drove me to my starting point at Walmer Bridge roundabout, south of Preston. I had really enjoyed staying with Chris and Alison after a break of too many years and they were wonderful hosts, providing food, drink, accommodation, transport and good company. We vowed to keep in contact, rather than wait for another twenty years to elapse!

I lingered at the roundabout and was soon joined by another Alison, a former work colleague, who had travelled from Lymm in Cheshire that morning. Back in January when I was advising colleagues of my plans to undertake my JOGLE walk, Alison had contacted me to say that she lived in the North West and would be interested in joining me for a day's walk. Being based in different offices, I had rarely seen her in recent years, so it was good to catch up on recent events at my former employer and to hear about Alison's recent transfer to another division.

After five miles, we were joined by my cousin Geoff, his wife Heather, their daughter Nicola and dog Coco, who lived a few miles away. We diverted from the main road to join the Rufford branch of the Leeds and Liverpool canal, which later connected to the main canal. Canals had been my staple diet for the last few days and the change in both scenery and pace of life from the busy A59 main road just a hundred metres away was both welcoming and dramatic.

I had tried desperately to purchase a route map for the Leeds and Liverpool canal. I'd bought an excellent map of the Lancaster canal and found it to be useful for both identifying my location and for highlighting the nearby landmarks. Although a few specialist online stores offered the Leeds and Liverpool equivalent map on their websites, none seemed to have it in stock. One site claimed to have one available and accepted my order and payment, but sent me an email on the following day to explain that the map publishers had gone into administration and explained that no copies of the map were currently available. I accepted defeat and would have to make do with my standard Ordnance Survey maps instead!

In glorious sunshine, we followed the towpath past fields and meadows and, increasingly, moored canal boats. This area is part of the West Lancashire plain and the flat land is fertile and agriculturally very productive, especially for vegetable crops, including potatoes, carrots, cabbages, Brussels sprouts and onions.

Geoff had lived in the area for most of his life, but admitted that he had never walked along this section of the towpath before! We stopped to refresh ourselves at the Farmer's Arms pub in Burscough, where the locals generously re-stocked my Cancer Research UK collecting jar. I enjoyed a cool pint of Pendle Pride and Alison shared her lunch with us.

The fine weather on this Saturday in July had attracted many walkers and cyclists to the canal towpath and numerous boaters to the canal itself, but their numbers were dwarfed by the crowds that frequented the gardens and patios of the plentiful canal-side pubs.

We continued as far as Haskayne, where further refreshments were required at the Ship Inn (due to the heat, I must explain), in my case a thirst quenching pint of Eugene's Lair. We sat at a table in the garden, which overlooked the canal, while on a large screen inside the pub, the Ladies' Final was underway at Wimbledon.

We returned by car to Geoff and Heather's house, my accommodation for the night, from where Alison was collected by her husband. We then had a mega barbecue to celebrate Geoff's birthday and finished the evening in the early hours after reviewing the family tree (the genealogical, not the arboreal sort!).

Day 31 – Aughton to Liverpool
Distance: 15.6 miles
Cumulative distance: 536.3 miles
Weather: Hot and sunny

To my native city along the canal in baking sunshine, a panoramic Sunday lunch with guests, new boots, and British sporting success

After a wholesome breakfast, Geoff drove us to the starting point for today's walk, where Heather joined me for the first few miles. We followed the canal for a short section, but as its route then added a sizeable loop around Aintree, home of the Grand National, I had decided to take a more direct route and to re-join the canal later on its journey to Liverpool. We joined a country lane which united us with the Trans Pennine Trail, a well-defined footpath which followed the route of the former Cheshire Lines railway. The Trans Pennine Trail is a long-distance path which runs for 207 miles across northern England from Southport on the West coast to Hornsea on the East coast entirely on surfaced paths, predominantly along disused railway lines and canal towpaths.

Heather finished her walk close to a garden centre in Sefton, where Geoff had arranged to collect her, while I continued along the Trail until it reached the canal at Netherton. The Trail turned left towards the Pennines, but I turned right along the towpath. I had a lunch appointment, so accelerated towards Liverpool, my birthplace and spiritual home. This was now the hottest day of my journey so far, but despite having a full load for the first time in several days, it wasn't a struggle – another telling sign of my renewed level of fitness.

On this sizzling July Sunday morning, the canal towpath was again bustling with activity. Along the way, I engaged in brief conversation with a diverse collection of walkers and cyclists, all attracted to the calming effects of the still water, teeming wildlife and a more leisurely pace of life.

After extensive experience of canal walking over the last few days, I had reluctantly reached the conclusion that canal fishermen (they are always men!) are the most unsociable group amongst canal users. Their natural pose is to sit on the canal bank with their heads in a fixed position staring directly at the tips of their rods, so a greeting to cyclists, dog walkers or long distance walkers is an unlikely event. I persisted with my attempts to hold a conversation or, at the very least, to get them to reciprocate a greeting, but all to no avail! Apologies to any fishermen who believe that they don't fit this image, but I didn't meet any!

The canal towpath would lead me right into the heart of Liverpool, passing a few landmarks from my student days on the way. I walked within a stone's throw of the terraced house in Bootle, which I'd shared with Chris and some other friends, then the offices where I'd had my medical prior to joining my long term employer, and the roads I'd jogged along as part of my training for my first marathon. Despite its proximity, I don't ever recall walking or running along the towpath during the four years I lived here – perhaps it wasn't accessible in those days.

I was astonished to encounter so much wildlife on the canal in the industrial outskirts of Liverpool. Under a bridge very close to the city centre, I spotted a pair of swans and seven cygnets and, nearby, a family of moorhens, presumably a sign that the canal has become less polluted in recent years and more suited to nature.

I arrived early at the restaurant, the Panoramic on the 34th floor of a building overlooking Liverpool's waterfront. The ground floor security guard looked at me suspiciously as I headed towards the lift carrying my weighty rucksack, resembling someone who had just walked 15 miles in the morning heat. The restaurant had kindly arranged for me to use the facilities in the disabled washroom and within minutes, after a thorough wash and a rapid change of clothes, I looked reasonably presentable. So much so that the receptionist didn't recognise me at first and commented on my major transformation. I waited for my guests in the cocktail bar, but couldn't forego my traditional thirst quenching drink – two glasses of Coke with ice and lemon.

I had Sunday lunch with my parents and an uncle and aunt who were visiting from Australia, but were returning on the next day via an extended tour of USA and Canada. The food and service in the restaurant were both first class, and the wonderful location offered stunning views across Liverpool city centre and beyond. In the foreground, the Albert Dock, the famous Liver Building and the Pier Head all seemed within touching distance. Further afield, I could clearly make out my accommodation for the following night on the Wirral peninsular and could even trace my walking route for the day after, as well as seeing the hills which form part of the Offa's Dyke path further in the distance.

I quickly checked into my accommodation, the Albert Dock Premier Inn (still no charity donation from them!), then hurried into the city centre shopping area for my major purchase of a new pair of walking boots. Donna, the shop assistant at Cotswold Outdoor could not have been more helpful, quickly locating the package which had been put aside for me and readily agreeing to stretch the boots overnight for me to collect the following morning.

I returned to the hotel to offload some used kit and to receive some fresh clothes and new maps, then switched on the TV just in time to see Andy Murray clinch the Wimbledon title, the first British player to win the trophy for 77 years. After all the excitement, I wandered downstairs for a quiet stroll around the Albert Dock.

The Albert Dock was designed by Jesse Hartley and opened in 1846, the first enclosed, non-combustible dock warehouse system in the world, and the first structure in Britain to be built entirely of cast iron, brick and stone. Two years later, the world's first hydraulic warehouse hoists were installed. It rapidly became a popular store for valuable cargoes such as brandy, cotton, tea, silk, tobacco, ivory and sugar, but following a gradual decline in shipping in Liverpool, due largely to the advent of containerisation and the emergence of stronger ports elsewhere in the UK, the dock was finally closed in 1972, the dock silted and the warehouses became derelict for over ten years.

After a major refurbishment programme, the warehouses were converted into hotels, offices and luxury apartments, shops and restaurants, and tourist attractions (including the Tate Gallery, Merseyside Maritime Museum and International Slavery Museum, and The Beatles' Story Exhibition). Today, the Albert Dock attracts around five million visitors each year and its lofty colonnades and statuesque columns make up the largest collection of Grade 1 listed buildings in the country.

Later in the evening, I met up in town with Jeremy and Sarah, some longstanding university friends, but also my hosts for the following night. They had married straight after university and we had remained in contact over the years. Sarah had later lodged at my house in Liverpool for a year while she studied for a postgraduate qualification – I recall that she regularly cooked a vegetable lasagne to die for! We had a few drinks and some food in a local bar, while catching up on our news.

Day 32 – Liverpool
Distance: 0.0 miles
Cumulative distance: 536.3 miles
Weather: Hot and sunny

**A leisurely day in Liverpool, catching up on a few
chores, being a tourist and reunited
with longstanding friends**

After a relaxing 'eat as much as you like' breakfast, I caught up on my emails and texts from the comfort of my hotel room, which offered a fine view across Duke's Dock to Liverpool's 'big wheel' (sponsored as 'The Echo Wheel of Liverpool' by the Liverpool Echo, the city's evening newspaper), the Echo Arena convention centre and the southern docks beyond.

I left the Albert Dock, thronged with tourists, and walked into the city centre to collect my new walking boots, freshly stretched overnight. They fitted like a glove, so it was a huge relief to have a pair of boots which would hopefully walk me from here to Cornwall. Of course, every walker knows the golden rule about not wearing a pair of boots for immediate action without gently breaking them in. Unfortunately, I didn't have any time to provide my boots with such a relaxed and luxurious introduction to walking life, so the breaking in process would have to be limited to a couple of hours of shopping and sightseeing around the city centre, before being thrust into live action the following morning. I did however make a customary visit to Boots the Chemists and stocked up on foot care products, just in case my new boots gave me any problems later.

I'd arranged to meet Jeremy at LIPA (Liverpool Institute of Performing Arts), where he was a member of the management team. The Institute was co-founded by Sir Paul McCartney (it is located in his old school) and offers degree courses to around two hundred students each year. Jeremy gave me a tour of the building, then we went for an *al fresco* lunch at a nearby restaurant and watched as dozens of university graduates, dressed in gowns and mortar boards, strolled by with proud parents, fresh from their graduation ceremonies. We also spotted two Everton and England footballers, Leighton Baines and Phil Jagielka, who were having lunch at a neighbouring table, but I resisted the opportunity for a publicity photograph.

Just a mile away from our lunch table, in Edge Hill, was the scene of Liverpool's worst tragedy of the Blitz. Liverpool was the most heavily bombed British city outside London during the Second World War and, being the country's largest west coast seaport, Liverpool and neighbouring Birkenhead were prime targets for attack. Atlantic convoy ships regularly arrived in the River Mersey bringing supplies of food and other cargoes from North America, which were critical to Britain's success in the war.

In November 1940, during the heaviest air raid to date, a parachute mine landed directly on a training centre in Durning Road, where around three hundred people were tightly packed into an air raid shelter in the basement boiler room. The three-storey building collapsed into the shelter below, crushing many of its occupants. Boiling water from the heating system and gas from fractured mains compounded the situation, and overhead fires made rescue work very dangerous. A total of 166 men, women and children were killed and many more were seriously injured. Winston Churchill later called it "the worst single civilian incident of the war".

With time to spare, I took the opportunity to have my hair cut, aware that this would probably be my last chance for some weeks. I was first in the queue, but to my frustration, the previous customer had seemingly opted for the entire menu of services, even though he already appeared to be rather follically challenged. He finally emerged from the tonsorial seat and, within five minutes, my neat trim had been completed.

Liverpool was buzzing with activity in the intense heat, with pavement cafes and bars thriving on the custom of office workers, shoppers and tourists, not to forget the new graduates and their guests. I'm sure that the blazing sunshine was responsible for a proliferation of extended lunch breaks and do not imagine that too much productive work was undertaken in the city offices that afternoon.

The history of Liverpool dates back to the first century, when a settlement first appeared on the banks of the River Mersey. By the time King John granted the town its Charter in 1207, it had grown into a thriving fishing village. Trade with Ireland and Europe developed, but it wasn't until the 18th century, as trade from the West Indies expanded, that Liverpool began to grow. International trade flourished, based on slavery and a wide range of commodities – including cotton, for which the city became the leading world market, supplying the textile mills of Manchester and Lancashire.

During the 18th century, the town's population grew from around 6,000 to 80,000. Substantial profits from the slave trade helped the city to develop and prosper and, by the beginning of the 19th century, 40% of the world's trade was passing through the docks at Liverpool. Rapid expansion continued, as growth in the cotton trade was accompanied by the development of strong trading links with India and the Far East.

The early part of the 20th century brought about economic changes, as a gradual fall in world demand for the region's traditional export commodities contributed to stagnation and decline in the city. Much of the city's housing stock was damaged or destroyed as a result of the heavy aerial bombardment Liverpool had suffered in the Second World War. The growth of containerisation brought about further decline of the docks and, by the 1980s, Liverpool's fortunes had sunk to their lowest point, with unemployment rates amongst the highest in the UK, the city's population declining and riots taking place in the Toxteth district. During this period the City Council was controlled by the far-left wing Militant group and the city sank heavily into debt.

Since its low point, there has been an economic revival in the city, with significant investment made, especially in the city centre. Liverpool was named as European Capital of Culture for 2008 and, with a focus on its cultural attractions, tourism has become an important industry.

Being in Liverpool felt like a homecoming for me. I was born in the city and lived there until I was nine years old, before I later returned as a student and stayed for another fifteen years. It was here that I bought my first property, met my wife and married. I had been determined to visit the city on my journey to Land's End, so I was delighted that my plan had succeeded. It was especially pleasing to see the city so vibrant, and even the fine weather had played a contributory role.

I briefly visited the Mathew Street area (where the Beatles played on 292 occasions at the Cavern Club) and sought out some of my old haunts, including a few city centre hostelries. To my surprise and pleasure, most were unchanged from my student days thirty years earlier, but sadly I had no time to venture inside to sample their products. Instead, I walked to the Merseyside Maritime Museum and visited the excellent and informative 'Emigrants to a New World' gallery, which told the story of the nine million people who sailed from Liverpool, then the largest emigration port in the world. They travelled to North America, Australia and New Zealand – the 'New World' – in search of a better life.

I returned to the Premier Inn, collected my rucksack, and checked out, then walked along the waterfront, a World Heritage Site, passing the renowned 'Three Graces' – the Royal Liver Building, with its two towers supporting the legendary Liver Birds, the Cunard Building, and the Port of Liverpool Building. I arrived at the Pier Head, where I would catch the infamous ferry across the Mersey to Birkenhead.

I had been faced with a dilemma when I included Liverpool in my JOGLE itinerary. My route across to Birkenhead was severed by the River Mersey, so I was left with several choices of how to continue my journey.

My favoured option involved walking through the two-mile long Mersey Tunnel, either along the road itself or, alternatively, through a deeper access tunnel, which I'd become aware of during a tour I'd attended some months earlier. I wrote to the tunnel authorities to enquire about special dispensation to undertake either option, but to my disappointment they declined, citing health and safety factors.

A second option involved cycling through the Mersey tunnel. This is permitted before the morning rush hour and later in the evening, but it transpired that cycling would not be permissible for my JOGLE journey to be verified as a walk.

The third option involved walking to the nearest bridge crossing at Runcorn. This would add an extra 24 miles to my journey, but the additional day required would necessitate multiple changes to the accommodation I'd already booked ahead, so I really wanted to avoid this option.

I consulted the experts at the Land's End – John O' Groats Association, who had already been most supportive in providing planning information in advance of my walk. Their suggested solution was to catch the ferry across the river, but to keep walking around on deck during the ten minute crossing. This option was considered to be consistent with the spirit of the walk, so I gratefully accepted it.

To my slight annoyance, on arrival in Liverpool on the Sunday, I'd discovered that the Mersey Tunnel was closed that afternoon for an organised cycle event to the Wirral. I felt sure that a lone long distance walker strolling out at the rear of the cyclists would not have created any additional health and safety issues, but that was history now.

It was from the Pier Head back in 1793, that a most distressing sight was witnessed. The Pelican, a privateer ship, was a small brig fitted with a number of cannon, designed to capture French merchant shipping. The ship had just been launched for the first time and was cruising along the river with well over one hundred people on board, including the shareholders and their families and friends. While they were enjoying themselves to the strains of music, the weather quickly deteriorated and the ship suddenly capsized opposite Seacombe and sank within minutes. It was discovered that several cannon, which had been improperly tied down, had broken free and these had effectively become iron missiles, which rolled across the deck and punched huge holes in the ship's opposite side. 102 people were drowned and the survivors either swam ashore or were rescued by boats.

I queued briefly next to the landing stage and then boarded a mid-afternoon ferry, with the tune of Gerry Marsden's 1965 hit "Ferry 'Cross the Mersey" ringing out in the distance. While the rest of the passengers enjoyed the views of the historic Liverpool waterfront from the comfort of the benches on the mid and upper decks, I followed my orders and walked around the deck, looking somewhat conspicuous. A trio of police officers was on board, apparently searching the decks for a man carrying a dark suitcase, but their efforts were in vain. Fortunately, they did not divert their attentions to the strange man carrying a large red rucksack, who was constantly on the move during the short river crossing.

The ferry follows a triangular route, calling initially at

Seacombe in Wallasey, then at Birkenhead Woodside, where I disembarked after a 20 minute journey. After a brief wait in Birkenhead, Jeremy collected me and drove me the few miles to their home, my accommodation for the night.

We had a delicious meal in the garden, joined by Jeremy and Sarah's sociable teenage daughters Rebecca and Rachel, and another longstanding university friend Paul, whom I hadn't seen for a few years. Later in the evening the old photographs from our university days in the last century were circulated, reviving memories of youthful innocence, embarrassing hairstyles and dubious fashion choices.

CHAPTER FIVE

Walking the length of Wales

Day 33 – Liverpool to Buckley
Distance: 19.6 miles
Cumulative distance: 555.9 miles
Weather: Hot and sunny

A varied walk to Wales in baking heat

Jeremy served an alternative to the standard breakfast fare, with fresh fruit, followed by a bacon muffin, then drove me to my starting point in Birkenhead. It already felt warm and, according to the local weather forecast, the temperature would rise much further still.

Birkenhead boasts a rich maritime history, with HMS Ark Royal and many other vessels built at the Cammell Laird shipyard in the town. Shipbuilding and ship repair both remain important elements of the local economy today. In 1860, the first street tramway in Europe opened in the town and Birkenhead Park, a large Victorian park, was the inspiration for New York's Central Park.

I walked out of town up a steep hill, which led me to pleasant residential suburbs, before eventually reaching country lanes close to Clatterbridge Hospital. I was heading for a country pub in nearby Raby to meet Roy, my Liverpool

Football Club companion who lives near Chester. I'd mixed up the date for our meeting and Roy had been expecting to meet me on the previous day. Fortunately, he had texted me in advance to confirm that my walk was still on schedule and I realised my mistake, so we were able to rearrange for today.

Roy had taken early retirement from the banking industry some years ago, but sadly lost his wife, Pat, to cancer. He now filled his days playing golf, following Liverpool Football Club, supporting the RSPB and spending time with his grandchildren.

The 17th century thatched building was decked with hanging baskets brimming with colour and, in bright sunshine, represented a picture postcard image. Over an extensive ploughman's lunch and a couple of pints of Liverpool Lou beer from the Baltic Fleet brewery, Roy and I talked about my experiences of the walk so far and his recent 'holiday' as a RSPB volunteer (I'd really needed his bird watching knowledge in earlier legs of my journey!). I'd already explained to him that I needed to depart for the afternoon leg by 1.15pm, but the relaxing environment, refreshing beer and good company took effect and it was nearer to 2.00pm by the time I set off.

I had plenty of miles to cover in the afternoon, following off road tracks around some picturesque Wirral villages. Trees initially provided welcome shade from the burning sun, but it became less sheltered as I headed down towards the estuary marshes. Here I joined the Dee Marshes cycle path, still brand spanking new following its recent opening. The path crossed the marsh on a raised wooden boardwalk, then ran adjacent to the MOD Sealand Firing Range and the railway line. This was one of my major route planning achievements – I had discovered it quite fortuitously from a search engine, which led me to the website of a Chester cycling club. This path helped to save some mileage on a long, hot day but, more importantly, enabled me to avoid Queensferry, a busy industrial area with a fast dual carriageway not designed to be used by pedestrians.

The route was a great success, but the heat slowed me down and significantly increased my water intake. To my despair, there were no opportunities to refill my water bottles at any point of the route. A further short cut didn't materialise, when I discovered that the open land I'd planned to cross to cut a large corner had been fenced off and planted with saplings. I crossed the River Dee on the pedestrian track alongside the Hawarden rail bridge, another fruitful short cut I'd identified during my route planning.

I had now reached Wales, the third country of my journey so far. The bilingual signs, including those on the cycle path, were the first indication that I'd crossed the border. To my relief I could see civilisation ahead, the busy town of Shotton. I desperately needed liquid refreshment.

The pedestrian path circumnavigated both of Shotton's railway stations, before depositing me on the high street. I was heartened to discover that the first building ahead of me was a pub. On closer inspection, it was the Central Hotel, a Wetherspoon's pub, so I hurried inside to buy a pint of Coke with ice and lemon to relieve my desperate thirst. Seeing my large rucksack, the barman enquired about my walk and insisted on giving me the drink on the house. He called the manager over, then she made a generous donation to my charity tin and tried to offer me food and more drink. I gratefully accepted a second pint of iced Coke, then several customers made further donations to the cause. The manager wanted to call ahead to the Wetherspoon's pub in Mold to arrange a meal and a collection, but I explained that I was staying with friends for the evening. I was pressed for time and had to leave the pub to continue my journey, but I was really struck by the experience. I'd only visited for ten minutes yet, touched by their hospitality and kindness to a complete stranger in my moment of need, I felt really inspired.

Physically refreshed and mentally uplifted, I continued my journey with renewed vigour. After some careful map reading around a series of off-road paths, I navigated my way to Buckley (Bwcle, in Welsh), "historic brickmaking town". The town was alive with activity, with young and old heading towards a funfair. I soon established that it was Jubilee Day.

Buckley Jubilee is an annual regional celebration, which takes place on the second Tuesday of July. The ceremonial march begins on "The Common", a large area of common ground owned by the people of the town and used for leisure and recreational purposes. The march then leaves the common, and parades through the town, with representatives from the local groups, Scout and Guide troops, and many of the local schools.

I phoned ahead to arrange my lift and Gordon duly arrived in his car to collect me. Gordon and Shelley are more university friends, who live near Mold with their son, Owen. My route passed about ten miles away from their house, so they had kindly offered to accommodate me. Meeting up with old student friends over the last couple of weeks had almost become a parallel agenda to the main event!

Gordon and Shelley's house was a beautiful converted barn, with a delightful hillside garden and panoramic views of the neighbouring countryside. As a child, Shelley had lived with her parents in the house just a few yards downhill from the barn, then some years later Gordon and Shelley had converted the barn to become their own home.

After a long day in the heat and a border crossing, I really appreciated a hot shower on arrival. On the chair next to my bed, Shelley had placed several envelopes addressed to me. On closer scrutiny, these were donations from her family and friends – another act of generosity. We had a tasty sausage dinner and later sampled a few bottles of Welsh Black beer from the Great Orme brewery.

Day 34 – Buckley to Chirk
Distance: 21.7 miles
Cumulative distance: 577.6 miles
Weather: Warm and sunny

A long undulating walk across some challenging paths to reach the Offa's Dyke path

There was further variety for breakfast, as I declined the full Welsh option in favour of cereal and boiled eggs. Gordon and Owen had agreed to join me for today's walk, so Shelley drove us back into Buckley for the start. Owen had just finished school and was preparing to go to university in the autumn, so had some free time on his hands.

Although it was warm, there was a light breeze, which made walking more comfortable. We followed some minor roads and managed to overlook a footpath which would have eliminated a corner from the route. Another one to add to the list of missed footpaths.

We followed the road through Pontblyddyn and Pontybodkin. I had driven through these villages countless times over the years, but close up and at walking pace they took on a very different personality. I discovered features which would go unnoticed by passing motorists, including a model of a railway goods wagon, which was displayed on a public lawn next to the road.

Shortly afterwards, at Coed Talon, we diverted from the road and joined the track of an old railway line. This was the Wrexham and Minera Joint Railway, which connected Mold with Brymbo. Passenger traffic on the line declined during the Second World War, with only two passenger trains a day in each direction, ostensibly for local children attending grammar school in Mold. Passenger services were ceased in 1950, but goods traffic continued until 1963, when the line was closed completely.

We re-joined the road at the end of the footpath and passed through the pleasant, peaceful villages of Llanfynydd and Ffrith.

After Ffrith we joined a woodland path, which was intended to be a short cut, but proved to be rather challenging and so became a long cut. Fallen trees were strewn across most of the path, so it represented an assault course. We clambered under, over and between trees, which was made more difficult by having a bulky rucksack which had to be manoeuvred at the same time. At best, it could be described as a little-used footpath, but we did wonder whether we were the first humans for many years to set foot here. We eventually battled our way out of the woods and joined a minor road.

Since student days, I'd enjoyed many day hikes with Gordon and Shelley. Typically, we'd be part of a larger group, hiking in the Lake District, the Peak District, Snowdonia or the Brecon Beacons. After many years of service for a packaging company, Gordon had been made redundant, but had now established himself as a self-employed gardener. Business appeared to be thriving and, apart from days when the rain lashed down incessantly, he didn't miss office life.

We took a wrong turn at lunchtime, largely due to one footpath appearing to follow a slightly different route to the version on the map. The end result was that we walked an additional mile, made worse because we had to re-climb the hill which we had just descended. On the bright side, it was considerably less than the 3.5 mile detour caused by my failure to consult the map at the Scotland / England border!

We descended into the Vale of Llangollen as far as Trevor, where we joined the Shropshire Union canal and walked across the famous Pontcysyllte Aqueduct, a World Heritage Site. The impressive aqueduct, which was designed by Thomas Telford, consists of a cast iron trough, supported nearly forty metres above the River Dee on iron arched ribs carried on nineteen pillars. The trough is over 300 metres long, 3.4 metres wide and 1.6 metres deep and the towpath is mounted slightly above the canal, which allows the water displaced by the passage of a narrow boat to flow easily under the towpath and around the boat. Pedestrians are protected from falling from the aqueduct by railings on the outside edge of the towpath. Every five years, the ends of the aqueduct are closed and a plug situated in one of the highest spans is opened to drain the canal water into the river below, for inspection and maintenance of the trough.

Fortunately, all three of us had a head for heights, so we were able to walk across the aqueduct without any difficulty. This was not the case when I'd steered a canal barge across some years earlier – all members of my party had descended into the bowels of the boat in fear of vertigo, despite the fact that we were towing another barge which had broken down en route.

Our final climb of the day was a steep one, but we were rewarded with fine views back towards the aqueduct and the Vale of Llangollen. As the road levelled off, I spotted a wooden signpost bearing a small acorn symbol. This was my introduction to the Offa's Dyke path, which would be my partner for the next week. Great oaks out of little acorns grow…

We met up again with Shelley in the car park of Chirk Castle and we parted. After the aches and pains incurred by my previous walking partners, I sincerely hoped that Gordon and Owen would be fit by the following morning, especially as Gordon had some gardening work to catch up with.

I continued on from the car park to complete the final section of my walk. I tramped through a field of overgrown nettles then, as I descended towards the road, a pheasant flew out from the undergrowth. It was a close contest as to which one of us was more startled.

It was nearby that the Battle of Crogen took place in 1165 and led to a defeat for the forces of Henry II against the combined might of the Welsh princes, led by Owain Gwynedd. Although outnumbered, the Welsh waited until Henry's army had entered the narrow Ceiriog Valley and then attacked, using local knowledge to their advantage. Many soldiers on both sides were killed in the battle and Henry's forces had to retreat.

I checked in to my B&B at Castle Mill and, after a much needed bath, Eric the owner drove me into Chirk, where I dined at the Poacher's Pocket. The service was slow, but the food was good value and I especially appreciated the Marston's Pedigree beer offered.

As an enthusiastic cricket supporter, I was keen to follow progress of the latest Ashes series between England and Australia. Today had been the first day of the First Test Match at Trent Bridge, Nottingham and England had scored only 215 runs in their first innings, losing their final four wickets for just 2 runs. However, the English bowlers had fought back strongly, with Australia reduced to 75-4 by close of play.

Day 35 – Chirk to Llanymynech
Distance: 13.4 miles
Cumulative distance: 591.0 miles
Weather: Warm and sunny

No water, personal pub hours, wonderful walking and more Welsh generosity

As today's walk was relatively short and tonight's accommodation was not available until 4pm, I decided to treat myself to a lie in and a later breakfast. This gave me the chance to review today's route and catch up on some emails.

During breakfast Mel, my B&B host, explained that the village's water supply had been disconnected during the night, leaving brown water flowing out of the taps. She kindly filled my water bottles with orange juice and also made a donation to my charity.

I left yet another welcoming B&B and was confronted immediately by a steep climb. Some of the stiles on the route presented a major challenge, having being conquered by prickly gorse and nettles – I had to perform a tricky pirouette to manoeuvre myself and my load over them. I walked for a mile with Graham, a long distance walker from Barrow in Furness, who was undertaking Offa's Dyke and sleeping in his camper van.

Offa's Dyke is a 177 mile trail which runs along the English-Welsh border from Prestatyn in the north to Chepstow in the south, broadly following the earthwork from which it derives its name. The footpath was officially opened in 1971 by Lord Hunt, of Everest fame.

From 757 to 796 AD, Offa was King of Mercia, the largest of England's seven kingdoms, although his span of control was even wider due to family alliances. His armies invaded Wales on two occasions, but each was unsuccessful and it appears that he then decided to build the Dyke as a permanent barrier.

The Dyke consists of a ditch and embankment constructed with the ditch on the Welsh-facing side. The original Dyke was about 27 metres wide and 8 metres from the bottom of the ditch to the top of the bank. Much of the Dyke can still be traced – in places it still retains most of its original features, but in other areas centuries of farming have led to its disappearance.

I'd read and been warned about the considerable number of energy-sapping stiles which are scattered along the length of the path and could only hope that the overgrown examples I'd encountered during the morning were not representative.

After rounding Selattyn Hill and Baker's Hill, I followed a road which led to Racecourse Common, a popular venue for horseracing until 1848. There is still evidence of the old racecourse, including the remains of the figure-of-eight course and grandstand.

I arrived in the village of Trefonen, ready for my regular pint of refreshing Coke. I walked into the Barley Mow pub and was surprised to be the only customer on this warm day. It was soon evident why – the pub didn't open until 5pm! However, on hearing about my plight, the sympathetic landlady broke off from her chores and opened the bar just for me. We chatted about my walk and, as I left the premises, she locked the door. What hospitality!

At lunchtime, I reached the summit of Moelydd, an impressive hill which offered 360 degree views for miles. The weather was perfect, the scenery wonderful and I felt in control. Shortly after my arrival, a German couple arrived at the summit, having become lost en route. I pointed them in the right direction, but then watched as they ignored my instructions and opted for a different path. Shortly afterwards, I saw them return after a second navigational error.

I spent almost ninety minutes at the summit as it was warm, the views were idyllic and I had time to spare. I phoned my niece Rosie, who had suffered from a chronic lung illness for some years, but was delighted to hear that she had recently made some encouraging progress. We chatted for almost an hour, but the Germans didn't re-appear during this time!

The path descended to Nant-Mawr and Porth-y-Waen, before crossing an old railway track and continuing right through the middle of a crop field. At the other side of the field I encountered the Germans again – they were taking a refreshment break, but I was pleased that they had been able to follow the path without further hitches.

The path climbed up through the woods of Llanymynech Hill, clinging to the edge of a golf course as it plateaued towards Llanymynech Rocks, a nature reserve. Offa's Dyke path criss-crosses the border between England and Wales, but I climbed over one notable stile, which was marked 'England' on one side and 'Cymru' (Wales) on the other!

I spotted numerous different species of butterfly up on the hill and around the reserve, including red admiral, painted lady, tortoiseshell, peacock and the rarer orange tip (the latter identified from my guide book!). In fact, butterflies had been prevalent during most parts of my journey from John O' Groats, but especially along the canal banks and public footpaths. This was a surprise to me, since in the spring I'd listened to depressing stories about the UK's butterfly population being in serious decline. 2012 had been a catastrophic year for most butterflies, with relentless rain and cold leading to a struggle for them to find food, shelter and mating opportunities. But in the hot, dry summer of 2013, the butterflies were fighting back with a vengeance, showing nature's remarkable powers of recovery.

I arrived in Llanymynech, my base for the night. In this border area, its claim to fame is that it sits in both England and Wales, with each side of the main street in different countries! As far as I could make out, it had three pubs, four takeaways and just one shop. Curious.

One of the pubs, the Cross Keys, was my accommodation for the night. I checked in at the bar and immediately sank two pints of the local brew, Station bitter from the Stonehouse brewery. I soon engaged in conversation with a few locals and sampled a pint of Glaslyn from Bragdy Mws Piws (Purple Moose Brewery) in Porthmadog. They were very interested in hearing about my walk and, with no effort, I had raised another £25 for Cancer Research UK.

The large screen TV in the bar was showing cricket – England versus Australia. It was the final session of the second day of the First Test match, so with a handful of the pub's regulars, I watched England start to regain momentum after a disappointing day. After succumbing to 117 for 9, the Australian last pair had put on an extraordinary partnership of 163 runs, giving the Aussies a first innings lead of 65 runs. By close of play, England had built up a lead of 15 runs for the loss of two wickets. It promised to be a close match.

I ate in the restaurant (tasty chicken kebabs in sweet chilli sauce with chips) and was not totally surprised to see the lost German couple dining there too – they were also staying at the inn!

Day 36 – Llanymynech to Montgomery

Distance: 20.0 miles
Cumulative distance: 611.0 miles
Weather: Very hot and sunny

A tough day in baking sun, a swim, a visit from my ex-boss and meeting my namesake

Predictably, I was greeted by the German couple at breakfast. They explained that they were scheduled today to walk to Welshpool in order to catch a train to Cardiff, where they would meet up with some family members. We said our farewells for the fourth and final time, while I crossed my fingers that they would not become disoriented on the way to the station and subsequently miss their train.

I checked out of the hotel and immediately joined the Montgomery canal. The towpath was carpeted with hundreds and hundreds of tiny frogs and I had to tiptoe judiciously to avoid crushing them with my size 10.5 boots. The canal had been abandoned in 1944, following a breach some years earlier, but some recent restoration work had been undertaken and further work was planned. The route left the towpath at Four Crosses and followed a scenic track along the River Severn for several miles.

An enterprising cottage owner had placed a small circular table on the path next to their garden gate, together with a neatly written sign which read "Jam made with fruit from this garden for sale £2". I was tempted to buy a jar of jam, but reluctantly had to accept that I could not afford to transport the additional weight in my rucksack. However, the homemade fruit cake which was also on display could be consumed today, so I placed my coins into the collection pot and carefully selected a slice.

I was confronted by herds of cows at half a dozen places en route. Most ignored me, but some seemed to be a little too interested for comfort. Very occasionally you hear reports about people being crushed by cows, so I decided to plan my escape routes, just in case. I soon drew up a list of alternative plans, which included climbing over a barbed wire fence, hurdling over an electric fence (not easily negotiated with a bulky backpack) or just running very quickly. Luckily, I did not have to put any of these into practice, but at least I was prepared!

I met a mother and her young son who were walking the entire Offa's Dyke path for charity. They were heading north and had been blessed with superb weather to date. After we'd been chatting for a while, the son suddenly interrupted and pointed out that they'd still be walking at 8 o'clock tonight if his mum and I didn't stop talking!

The baking sun was increasing my water consumption, so I called into the Green Dragon Inn in Buttington at opening time for an iced Coke and a water bottle refill. I'd driven past this pub many times on the way to North Wales, so it seemed strange to visit it for the first time. The pub is situated right next to the railway level crossing, but the trains between Birmingham and Aberystwyth or Pwllheli are infrequent, so it was a surprise to hear a train pass by. Just four days after my visit, the same train was involved in a collision with a tractor and trailer at a private level crossing a few hundred yards up the line. The train, carrying over one hundred passengers, had been travelling at 70 miles per hour, but managed to brake quickly to minimise the impact. Miraculously, only two passengers sustained minor injuries. The driver's compartment of the train was badly damaged and the train itself was partially derailed.

Back on the footpath, I passed a little wooden seat which bore the inscription:

> "There was a crooked man
> who walked a crooked mile
> he found a crooked sixpence
> upon a crooked stile"

I later discovered that this verse originates from the time of King Charles I. The 'crooked man' is believed to be the Scottish General Sir Alexander Leslie, who signed a covenant securing religious and political freedom for Scotland and the 'crooked stile' referred to is the border between England and Scotland. The full verse concludes that 'they all lived together in a little crooked house', which is a reference to the fact that the English and Scots had at last come to an agreement. However, it puzzled me why the verse appeared here on a wooden seat close to the English and Welsh border!

I spent the next hour climbing steeply up to Beacon Ring, a hill offering splendid views of Welshpool and surrounding hills. I somehow managed to lose the official footpath close to the summit of the Beacon Ring and had to scramble over a stone wall, wade through a field of dense, long grass, and then climb over a barbed wire fence to re-join the path.

The heat became more intense, especially with no breeze and minimal shelter. After the early days of my walk, when my right boot was troubling me, today was probably the toughest walking day to date. However, the local forecast for the next few days predicted even hotter weather, so I would have to grin and bear it.

I left the Offa's Dyke path and walked the final few miles along the main road, before I eventually arrived in Montgomery (it was signposted in its Welsh form as Trefaldwyn, which caused me some confusion). I had imagined Montgomery to be a large county town, but it was little more than an attractive main square and some charming timber-framed townhouses, surrounded by a few streets. At the top of the hill, the ruins of the thirteenth century castle overlooked the town. Surprisingly for such a small place, it boasted a Michelin starred restaurant, only the fourth in Wales. I easily located my accommodation at the Dragon Hotel, a historic seventeenth century former coaching inn situated in the main square, and wandered inside.

The heat had taken its toll and I was desperate for liquid refreshment and a hot, relaxing bath. Having soon addressed both needs, I took advantage of the hotel's small indoor swimming pool – I had transported my swimming trunks for six hundred miles, so I certainly wasn't going to miss this opportunity to use them!

The hotel had been taken over by new management a couple of days earlier, so it was amusing to observe the inexperienced team struggle to operate the computer system. One of the new managers was serving at the hotel bar, but seemed more intent on adjusting the nameplates on the cask beers, rather than attending to the growing queue of thirsty customers. He barked out instructions to a young female waitress, but it was clear that he had burdened her with far more than she could reasonably be expected to cope with.

During dinner in the hotel restaurant, I was joined by Jeff, my last line manager before I finished work. He'd just arrived after a tricky journey from Windsor by road and taxi, and was staying at a nearby B&B, but would be joining me for the following day's walk. Jeff had been a colossal source of support during my final months at work and was my sounding board during the conception and embryonic development of my journey. That his initial reaction to my crazy idea did not involve him falling off his chair nor referring me for counselling, was an important factor in my decision to proceed and it seemed fitting that he was able to join me for part of the journey.

After dinner I was joined by my namesake, Russell George. I'd better explain! A couple of years earlier, I was driving with my family through mid-Wales late one Friday evening and my son Daniel exclaimed that he'd spotted a banner bearing my name at the roadside. I suggested that he'd probably misread the name but, a short distance further down the road, I identified another large banner – Daniel had been right! This was nothing to do with a personal publicity stunt, but rather the Welsh Assembly elections, which were due to take place later in the month, and a certain Russell George was standing for the Montgomery constituency. We were neither known to each other, nor related – he was a local councillor in neighbouring Newtown and he subsequently went on to win the seat quite comfortably to become one of the Welsh Assembly's 60 members. When I was planning my walk and realised that I would be staying in Montgomery, I thought it would be interesting to make contact with him, at the very least to inform him that I wasn't an imposter visiting his constituency! He readily agreed to meet and had contacted me a few days earlier to confirm the arrangements.

Russell George AM (Assembly Member) drove over to my hotel in Montgomery after an earlier evening engagement with the Montgomeryshire Area Scout Council. He was very interested to hear about my walk, especially as he had participated in a one day 42 mile charity walk in his constituency in the previous year, and had battled through the pain barrier to complete the course. We sat at an *al fresco* table and chatted for a few hours about Welsh politics and life as an Assembly member. He told me a story about one of his visits to 10 Downing Street, where he'd been left alone to wander around the house with a mug of tea. Apart from sharing a name, we discovered another coincidence – his cousins, who now run his family's original agricultural business, share the same names as my children, Daniel and Hannah. Jeff joined us later and we all enjoyed a final drink in the balmy, late evening.

In the Test Match, thanks to a late unbeaten partnership, England had closed the day on 326-6, to extend their lead over Australia to 261 runs. Everything was set for a thrilling finish.

Day 37 – Montgomery to Knighton
Distance: 20.6 miles
Cumulative distance: 631.6 miles
Weather: Very hot and sunny

A very tough day of steep ascents and descents in the blazing heat, wonderful hospitality and a rescue

Jeff met me outside the hotel and we set off knowing that we had a challenging day ahead of us, even before hearing that it was going to be the hottest day of the year.

Jeff is Canadian, but had lived with his wife and children in England for over five years. In that time, he had visited more areas of the UK than most of its own residents manage to visit in a lifetime and, having recently taken the UK citizenship test, his knowledge of Britain would put most natives to shame.

We set off at a fair pace along local roads, then re-joined

Offa's Dyke path at Brompton Crossroads, where some rusty petrol pumps hinted at a bygone era. We benefited from the welcome shelter of woodland for a while, until the trees disappeared and the path followed the ridge of the earthwork itself, a feature of this section of the route.

It wasn't long before we reached the infamous Switchbacks, a series of steep hills and steep descents. On a normal day they would have been a challenge, but in today's blazing heat they were really punishing, especially with a loaded rucksack. The uphill sections were quite strenuous, but the steep downhill sections placed a pronounced strain on knees and ankles and it was a constant battle to stay upright.

The intense heat and the physical exertion resulted in us drinking litres of water and by mid-morning we had exhausted our supplies. As we crossed a remote road south of Churchtown, we came across a collection of un-signposted buildings which appeared to be part of a young people's outdoor activity centre. Desperate for our water bottles to be re-filled, we wandered into the grounds and tried to attract the attention of somebody. We eventually located an adult, who explained that the centre catered for children in care and that access was not permitted to the public. However, he recognised our predicament in the fierce sun and escorted us to the kitchen, where the staff kindly re-filled all our empty containers.

We had embarked on another steep descent, when a group of two middle-aged couples approached us from the opposite direction and handed over a generous donation to my charity. Expressing surprise, I enquired how they knew that I was walking for charity.

"We saw you from our hotel bedroom window in Montgomery earlier this morning and read the sign on the back of your rucksack. And we started our walk from further south today, so we guessed that we might see you at some point!"

At Newcastle-on-Clun, we decided to divert to the Crown Inn for an iced drink. After experiencing a number of pubs not being open for business when I needed them most during the earlier days of my walk, we joked on the way that this one couldn't possibly be closed on a hot Saturday afternoon, but sadly our worst fears materialised. We looked at each other in disbelief and considered our options, when human kindness intervened. A nearby resident had witnessed our plight and apologised profusely for the lack of service provided by his local hostelry. He then invited us to join him and his wife in their garden, where he brought us several jugs of iced juice and offered us food (we declined the latter). He even made a generous donation to my charity. So it's a big thumbs down to the Crown Inn (we later spotted several other thirsty and frustrated walkers who shared our disappointment) and a mighty three cheers for Derek and his family for showing immense kindness to two hot and sweaty complete strangers.

In the extreme heat and without the benefit of over a month of long distance walking, Jeff's legs decided that they would be punished no further. I persuaded him to continue a little further up the road, until we reached a remote farmhouse bed and breakfast, the only sign of any civilisation indicated on the map. Here we hatched a cunning plan, which involved me walking eight miles to Knighton carrying Jeff's smaller backpack, collecting Jeff's car and driving back to collect him. In the meantime, he could relax in a field next door to the B&B in an otherwise remote location. This plan would enable me to reach my destination on foot and within the rules of my walk, but would allow Jeff to avoid a lengthy walk and give him time to recover.

With a much lighter load and the benefit of downhill terrain, I walked at a furious pace. The desolate road crossed over Weston Hill, then meandered around Llanfair Hill, Cefn Hepreas and Cwm-sanaham Hill, before reaching the valley and following the River Teme into Knighton. The journey had taken me less than one and three quarter hours, which left me enough time to pop into a local hostelry for a rapid iced Coke before locating Jeff's car, which was parked next to the Visitor Centre.

I had some concerns about driving back from Knighton to collect Jeff. I hadn't driven for a month, which didn't really trouble me, but I deduced that, being Canadian, Jeff probably drove an automatic car – I dislike automatics and hadn't driven one for at least ten years. On the last occasion, I'd picked up a hire car at Glasgow airport and found myself jolting down the nearby M8 motorway as I tried to master the controls. Most worryingly right now, I had left my light casual shoes in my rucksack with Jeff, so would have to drive in my walking boots, which would make it more difficult to control the pedals. Despite my concerns, I drove very cautiously back up the deserted roads I'd recently descended and made it safely to meet my walking companion. It was a relief to find that the respite had resulted in a significant improvement in Jeff's condition and he was in good spirits when I arrived.

Jeff dropped me off at my B&B, where I had a refreshing cup of tea with the friendly owners, Bernadine and Mike. After a quick shower, I walked into the town centre and tried to dine at the pub recommended to me by my hosts. However, the locals were out in force on this hot Saturday evening and it was evident as soon as I entered the pub that I would have a long wait. I opted instead for the local Indian restaurant, where I had a choice of tables to dine at and, consequently, very efficient service.

Knighton is a picturesque market town set in the lush rolling country of the Marches. "Marches" means boundary or disputed country; this part of the country certainly had a turbulent past. This was another town with dual nationality – part is in Shropshire, England and part in Powys, Wales. Knighton is rich in history with half-timbered houses and winding streets known locally as 'The Narrows'. There is evidence of a settlement in the area dating back to the Stone Age, but the current town is mostly medieval in origin.

I read with amusement about one local custom. Apparently, until the mid-1800s, it was possible for a man to obtain a divorce by bringing his wife into town to the place where the clock tower now stands, parading her with a halter around her neck, arm, or waist, and then publicly auctioning her to the highest bidder. For all I know, the practice may still take place on eBay today!

Back at my B&B, I reflected on what had been a challenging day. It had undoubtedly been the hardest day's walking of my entire journey, with tiring ascents and descents coupled with intense heat. Jeff had been unfortunate to choose this day, but I concluded that he should be pleased with the distance he achieved in these difficult conditions. However, it did concern me that most of my walking companions to date had experienced injuries to some degree. With more walking partners scheduled to join me, I didn't want to continue this trend!

In the day's events at the Test Match, England had completed their second innings, scoring 375 runs and setting the Australians a victory target of 311 runs. By close of play, England had reduced the Aussies to 174-6, so England were favourites to win the match on the final day.

Day 38 – Knighton to Kington

Distance: 14.1 miles
Cumulative distance: 645.7 miles
Weather: Warm and sunny

A panoramic walk, more comfortable weather conditions and another walking companion

I had a leisurely breakfast chatting to my host Bernadine, who kindly donated a free packed lunch to the cause. She was eager for me to notify her when (if, maybe?) I finally reached Land's End. Although I had now walked for well over six hundred miles, my ultimate destination was still over three hundred miles' distant, and I would continue to focus resolutely on the day's walk ahead of me.

I walked down the hill to the town centre and headed for the Offa's Dyke Visitor Centre, where I met Graham, my walking companion for the day. Graham is a self-employed security consultant, who I'd worked with previously. He had travelled by car from his home near Windsor the previous evening, but had stayed overnight in accommodation a few miles away.

We walked away from the town centre and tried with difficulty to locate the Offa's Dyke path. After a few unsuccessful attempts we eventually found it and followed the track as it climbed unhurriedly around the golf course until we encountered fine views of patchwork green fields and meadows. This was to be the theme of the day. After crossing Hawthorn Hill and its near neighbour Furrow Hill, we adjourned for a short break next to the River Lugg and cooled ourselves in the clear waters.

Graham's family called him on several occasions to check

on his progress – if there had been any doubts about his ability to complete this undulating walk in challenging weather conditions, he quickly dispelled them and proved that his fitness level could not be questioned.

Fortunately, the weather conditions were more favourable than on the previous day, with a little cloud cover helping to reduce temperatures and a pleasant breeze providing welcome relief. The path included a few ascents, but they were not as challenging and the descents were not as punishing. For a sunny July Sunday, we were intrigued that we didn't encounter more walkers on this very scenic part of Offa's Dyke path.

As we ascended the gorse covered slopes of Herrock Hill, I kept abreast of the exciting developments in the Test Match cricket via my smartphone. Just as we reached Herrock Hill Common, England sealed dramatic victory over Australia by 14 runs, the narrowest of margins. The Australian final pair had threatened to steal victory from the jaws of defeat, but the English bowlers managed to take the crucial final wicket just in time.

After Rushock Hill, the path descended gradually across farmland. It was not well sign-posted in this area and on several occasions we had to speculate which way the path led. Only when we arrived at a sheepfold were we convinced that we had followed the correct path.

Close to the end of the route, at Bradnor Hill, we reached a golf club. My Offa's Dyke guidebook had commented that the club was "surprisingly friendly towards walkers" so, intrigued and desperate for a drink, we decided to find out for ourselves. After a couple of pints, I can vouch that the guidebook was completely reliable as we chatted with a few members who informed us that, at 1100 feet above sea level, this was the highest eighteen-hole golf course in England.

A few minutes later, we arrived at the Royal Oak Hotel in Kington, my home for the night. Graham ordered a taxi to take him back to Knighton to collect his car and, to our joint surprise, it arrived within twenty minutes, leaving just enough time for us each to down a pint of the local ale.

One of the features of the Offa's Dyke walk is that it constantly weaves between England and Wales. As a consequence of this, I was never completely certain which of the two countries I was walking in during most stages of my journey. This confusion was further muddied in towns such as Llanymynech and Knighton, which were divided between England and Wales. In truth, none of the places where I stayed portrayed any dominant characteristics of either nationality, which left me to conclude that each had been diluted over time to form a hybrid Anglo-Welsh identity.

The exception to this rule, however, appeared to be Kington. It was very noticeable how the border accents of the last few days had been replaced by the Herefordshire "burr" and the town itself, despite being just two miles from the Welsh border, had a genuinely English feel to it, being dominated by pubs and antique shops. Curiously, although it lies on the western (Welsh) side of Offa's Dyke, Kington has been part of England for over a thousand years.

I dined at the hotel and opted for the local Herefordshire dish on the menu – pork, apple and cider pie. Back in my room, there was a quiz taking place in the pub's beer garden, just outside my open window. I dozed off to the gentle lull of the quiz master's Herefordshire accent, as he posed increasingly more difficult questions to a boisterous crowd.

Day 39 – Kington to Hay-on-Wye
Distance: 15.6 miles
Cumulative distance: 661.3 miles
Weather: Hot and sunny

A wonderful ridge walk and arrival in the capital of second hand books

After a full night's sleep (a surprisingly rare event on my journey), I checked out of the hotel and started the gradual climb up to the Hergest Ridge, an open common on which wild ponies and sheep grazed.

The musician Mike Oldfield, who once lived nearby in a large house close to the golf course, named his second album after Hergest Ridge (pronounced "Hargist", with a hard g), following the spectacular success of Tubular Bells. Hergest Ridge entered the UK album charts at number one but, unusually, was then displaced by its predecessor, Tubular Bells. His next album, Ommadawn, also included a reference to this area, with the lyric "… if you feel a little glum, to Hergest Ridge you should come."

I reached a broad, grassy path which teasingly continued to ascend, but offered superb views of the Shropshire hills and the Black mountains. This was one of the best walks of my entire journey, combining a gentle, verdant path with perfect weather conditions and an impressive panorama.

I met a group of four people, three of whom were holding up large umbrellas, not because there was any prospect of rain, but rather as protection against the sun as they walked. Later on I encountered John and Judith from Chester, who had planned a number of long distance walks this summer, including the West Highland Way, and insisted on taking my photograph.

The path descended into the tiny village of Gladestry,

where children at the nearby primary school seemed bemused by my large rucksack. My guidebook referred to a shop in the village, so I'd planned to buy some lunch there but, unfortunately, the shop appeared to have closed down since the book was written, leaving me without any fresh food.

The trail followed a narrow lane beyond Gladestry, where I encountered Postman Pat. Well, he might have been named Pat, but he definitely drove a red Royal Mail van and he unquestionably looked the part. I squeezed into the hedgerow to allow him to pass, then he turned into the driveway of the next house to deliver their mail. In the meantime, I progressed a little further up the road until he re-appeared behind me, and then I had to wedge myself into the bank again, while he drove by towards the next house. This procedure continued five times until the trail conveniently turned away from the road.

Very occasionally, at remote locations along the Offa's Dyke path, my map indicated a tap symbol. This represented a supply of water, kindly provided by a sympathetic local farmer for the benefit of thirsty walkers. I noticed that a tap was imminent, which was a godsend as I was now down to my final emergency bottle of lukewarm water. I immediately spotted the tap next to a farm building, so hurriedly extracted my three empty containers from my rucksack, poured away the remaining lukewarm water and turned on the tap. A brown liquid emerged, so I allowed the tap to run for a minute. To my despair, the tap water remained brown and, on closer inspection, seemed to have a type of algae in it. I now had nothing at all left to drink, the midday sun was blazing, and I was a long way from civilisation.

My frustration at losing my water supplies disappeared a few yards further along the track, where a laminated A4 poster attached to a gate attracted my attention:

Disgwylfa Hill is a gift from God
Or whomever you believe in
Please cherish it as we do
Don't dump your scrap or tin

We wish to preserve the beauty
Of this green and pleasant land
So don't be selfish have a heart
And help us make a stand

This is a heartfelt message
To all you lazy dumpees
Take away your rubbish and litter
Don't leave it here, PLEASE

For those of you who do not care
And ignore our message too
Just remember that these hills have eyes
And they are watching YOU

I appreciated the scenery around Disgwylfa Hill and took special care not to dump any scrap or tin, but I could not detect any eyes watching me. Perhaps a few similar, but shorter, verses should be prominently displayed on the highway to deter road users from discarding their litter!

I was in serious need of food and drink, but recognised that the official path would not provide the prospect of either before Hay-on-Wye. I consulted my map and decided to divert from the trail. Instead, I took a detour of several miles through Clyro, which offered a shop and a pub, both of which were open. I drank a pint of iced Coke at the Baskerville Arms – Sir Arthur Conan Doyle is said to have stayed at nearby Clyro

Court (built by the Baskerville family) prior to writing 'The Hound of the Baskervilles'.

I eventually arrived in Hay-on-Wye, town of books, early in the afternoon and ate a late picnic lunch overlooking the River Wye. The town lies just inside the Welsh border and boasts not one, but two Norman castles.

I checked into my B&B, the aptly named Rest for the Tired, situated unsurprisingly above a second hand book shop. My room was on the top floor and I had to crouch to get through the doorway, which was under five feet in height!

After a snooze, I wandered around town and quickly confirmed that this was undoubtedly the second hand books capital of the UK. Every other shop seemed to sell books, with some specialising in specific themes, such as murder and mystery or transport. Unfortunately none of the book shops were open at this time, but I made a mental note to return one day.

Hay-on-Wye has also been the venue for a literary festival since 1988, attracting around 80,000 visitors over ten days in June to see and hear well known literary names from all over the world.

I dined at Kilverts, named after Francis Kilvert, curate of Clyro parish church from 1865 to 1872 and a prominent diarist of the period. The pub was holding a Welsh beer festival so, to accompany my moussaka, I sampled Butty Bach from Wye Valley brewery and Porters 06 from Otley brewery, Pontypridd.

Back in my room in the eaves, I noticed that the literary theme continued – there was a shelf laden with books on the floor and the television was supported by several hardback editions.

Day 40 – Hay-on-Wye to Llanthony
Distance: 13.0 miles
Cumulative distance: 674.3 miles
Weather: Warm and sunny

Company, another pleasant ridge walk and recuperation at the Priory

After a comfortable night's sleep at the Rest for the Tired, I had a leisurely breakfast with my host, before David, my walking companion for the next couple of days, duly arrived. I checked out while David parked his car nearby, and the B&B owner kindly made a donation to CRUK.

David had travelled from Buckingham very early that morning. I had worked with him previously on a number of projects, before he left to join Whitbread, the owners of Premier Inn (still no response to my requests for a charitable donation from them!). David, a proud Yorkshireman, had been an experienced hiker in his youth and had been keen to join me at some stage of my journey, but he had undoubtedly chosen two of the hottest days.

The first part of the walk included a gradual climb away from the town centre, then a steeper ascent towards Hay Bluff, described as "a large wedge of a mountain overlooking the pretty town of Hay-on-Wye", before we joined the Hatterrall Ridge at a height of 700 metres. The hill was shrouded in mist as we ascended, but this soon lifted. The reward for our efforts was a fine ridge walk, frequented by wild ponies and offering panoramic views of the surrounding Black mountains, the easternmost of the four ranges of hills that comprise the Brecon Beacons National Park. With the mist removed, temperatures rose rapidly, but a welcoming breeze provided some comfort.

The Army was conducting a training exercise in the area and we spotted a number of very focused, but exhausted young recruits carrying full packs as they struggled at pace along the ridge. Their superiors had set up a small tented checkpoint further along the ridge but, apart from acknowledging our presence, they were not inclined to engage in conversation with civilians. A few days earlier, in the nearby Brecon Beacons, two Territorial Army soldiers had died and a third was left critically ill (he later died) when they collapsed during gruelling military training on the hottest day of the year. The soldiers had been taking part in an exercise in the Welsh mountains, where the Army carries out infantry training and selection for the elite SAS.

We followed the ridge for about six miles along a level and well-defined path. The ridge also acts as the border between England and Wales, in keeping with much of the Offa's Dyke trail. Over recent days on Offa's Dyke, I'd become a great advocate of ridge walking – it offered easy terrain, wonderful panoramas, and a gentle breeze, which combined to leave me feeling quite uplifted.

After a well-earned picnic lunch, we began a precipitous descent towards Llanthony, in the Vale of Ewyas, a deep and long glacial valley, described by long distance walker John Hillaby as 'the Glencoe of the Welsh Border, a place marked indelibly by conflict'. Llanthony is dominated by the ruins of the 12th century Priory, which provided a stunning sight from our promontory. The descent down to the valley was steep, but we reached our base by mid-afternoon. We had time to check in early to our accommodation, the Half Moon Inn, before strolling up the road to visit the impressive Priory ruins and to sample the Priory Hotel's beer, the appropriately named Reverend James, from the Brains brewery. The beer was apparently named after one of the original owners of the

Buckley brewery, the Reverend James Buckley, a businessman with two conflicting roles – saving souls and satisfying thirsts.

Llanthony Priory dates back to around the year 1100, when Walter de Lacy is said to have discovered a ruined chapel of St. David here. With a band of followers, a church was built on the site and, by 1118, a group of monks from England founded a priory of Augustinian canons, the first in Wales. After persistent attacks from the local Welsh population, the monks retreated to Gloucester, but in about 1186 Hugh de Lacy provided funds to rebuild the priory church, and this work was completed by 1217. After the Dissolution of the Monasteries led by Henry the Eighth, the buildings gradually fell into a state of disrepair. Today, the remains of the priory are a Grade 1 listed building and a popular visitor attraction.

David's feet had attracted some unwelcome blisters during the course of the walk, so he treated them while I washed some clothes in the bedroom wash basin. With my daytime changeable 'wardrobe' consisting of only three Cancer Research UK tee-shirts, three pairs of underwear and three pairs of walking socks, it was a constant struggle to wash and dry my clothes. I'd just about managed so far, assisted by collecting freshly laundered replacements in Carlisle and Liverpool. After being exposed to a full day of walking, most recently in extreme heat, my tee-shirts looked weathered and bore the scars of my en route experiences, including blood from my fall in Dornoch and mango juice from a breakfast time mishap. It was probably time to consider acquiring a replacement set!

We dined in the pub, a few short steps downstairs, and I enjoyed a very generous portion of lasagne and chips. We both complemented our meals with pints of Son of a Bitch from the Bullmastiff brewery and sat with a sociable group of committed senior walkers from South Wales, sharing our long distance footpath walking experiences. One of them recounted the story of his cycle ride from Land's End to John O' Groats, when he fell off his bike on the final day in northern Scotland and broke his leg. I couldn't imagine anything more demoralising at the end of a long journey and sent myself a mental reminder to be extra vigilant on the South West Coast path if I made it to the final stages of my expedition.

Day 41 – Llanthony to Monmouth
Distance: 22.5 miles
Cumulative distance: 696.8 miles
Weather: Hot and sunny

A long walk in hot sunshine, a diversion from Offa, cruelly deprived of liquid refreshment, and rooms in a restaurant

On hearing about the charitable nature of my walk, the generous landlord of the Half Moon Inn had offered a much discounted rate for dinner, bed, breakfast and packed lunch, so we sought him out to thank him personally, before our departure for what we knew would be a challenging day's hike.

Unusually, we had the luxury of two choices of route available to us. The first involved a steep three hundred metre climb up the hillside to re-join the Hatterrall ridge for about three miles, then descending on the Offa's Dyke path shortly afterwards. The alternative was to follow the road down the valley, then to plot our own route to re-join Offa's Dyke later in the day. Having already experienced the stunning views from the ridge and reflecting on the challenges already facing us (a long walk in oppressive heat and David's tender feet), we opted to save energy by taking the latter option.

Taking the less demanding road route was not quite as straightforward as we had imagined. My National Trail maps covering Offa's Dyke had proved to be a most reliable navigational guide for following the path thus far, but regrettably the narrow strip covered by the map did not extend to include the road we were now following nor, more significantly, the connecting roads we expected to join later. To compound matters, the valley we were descending offered no communication signals, so I was unable to use GPS to check the route. Undaunted, after walking for just over six miles we reached a main road at the delightfully sounding Llanvihangel Crucorney, home to the Skirrid Mountain Inn, which dates from at least 1110 and is one of the oldest pubs in Wales.

We temporarily joined the Beacons Way, a 95 mile footpath across the Brecon Beacons National Park, then followed another footpath and walked along some narrow, hedgerow-lined country lanes.

The temperature soared rapidly and, at first, we managed to locate a sheltered path and a little welcome breeze. Gradually, however, the breeze disappeared and shelter became less prevalent as we negotiated the undulating landscape. We consumed litres of water between us, but our hopes of a refreshing cool drink were raised in the early afternoon when a roadside pub sign appeared in the most unlikely of locations. With bated breath, we followed the winding driveway up to a collection of buildings, only to have our hopes cruelly dashed – the pub was closed.

We finally re-joined the Offa's Dyke footpath shortly afterwards, where the prominent tall pointed spire of St Teilo's church provided an obliging landmark as we crossed a patchwork of fields towards the hamlet of Llantilio-Crossenny. Shortly afterwards, the path deviated through a vast orchard, where thousands of apple trees bore many thousands of tiny apples, on their lifecycle to be transformed into Bulmer's cider. We'd have paid good money for a glass or two of cider at that moment!

The path accompanied the banks of the River Trothy for a mile before we reached the densely forested King's Wood, where we were confronted with a gradual climb towards the summit, which unfortunately offered only limited views of neighbouring countryside due to the tall trees surrounding it.

We descended out of the wood and along the edge of several parched fields of potatoes. By late afternoon we were weary and thirsty – the remains of our early morning cool water supplies had now transitioned to lukewarm. After nine hours of walking, we eventually reached Monmouth, where we each downed two pints of iced Coke at the first pub we encountered. It had been another tough day's walking, not particularly due to the route or the terrain, but more due to the extreme heat and lack of shelter, and partly to the absence of any shops or refreshment opportunities en route. My winter training walks had not equipped me for this!

My Bradshaw's Guide advised me that Monmouth was once famous for its woollen caps, "the most ancient, general, warm and profitable covering men's heads on this island". A brief survey of the shoppers in the town's high street did not reveal a single woollen cap, but the extreme heat may have been a contributory factor to its absence.

Tonight's accommodation, situated at the furthest end of the main shopping street in the centre of Monmouth, was a restaurant with rooms, a first for my journey. My room was located on the top floor overlooking the narrow street below. After a quick shower and a slightly longer nap, we dined in the ground floor restaurant and enjoyed a fine meal, which was decidedly more *haute cuisine* than my usual pub dinners. Whilst recounting my journey to David, I noticed that I twice referred to it as a 'holiday' – was this a Freudian slip? With almost 700 miles completed and my blisters and injuries a distant memory, my body and mind were now 'in the groove' and I actually had been enjoying myself for the last two weeks.

After dinner, we slipped outside to the Punch House Inn, located in Agincourt Square, where a statue positioned on a raised balcony reminded us that Henry V was born here in Monmouth in 1387. As we sat outside with our beers, we engaged in conversation with a mobile communications specialist who hailed from France, but lived in Ireland. His accent was a rich blend of French and Irish, not one I'd ever experienced before!

David would return to civilisation in the morning with a few more aches and pains than he arrived with, but hopefully some positive memories of his two days of walking. For my part, it was great to have had good company during a challenging part of the journey.

Day 42 – Monmouth to Chepstow
Distance: 16.5 miles
Cumulative distance: 713.3 miles
Weather: Very hot and sunny

Farewell to Offa, several refreshment stops along the Wye valley and a room with a view

I awoke feeling tired, not ideal preparation for a long distance walker! Along with most of the UK's population, the oppressive heat had prevented me from acquiring a comfortable night's sleep and at 4 o'clock in the morning I was still frustratingly awake. The heat was not the only culprit – a bank cash machine was located in the street below my open bedroom window and the monotonous beep-beep-beep-beep of pin code entry and service selections resonated at frequent intervals, as wads of crisp notes were hastily withdrawn by Monmouth's cash starved, 24/7 citizens.

After breakfast, I left David to wait for the taxi that would transport him back to Hay-on-Wye to collect his car, while I headed out of the town centre, crossed the bridge over the River Wye and began the steep climb out of Monmouth up to The Kymin, a local National Trust beauty spot which, at a height of 850 feet, offered superb views of the town and neighbouring Wye valley. It is claimed that nine original counties are visible from the summit, but I did not seek to confirm this fact.

Close to the summit stood two buildings, a square Naval Temple, which was constructed in 1800 to celebrate Britain's success in the Battle of the Nile in 1798, and The Round House, once a naval banqueting house to which Admiral Lord Nelson brought his lady friends (that's according to a local I encountered at the summit!). The Kymin Club, whose membership consisted of wealthy gentlemen from Monmouth and its vicinity, met here regularly "for the purpose of dining together and spending the day in a social and friendly manner". There's nothing wrong with that, surely!

The path gradually descended through farmland to the main road at Lower Redbrook, where I was almost felled by a tennis ball which appeared from nowhere above me. I quickly realised that its source was the primary school playground, which was situated on a steep bank above the road. With my rucksack attached, I struggled to throw the ball back up over the fence, but managed at the third attempt. Another boy shouted down and asked if I could recover a football, which lay in the roadside on the opposite side. This time I jettisoned my rucksack and successfully kicked the ball back goalkeeper-style up over the fence.

The path continued through dense woodland for a couple of miles until I reached the bridge at Bigsweir, where there was a choice of routes. The more challenging option took a higher route through woodland to St Briavels Common, while the easier low level path followed the River Wye. I chose the latter, in part because it provided more liquid refreshment opportunities, but also because it would give me the chance to see Tintern Abbey at closer quarters.

It was another very hot day with little breeze, but the riverside path did provide some shelter from the sun. I walked for a few miles with Les and Anne, a couple from Thornbury who explained some of the local history and enthused about their regular visits to Hebridean islands.

At Brockweir, I parted from Les and Anne, but also took an important decision to finally end my relationship with Offa. I'd flirted with other footpaths in recent days and today the Wye Valley path offered more interesting side shows, including Tintern Abbey and the River Wye itself, not to mention the prospect of further sustenance en route. Nevertheless, I'd been faithful to Offa for most of the many sunny days since uniting with him at the Llangollen canal, we'd been trusted travelling companions and our parting was on good terms. He had set me difficult and unexpected challenges along the way, but I had overcome each one and now considered myself ready to move on.

I passed through the Old Station at Tintern, which now provided a restored station, signal box and three restored railway carriages, which contained various exhibitions and memorabilia stalls. It was evidently a popular and successful visitor attraction, which had accumulated numerous tourist awards. I stopped at the tea rooms for an iced Coke and managed to find a vacant bench seat on the old platform to quench my thirst.

I continued in the blazing heat through Tintern village and soon reached the splendid remains of Tintern Abbey, the first Cistercian foundation in Wales and only the second in Britain. Little is left of the original building first constructed in 1131, but despite a further four hundred years of re-building, the original design is still in existence.

I had to stop at a pub next to the Abbey for another iced Coke. As I was departing, I met a friendly couple from Galway in Ireland, who were fascinated to hear about my walk and insisted on taking a photograph of me. We would probably have chatted for hours, but the man's wife reminded him that they had left their daughter sheltering from the intense sun in their parked car.

I needed another refreshment stop at St Arvans a few miles down the road, so found a village pub, where a group of cyclists were taking shelter from the heat. Unfortunately my customary iced Coke was not available, so I was forced to have a pint of Reverend James beer instead.

The next landmark on my route was Chepstow race course, where the Welsh National is run in late December each year. During the Second World War, the entire site became RAF Chepstow, with the grass in the centre of the course used as a runway. Being a non-race day, and with no other events taking place, today the race course and its buildings exuded solitude.

I approached the centre of Chepstow via a scenic footpath

which passed the castle, the oldest surviving stone fortification in Britain apparently. My hotel, the Castle View, predictably offered fine views of the castle from my bedroom window.

I briefly caught up with the day's proceedings on the first day of the Second Ashes Test match at Lords, where England had recovered from a poor start to reach a comfortable position of 289 for 7 wickets at close of play, despite losing three late wickets.

After a relaxing bath, I wandered down the high street. An ear-splitting alarm emanated from one of the buildings, and a small crowd gathered close by to share their frustrations, but nobody seemed able to stop the piercing sound.

I dined at Mamma Mia's, an Italian restaurant, where the food was delicious, plentiful and good value, and the service friendly and efficient. This would be my journey's last dinner in Wales – my return to England was now imminent.

CHAPTER SIX

Over the border to England and heading to Cornwall

Day 43 – Chepstow to Gordano

Distance: 16.2 miles
Cumulative distance: 729.5 miles
Weather: Hot and sunny

A day of bridges, overgrown paths, an accommodation mystery and thirst inducing heat

The hotel receptionist kindly allowed me to raid the ice machine in the hotel kitchen to fill some of my water bottles. With luck, this would enable my drinking water to remain cool for an extra hour or so. I checked out, then set off through the town and followed a long residential road in the direction of the Severn Bridge.

Fortunately, there are cycle and pedestrian paths alongside the M48 Severn Bridge, which provided me with a direct route to cross the River Wye and the River Severn estuary without having to make a thirty mile diversion in the wrong direction to the next available crossing in Gloucester.

The bridge actually consists of four bridges (the Wye

Bridge, the Beachley Viaduct, the Severn Bridge and the Aust Viaduct). It was opened in 1966, replacing a car ferry which operated between Aust and Beachley. The toll for a car to cross the bridge was set at two shillings and sixpence (12.5 pence in today's currency), but this represented a saving of seven shillings on the equivalent cost of using the ferry. At the time of my crossing, the toll had risen to £6.20, but it is only charged to traffic travelling westwards from England into Wales.

The Severn Bridge is owned and operated by Severn Crossing plc, a consortium of two civil engineering companies and two banks. They were originally given a twenty year concession as part of the deal in which they funded and developed the Second Severn Crossing, a suspension bridge a few miles to the south which carries the M4 motorway and was completed in 1996. The ownership of both bridges is expected to revert to the UK government in 2018, by which time the construction and maintenance costs will have been recovered through toll income. No doubt there will then be demands from motorists for the tolls to be reduced.

It took me around half an hour to walk over the bridges from start to finish, but a light breeze made it a pleasant crossing. Apart from a single cyclist travelling in the opposite direction, I had the footpath and the cycle track completely to myself. Occasionally a heavy goods vehicle would thunder past me, creating powerful turbulence and requiring me to hold my hat firmly against the top of my head. It was a somewhat surreal and uplifting experience being a lone pedestrian traveller across this mighty feat of civil engineering.

At the end of the bridge, back on English soil in the village of Aust, I joined the final stages of the Severn Way, yet another long distance path which runs for over two hundred miles from the source of the River Severn at Plynlimon in Mid Wales to its mouth in Bristol. The path was well maintained and clearly signposted as it followed the coast across fields, passing underneath the impressive structure of the Second Severn Crossing and beyond to Severn Beach, created as an unlikely seaside resort in 1922 following the arrival of the railway. After a while, the path rapidly deteriorated into overgrown nettles and brambles, as if the maintenance budget had expired suddenly mid-project or, possibly, because the footpath had crossed a boundary to become the responsibility of a neighbouring, but less pedestrian-friendly, local authority. To save my calves from further damage, I crossed over a single track railway line, took a short cut over some private land and joined a main road.

To try to restrict my time in the heat, I'd tried to find out what time my B&B for the evening would allow me in. Oddly, their website was constantly unavailable and the telephone line would not connect, so I left a message on a mobile phone. I really didn't want to be without a bed! Late in the morning I received a call from the owner to say that she'd just sold the business and new owners had taken over. This at least explained why I hadn't been able to make contact, but it hadn't yet confirmed my accommodation arrangements.

On my right was the Severn estuary, where over four hundred years ago, a huge tidal wave had wreaked havoc, resulting in severe loss of life. In January 1607, the Bristol Floods caused devastation across a wide area, with eyewitness reports of the disaster telling of "huge and mighty hills of water" advancing at a speed "faster than a greyhound can run". The tidal wave resulted in the drowning of an estimated two thousand people, with houses and villages swept away, around 200 square miles of farmland flooded and livestock destroyed, ruining the local economy along the coasts of the Bristol Channel and Severn Estuary. The impact was particularly severe on the Welsh side, extending from Carmarthenshire to above Chepstow in Monmouthshire, but the coasts of Devon and the Somerset Levels, as far inland as Glastonbury Tor, were also affected.

The cause of the flood remains disputed. Contemporary written evidence referred to "God's warning to the people of England by the great overflowing of the waters or floods", but subsequent scientific explanations pointed to the floods being caused by a storm surge, arising from a combination of extreme weather conditions and a high tide. However, more recent research has suggested that it may have been a tsunami.

My route drew me closer to the industrial landscape of Avonmouth, home to a large port, numerous chemical manufacturing plants and a gas-fired power station. Suddenly, I started to miss the undulating countryside of Offa's Dyke, which I had only recently sacrificed.

In the uncomfortable heat, with no breeze and limited shelter, I managed to keep myself refreshed. Firstly, at a burger bar on an industrial estate, where I bought a couple of cans of iced drink and later at a Co-op store in Avonmouth town, where I consumed a large carton of cool smoothie drink. I lost count of how many litres per day I was drinking in this extreme weather, but it must have been approaching ten litres.

My second bridge of the day (or fifth, if you count the Severn Bridge as being four) was the M5 Avonmouth bridge, which enabled me to cross the River Avon via a cycle track which runs parallel to the motorway, and brought me to Somerset, the third last county of my epic journey. As I accessed the bridge, a local man read the sign attached to my rucksack and shouted out "Fair play to you, mate" in a recognisable Bristolian accent. It was a Friday afternoon in mid-July and the motorway traffic level was building rapidly. The forecast of continued fine weather over the weekend had led to an early exodus from work, while many drivers were rushing to avoid the evening congestion as they headed to holiday destinations in Devon and Cornwall.

The M5 cycle path thankfully enabled me to avoid another long detour and it led me to within a mile of my B&B, which was situated on a main road. I rang the doorbell with slight trepidation, not quite knowing whether a bed awaited me. It was a great relief to discover that I had been expected after all, although the new owners did not seem to be aware that I had paid a deposit in advance. A quick telephone call to the previous owner soon resolved that issue. For some reason, they also seemed surprised that the previous owner had offered a cooked breakfast, but they readily agreed to provide one for me.

I opened all of the windows in my bedroom and en suite bathroom to create a flow of air, which would hopefully provide some comfort in the stifling heat. This appeared to work effectively, but the substantial downside was that the noise of the passing traffic was relentless. Cars and heavy goods vehicles thundered through the last remnants of countryside before the motorway junction, just over a mile in the distance. Despite the uproar from the late afternoon traffic, within minutes I had fallen asleep on the bed.

After a refreshing shower, I ventured out into the early evening heat. It took several minutes before a fleeting break in the constant flow of traffic allowed me to cross the road safely. I quickly diverted down a more serene side track, which ultimately led me to the pleasant village of Easton-in-Gordano (known locally as E-I-G), which was mentioned in the

Domesday Book. One of the village landmarks is the King's Arms pub, where I dined on whitebait and a tasty chilli, washed down with a couple of pints of Doom Bar.

The England cricket team had also enjoyed a successful day in the sun. Having reached a promising first innings score of 361 all out, they had bowled out the Aussies for a mere 128 runs. Despite a late evening collapse to 31 for 3 in their second innings, England had accumulated a healthy lead and the prospect of a second successive victory looked encouraging.

Day 44 – Gordano to Stone Allerton

Distance: 20.4 miles
Cumulative distance: 749.9 miles
Weather: Warm with sunny intervals

Cloud cover, the Strawberry line, company and warm hospitality

As a development of the ice cube idea from my hotel in Chepstow, I left my water bottles in the freezer overnight, courtesy of the guest kitchen at the B&B. Of course, I'd now have to wait until they had partially defrosted before I could take my first drink en route!

After checking out, I joined a footpath right outside the house and climbed up through Summer House Wood and farm fields to reach open land near to Failand Church. The pleasant rural scenery offered a stark contrast to the blighted industrial landscape of Avonmouth, just a couple of miles away. I had to pass through a field of cows, but retained a sensible distance by skirting around the boundary wall until I reached a quiet country lane, bordered by farmland. After passing the outskirts of Failand village, the road descended steeply down Belmont Hill, close to Tyntesfield Park, a National Trust Victorian gothic house and estate.

One of the real symbols of rural Britain is the traditional black and white fingerpost direction and distance sign, which is prevalent in many areas. Here in Somerset, they were widespread and I passed a perfect example bearing five fingers at the bottom of Belmont Hill. Fingerpost signs date back to the seventeenth century, but the 1964 Traffic Signs Regulations encouraged local authorities to replace fingerposts with new signage and forbade the creation of new fingerpost signs. Only from 1994 were new fingerpost signs permitted, but without the use of fractions of miles in the distances. By 2005, concern regarding the loss of heritage was reflected in Department of Transport and English Heritage guidance, which stated that "all surviving traditional fingerpost direction signs should be retained in situ and maintained on a regular basis".

After passing through the village of Flax Bourton, my route joined the busy A370, the main road to the coastal resort of Weston Super Mare. Before long, the clear skies had given way to cloud and, coupled with a breeze, for an hour or so, the temperature for walking became comfortable once more, for the first time since I'd left the Lake District.

I followed the road for several miles as it bordered Brockley Wood, close to Bristol International Airport, until I reached Congresbury, where another of my planned short cuts materialised. I headed for the church, where major renovation work seemed to be underway, walked through the churchyard and along a footpath next to a stream, which soon connected me with the Strawberry Line footpath.

This was once part of the Great Western Railway Cheddar Valley line, which ran between Yatton (north of Congresbury) and Witham (in East Somerset). The line was referred to as the Strawberry Line because it was used to transport large volumes of Cheddar strawberries to London and beyond. Like similar lines, it became one of Dr Beeching's casualties and finally closed in 1964. Much of the line between Yatton and Cheddar is currently a railway walk and cycle trail.

I'd planned to visit the Thatcher's cider farm shop highlighted at Sandford on my map, but it had either been closed or relocated, so I stopped at the nearby Railway Arms pub instead. Being in cider country, I thought I should try out the local brew so enquired of the landlady which of those on offer she would recommend. She readily poured three different ciders into small glasses for me to sample and, after a thorough tasting process, I opted for a pint of the traditional variety.

The original Sandford station site had been retained and developed as Sandford Station Retirement Village, which included over one hundred retirement homes and a Pullman restaurant. I pictured a community of retired train spotters, enjoying their final years adjacent to the old railway. The station itself had been restored as a railway heritage centre and was open to the public.

I'd arranged to meet my sister Wendy and her husband Chris further down the line, so I was regularly scanning the horizon to see if I could spot them. I soon pinpointed two likely contenders and was about to wave when, on closer inspection, I realised that the lady wearing tight fitting, brightly coloured hot pants was probably not my middle-aged sister! We did manage to locate each other ten minutes later and walked a short distance to the village of Winscombe, where we called into a pub for lunch. Chris had arranged to collect some friends from the airport, so Wendy and I followed the path to the charming market town of Axbridge, where we left the Strawberry Trail. We walked through the main square, with its half-timbered medieval buildings, and plotted a route across the drainage canals and farm fields to their house.

The Somerset Levels are an extensive low lying area of drained wetland and coastal plain, which border the Severn estuary and cover an area of around 250 square miles. The Levels are criss-crossed with thousands of drainage channels, known locally as rhynes (pronounced 'reens'), which are used to turn sea level wetland into pasture. The layout of the rhynes is based on a careful balance – if fields are too large, they are more difficult to drain and are therefore more prone to flooding, whereas too many draining channels reduce the available land. Water levels are controlled by sluice gates and pumps, enabling the pasture to be managed effectively. This system has operated for hundreds of years and enables local communities to farm the land, but the downside is that the land can be prone to extreme flooding, especially during the winter months.

My hosts provided a very warm welcome. We relaxed in their large garden then had a delicious barbecue dinner, rounded off inevitably by local strawberries and clotted cream. Chris had taken up my challenge of trying to locate local beers with obscure names, some of which we sampled. From the local Cheddar Ales ("nestling on the slopes of the Mendip Hills, within a stone's throw of the famous Cheddar Gorge") came Potholer golden ale and Gorge Best bitter, while from Badger Ales we tried Hopping Hare.

England's cricketers had continued to outperform Australia in the Test Match. They had batted all day, scoring over three hundred runs and losing just two wickets. The stage was set for an English victory, with two days remaining.

Day 45 – Stone Allerton to Watchfield

Distance: 7.0 miles
Cumulative distance: 756.9 miles
Weather: Hot and sunny

A leisurely Sunday morning stroll and an afternoon relaxing in the pool

After an unhurried breakfast, which included the journey's first egg and bacon sandwich, we prepared for a family walk. Although it was technically a rest day for me, in keeping with two of the earlier ones, I had decided to bring forward some of the following day's mileage.

I was fortunate to have company again, with Chris, Wendy, their two charming teenage daughters Lindsay and Rachel, and dogs Molly and Dixie all joining me.

The early clouds soon dissipated and the temperature quickly matched the highs of recent days, but with only a light daysack to carry, the heat was not as draining as normal. We walked along bridleways and footpaths, weaving our way between the rhynes. On my map, the rhynes resembled a pattern consisting of thousands of tiny rectangles of various sizes, with only the occasional road or settlement disrupting the pattern. I was beginning to discover that no route in this area offered a direct line to the final destination. Instead, I had to become adept at finding the most efficient zigzag course, but this inevitably involved a more meticulous examination of the map and increased the distance walked.

At one stage we were confronted by a herd of around twenty cows, lined up in military formation next to the gate which we were about to open, blocking our route across the neighbouring field. Fortunately, with undeniable assistance from Molly the dog, and much to the relief of the girls, we managed to distract the cows and were able to continue our journey across the field. The drainage channels provided wonderful cooling opportunities for the dogs, but unfortunately when they emerged from the water, they shook their bodies vigorously and showered us from all directions with a muddy brown solution.

We ended our Sunday stroll at a pub in the village of Watchfield, where welcoming liquid refreshments were taken. The original plan had been to eat lunch at the pub, but the last remains of the Sunday carvery lunch did not really appeal to us, so we opted to have a late salad lunch back at the house. Chris had earlier left his car at the pub, so we didn't need to retrace our steps on foot.

I then enjoyed the most relaxing few hours of my entire journey to date, spending most of the afternoon in the heated outdoor swimming pool, soaking up the sun's rays, imbibing the occasional beer and tracking England's humiliation of Australia in the 2nd Test match. England had bowled out Australia for 235, giving them victory by a colossal margin of 347 runs, to take a 2-0 lead in the five match series.

When the sun disappeared gracefully beyond the horizon and the temperature started to fall, we retired indoors to enjoy a delectable meal and sampled the remaining bottles of local beer.

As I re-loaded my rucksack for the final stages of my journey, I had to remind myself that my afternoon chill-out had been only a temporary nirvana, and that there were now twelve consecutive days and a walking distance of nearly two hundred miles between here and Land's End.

Day 46 – Watchfield to Taunton

Distance: 18.0 miles
Cumulative distance: 774.9 miles
Weather: Hot and sunny

Negotiating a route across the Somerset Levels, savaged by brambles and nettles, then recovery at a farm

I said goodbye to my hosts after a really welcoming and enjoyable stay, where the helpless long distance walker's every need was catered for. Chris kindly drove me to where we'd finished yesterday's walk and I set off to navigate my way through the Somerset Levels.

This area had undoubtedly provided the most difficult route planning challenge of my entire journey. As I'd discovered in the last couple of days, the Levels are criss-crossed with drainage channels, as much of the land is at or below sea level and, apart from the M5 motorway, there are no direct routes through the area and very few places where a long distance walker can overcome the key obstacles (main drainage channel, motorway, river, railway, and canal) which prevent access to Bridgwater and beyond.

The first section of the route was straightforward enough, following a 'B' road which traversed the Levels to the village of Woolavington. Here I joined a narrow country lane, which was initially populated with neat residential properties, but quickly returned to open farmland. I briefly joined the A39 main road, which was my passport to crossing the first two obstacles, the King's Sedgemoor Drain and the M5 motorway.

As soon as I'd left the motorway behind, I deviated down a minor road which would enable me to bypass Bridgewater,

Somerset's major industrial town. A few hundred yards along the road, in the residential district of Sydenham, I spotted a man walking along the pavement towards me carrying a glass and a bottle. As he approached, I stood aside to allow him room to pass, but he stopped and I was astonished to discover that these items were destined for me – he'd driven past me a few minutes earlier, dashed into his nearby house, and returned bearing refreshments! I thanked him for his kindness and continued towards the trickiest part of my route, which would enable me to conquer my three remaining obstacles, the River Parrett, the railway line, and the Bridgwater and Taunton Canal. I followed a road through a small industrial estate, then turned onto a narrow track that led to the river, where a footpath brought me to a railway bridge. Fortunately the bridge had a pedestrian crossing attached, so the river and the railway were traversed simultaneously and, within minutes, I crossed the canal at the Crossway swing bridge. All obstacles successfully negotiated!

I was given a brief glimpse of Bridgwater's industry, as my route passed by a recycling plant, an agricultural feeds depot, an Argos warehouse, and the rear of a motorway services complex. With my water supplies on the wane, I was grateful to stop at the Compass Tavern for a refreshing drink and temporary shelter from the heat. As I was leaving, an elderly gentleman jogged after me and made a donation to CRUK.

I reached North Petherton, which only became a town in the late 20th century, prior to which it laid claim to being the largest village in England. Ready for food, drink and refrigeration, I popped into the town's Tesco Express. The chill counters provided the most welcoming respite from the heat outside and I lingered there to cool down. I purchased a 'meal deal' lunch and turned off the main road into a quiet country lane.

After a couple of days on the Levels, my route started to climb again. I was soon immersed in rural Somerset, with pretty thatched cottages, towering hedgerows brimming with birds and insects, a patchwork of crop fields and gently undulating hills.

I left the road and followed a well-defined footpath around the edges of a crop field, until the path re-joined another minor lane. At this point, in front of a large property which overlooked King's Cliff Wood, I removed my rucksack and parked myself on a newly mowed lawn. Sheltering from the unrelenting heat under a neighbouring willow tree, I consumed my picnic lunch.

Shortly after lunch, I encountered the most overgrown footpath of my entire journey. Although it wasn't signposted, it was clearly marked on the Ordnance Survey map and it offered a worthwhile short cut, broadly forming the shortest side of an isosceles triangle. The footpath (or ex-footpath, to be more precise) was only a few hundred metres in length, but the brambles and nettles were taller than me. I battled through this Somerset jungle, but the bramble thorns became entwined in my rucksack and pressed into my arms and neck as I tried to advance, while the nettles attacked my bare legs. I finally emerged exhausted, with my neck, arms and legs now transformed into a patchwork of cuts and scratches. I reflected that I should have carried a pair of secateurs in my first aid kit, on the basis that prevention is better than cure.

To my great relief, the path eventually re-joined a minor road, where it was as overgrown and un-signposted as the starting point at the other end. I continued along tranquil country lanes, offering fine rural views of rolling hills and the town of Taunton in the valley below. The road descended steadily towards the conservation village of Cheddon Fitzpaine and my arrival coincided with end of term at the local primary school. Dozens of jubilant schoolchildren joined waiting parents at the school gates, ready to embark on their six week summer break.

My latest accommodation, a friendly farmhouse B&B, was situated nearby. A few months earlier, another farmhouse B&B which I had originally booked had contacted me to cancel due to flood damage, so I'd had to revise my original route for this late replacement. I strolled into the well-stocked farm shop and was greeted by Mary, the farmer's wife, who looked after the accommodation side of the business.

Pyrland Farm is situated in the Vale of Taunton, nestling under the Quantock Hills. With two hundred cows, as well as chickens, ducks, orchards and vegetable gardens, the farm shop was undeniably a haven for fresh, wholesome, home grown food.

Unfortunately, the B&B did not serve evening meals – how appetising it would have been to enjoy Pyrland roast beef, served with farm grown potatoes and an assortment of freshly picked vegetables, followed by local strawberries and clotted cream. Somewhat unusually, there were no pubs, restaurants or takeaways nearby, so I had to walk a mile to the local Co-op store to buy a microwave dinner. The microwave oven was located in the B&B's dining room, so I cautiously cooked my pasta dish, ensuring that I left behind no mess or lingering smells, and consumed it with two bottles of Barn Owl beer from the Cotleigh brewery in Somerset.

Day 47 – Taunton to Sampford Peverell

Distance: 18.7 miles
Cumulative distance: 793.6 miles
Weather: Cloudy at first, hot and sunny later

Intensive map reading, a delightful picnic and yet another canal towpath

I was awoken at 2.30am by the thunder and lightning, which

had been accurately forecasted by the Met Office. The rain lashed down onto the yard outside my bedroom window, the first downpour for several weeks. Thankfully, it was calm and dry by the time I was seated in the dining room enjoying my full English breakfast. Mary, my host, kindly donated some lunch items from the farm shop when I checked out.

The cuts and scratches on my neck, arms and legs were visible and, to unsuspecting pedestrians, I probably resembled a self-harming hiker. I made a vow to avoid any markedly overgrown footpaths for the rest of my journey.

I followed a fast, direct route through residential areas around Taunton and completed a productive short cut around the hospital. After the main road crossed over the railway, I joined the West Deane Way, a 45 mile circular route which featured prominently on my Ordnance Survey map, and which purported to provide a reasonably undeviating route for part of my day's journey. Unfortunately, what did not feature prominently were signposts. For the next few hours I had to employ my finest map reading and navigational skills to plot the route of the footpath.

The first section of the footpath was unproblematic as it traversed farmland between the placid River Tone and the London to Penzance mainline railway. In a few days' time, my son, Daniel, would be able to witness the exact same scenery as a train passenger en route to accompanying me on my journey to Land's End.

At Bradford-on-Tyne, the footpath joined a minor road next to the elegant 14th century stone bridge. My progress was temporarily thwarted at the railway level crossing, when the barriers descended in a seemingly pre-meditated routine just as I approached.

A short distance from here, back in 1991, was the site of a

major chemical incident on the railway. A train loaded with some 50,000 gallons of highly flammable liquids (kerosene, petrol and diesel) was derailed, causing a large scale explosion and fire. The fire service took two days to extinguish the fire and there was significant environmental damage. The cause of the accident was put down to an axle failure on one of the wagons.

The country lane continued past an assortment of farm buildings and a fruit farm, which displayed pallets stacked with punnets of appealing strawberries. The West Deane Way diverted onto a farm road and, after skirting around the edge of a field next to the farm, the signposts abruptly disappeared.

I wandered across a field in the general direction of my planned destination, but there was no evidence of a defined path and I soon found myself wading through a field of knee-high barley. I'd learned that the best approach during moments like this was not to panic, but calmly apply a combination of logic and technology to escape the predicament. GPS, in particular, provided considerable assistance during these periods of short term route uncertainty. My smartphone would indicate my current position on the map and I could usually identify a landmark on the intended route ahead. The challenge was to pick a direct route between the two points, but to avoid any rivers, buildings, high walls and fences, or other man-made obstacles which would be difficult to negotiate carrying a large rucksack. On this occasion, I had re-established the footpath within ten minutes.

Despite the occasional navigational setback, the route was scenic and rural, passing through farmland, woodland and gently undulating hills, although at one stage it did pass ominously close to a sewage works. The path loosely followed the remains of the Grand Western Canal, which ran from

Taunton to Tiverton in Devon, but there was little visible evidence of any canal features on this section. Signposting continued to be sparse, but with a few short unofficial diversions, I managed to reach the picturesque village of Greenham, where I removed my load and consumed a delicious picnic lunch of cheese and bacon quiche, tomatoes and home grown strawberries, courtesy of Mary from Pyrland Farm.

Just beyond Greenham, I managed to lose the path for a final time and had to resort to climbing over a barbed wire fence, following the road for a short distance before re-joining the footpath, which had now transformed into a towpath alongside the operational section of the Grand Western Canal. The towpath would form the final five miles of the day's walk and, fortunately, no further opportunities to get lost!

Originally part of an ambitious scheme to link the Bristol Channel with the English Channel, the Grand Western Canal was proposed as a way for shipping to avoid the long and perilous journey around the Cornish peninsular, and as a route for transporting goods, including coal from South Wales, into the heart of Somerset and Devon.

The section from Tiverton to the limestone quarries at Westleigh (also known locally as the Tiverton Canal) was completed in 1814, but the costs had escalated hugely due to the use of steep embankments and deep cuttings to keep the canal on a level contour.

This massive overspend delayed construction of the next section to Taunton for many years, but eventually it was completed in 1838. By then, any plans to link the canal with the English Channel had been abandoned, but for a short time the canal was profitable, mostly carrying coal and limestone, much of which was burnt in limekilns and used for improving agricultural land.

The arrival of the Bristol & Exeter Railway deprived the canal of much of its trade, and in 1865 the northern section to Taunton was sold to the railway company and subsequently abandoned – this had been my route earlier in the day. Apart from a small lily-cutting business, the canal was redundant until the 1960s, when proposals to develop the canal into a landfill site or a road were presented. However, the local community wanted to preserve the canal and started a campaign. This was ultimately successful and, in the early 1970s, the canal became a Country Park. Since then the canal has undergone a major programme of dredging and relining and is now a popular visitor attraction and flourishing local amenity.

A few miles further down the towpath, I reached Devon, the penultimate county of my epic journey. I was now not far short of completing eight hundred miles and journey's end was just ten days' walking distance away. Nevertheless, I pledged to carry on taking each day at a time!

Tonight's accommodation, the Globe Inn at Sampford Peverell, was a traditional Devon village inn, which backed on to the canal. On arrival in my bedroom, I removed my boots and socks – the carpet was instantly sprinkled with over a thousand tiny seeds, souvenirs of my time spent tramping across arable fields. After the previous day's brambles and today's barley, the hot bath was most appreciated!

Before dining, I spent half an hour trying to rescue a couple of painted lady butterflies, which had become trapped between the casement window and the net curtain in my bedroom. It was a game of patience, but I eventually enabled them to fly to their freedom.

In the pub's well populated restaurant, I enjoyed a very generous portion of lasagne, chips and salad, accompanied by a pint of award winning Otter bitter from the Otter brewery near Honiton, Devon.

Day 48 – Sampford Peverell to Black Dog

Distance: 16.8 miles
Cumulative distance: 810.4 miles
Weather: Cloudy with sunny intervals

An enjoyable walk across rural Devon in weather conditions more suited to walking

I walked downstairs to have breakfast, but found no signs of life. The internal door to the pub/restaurant was locked, as was the main public entrance on the street. I was perplexed and briefly returned to my room, but fifteen minutes later the chef arrived apologetically – it transpired that he had overslept! He did redeem himself with a fine breakfast though.

I re-joined the canal in the village and finally spotted the first canal boat. As on a previous towpath (the Montgomery canal in Wales), I had to tread cautiously to avoid squashing thousands of tiny frogs which lined the route. After about a mile, the footpath took a temporary detour through the village of Halberton.

In November 2012, exceptionally heavy rainfall caused a major breach in the Grand Western Canal's banks here, necessitating nearby homes to be evacuated. Two temporary dams were installed which allowed the rest of the canal to remain open and around four hundred fish were returned to the canal from a flooded field, but many more fish were lost.

Devon County Council agreed to pay for repairs to the canal, in time for its 200th anniversary and, a few weeks before

my arrival, a three million pound project to repair the breach
started in earnest. The repairs would involve rebuilding the
failed embankment and raising the level to reduce the risk of
overtopping in the future, and further improvements to the
water management, including the installation of a water level
monitoring and alarm system.

I re-joined the towpath close to a large field, the venue of
the Mid Devon Show, which was due to take place three days
later. Advertised as "the best one day agricultural show in the
West", it promised a fun day out for all the family, including
farm demonstrations, arts, rural crafts, food & drink and
entertainment. Preparations at the showground were well
advanced as I walked along the site's boundary next to the canal.

The towpath ended at the Tiverton canal basin, where a 75-
seater horse drawn canal boat called the 'Tivertonian', provided
leisure trips to visiting tourists. I opted instead to visit The
Duck's Ditty Café Bar, a colourfully painted canal barge, which
was decked with beautiful floral displays. Here, I treated myself
to a first ice cream of the journey, a delicious blackcurrant and
clotted cream cone.

I followed Canal Hill down towards Tiverton's main retail
street, which was bustling with lunchtime shoppers. Tiverton
grew from the wool trade in the sixteenth and seventeen
centuries, before lace making brought new prosperity in the
nineteenth century. The town's economy declined in the latter
half of the twentieth century, but had experienced something
of a revival in recent years.

I weaved my way out of the town centre, before climbing
steeply to the west along Baker's Hill. Before long I was in
rural Devon, in its own way almost as remote as the imposing
mountains of the West Highland Way or the undulating hills
of Offa's Dyke. On two occasions, the narrow, steep-banked

country lane I was following petered out into a muddy track, which was clearly signposted as being unsuitable for motor vehicles. I didn't meet a soul for five miles, but was treated to fine views of rolling hills and farmland. I passed through the remote villages of Pennymoor and Puddington, both endowed with charming thatched cottages.

For the first time since Carnforth, early on Day 28, weather conditions completely favoured the long distance walker. For much of the day the temperature was around 21 degrees and a refreshing breeze provided comfort. This brought to an end almost three weeks of walking in high temperatures, which had been an endurance test I hadn't planned for.

I reached tonight's accommodation, the thatched Black Dog Inn, located in the small village of the same name, just before it closed after lunch. This gave me time to down a pint of iced Coke in the homely bar, before being shown to my room. The beautifully designed and well equipped en suite bathroom was more fitting of a luxury hotel, and the multi-directional shower offered a novel way to refresh my tired body, another first for the journey. Thought had even been given to the design of the bedside lamps, which were incorporated into a sculptured black dog, while from the super king sized bed there were scenic views across Dartmoor.

Afterwards, for the second time in twenty four hours, but in different inns, I managed to rescue two butterflies which had flown in through the open window. The Devonshire butterflies were clearly thriving in the fine British summer.

The sumptuously presented dinner at the inn was amongst the best of my entire journey. I had peppered steak with a variety of fresh vegetables and home cooked chips, followed by plum tart and clotted cream, washed down with Exmoor ale. Afterwards, I sat in the bar and chatted with my hosts, Dave and Alli. To my amazement, Alli confessed that she was not a trained chef! I'd wondered why the pub and the restaurant were not particularly busy on a pleasant July evening, especially given the welcoming service and the excellent food on offer. Dave explained that they had been affected by the economic recession, with fewer people dining out and more drinking supermarket purchased beers at home, but also believed the inn's remote location made it difficult to attract passing traffic. I couldn't help thinking that this hard working couple deserved more custom and, as I provided a glowing review of the inn to a feedback website, I was pleased to note that most of the other reviewers had shared my opinion.

Day 49 – Black Dog to Okehampton
Distance: 18.7 miles
Cumulative distance: 829.1 miles
Weather: Cloudy and warm, with sunny intervals

A pleasant rural walk through Devon villages, successfully managing to avoid the rain

After a hearty breakfast, I said farewell to my welcoming hosts (who kindly made a donation) and set off down the road. I soon joined the Two Moors Way, another long distance path, which links Dartmoor and Exmoor. The path took me across farmland and through wooded glades.

At one point a herd of around thirty cows followed me across a field. I could see my escape route at the kissing gate which led into the next field, but that was some one hundred yards distant and the cows were by now gathering pace as they approached me. To make matters worse, the terrain was uneven, so running with a heavy rucksack was not a viable option. I took control of the situation by turning round sharply and shouting loudly at the bovine creatures. This behaviour took them by surprise and they immediately stopped in their tracks and a few of the less confident ones in the herd retreated. This gave me the headroom to make a dart for the kissing gate, which I reached with some relief.

The footpath passed through the pretty, sleepy village of Morchard Bishop (winner of the 2013 Best Kept Village in Devon – new entry category), where a senior resident confidently informed me that rain was imminent. I couldn't immediately recall when I'd last experienced rain on my journey, but after some consideration, I established that it was on Day 26 in Kendal in the Lake District over three weeks ago.

Just outside Morchard Bishop, the path weaved its way through an alpaca farm. I'd never seen these animals at close quarters before, but they seemed oblivious to my presence. They originally hail from South America, but are increasingly bred in the UK. Alpaca fleece is used for making knitted and woven items and is similar to wool, but it is not prickly and contains no lanolin.

I left the Two Moors Way and joined a series of very narrow minor roads which passed through some pretty Devon villages with thatched cottages and impressive floral displays.

In Morchard Road village, I bypassed the delightfully named pub, the Devonshire Dumpling, and a few miles further west I passed through Down St Mary, which until recently had been home to a vineyard.

I stopped for liquid refreshment in the elevated village of Zeal Monochorum. There is some dispute over the origin of its name, but the consensus view was that it translated to "cell of the monks", as the manor once belonged to Buckfast Abbey.

The weather forecast had indicated scattered heavy rain showers and my newly installed Rain Alarm smartphone app (which my brother-in-law Chris had alerted me to) showed that I was completely surrounded by rain clouds, but amazingly I managed to avoid them and so postponed donning my waterproofs for at least another day.

I followed minor roads to North Tawton, which boasts an impressive square, narrow streets and a collection of ubiquitous thatched cottages. Technically North Tawton is classed as a town, but its ambience seemed more in keeping with that of a village. Here I took a shortcut at Barton Hill and joined a 'B' road.

At Belstone Corner, the road crossed the railway next to Sampford Courtenay station. This line was originally a casualty of the Beeching cuts, but re-opened to passenger traffic in 2002 as part of the Dartmoor Railway, which runs from Okehampton to Exeter.

Sampford Courtenay played a major role in the extraordinary Prayer Book Rebellion, which took place in 1549. The government of Edward VI, the boy king, had imposed changes to traditional forms of worship, including the introduction of a new Book of Common Prayer, where English replaced the more familiar Latin. This did not go down well in largely Catholic Cornwall and was viewed as an assault on the rural way of life. Rebellion quickly broke out, with the villagers of Sampford Courtenay demanding an immediate return to the old ways. Such was the strength of the opposition that a mighty force of Cornish rebels united with those from Sampford Courtenay and set off to besiege Exeter, the regional capital. The rebels failed to seize the town and several thousand were killed in the ensuing battles. A few weeks later, in the final battle, fought at Sampford Courtenay, the royal army of some 8,000 men finally crushed the insurgents. It is estimated that between 500 and 600 rebels were killed in this battle alone, with losses in the overall Rebellion numbering around 5,500. Speaking about the Rebellion in 2007, the then Bishop of Truro stated that "there is no doubt that the English Government behaved brutally and stupidly and killed many Cornish people… I am sorry about what happened and I think it was an enormous mistake."

On the outskirts of Okehampton, major house building activity had taken place and was still in progress. West Devon Borough Council's twenty year strategy had set out the long term vision for the development of Okehampton. The core strategy had identified the town as a key growth area with potential to accommodate nine hundred new homes in the east of the town, together with supporting infrastructure.

I arrived early in Okehampton's town centre, so stopped to eat my packed lunch in the weakening sun and paid a visit to the Tourist Information Centre, where I picked up a trail guide for my next day's walk.

Positioned on the north edge of Dartmoor National Park, the market town of Okehampton can trace its roots back to the Iron Age and it is evident that the Romans built a fort nearby, sometime after the invasion of Britain in 43 AD. The town's motte and bailey castle was built in the late eleventh century, following the Norman Conquest, and its remains are now a tourist attraction.

As I arrived at my B&B, dark clouds gathered overhead and a few raindrops started to fall. Ali, my host, was very welcoming and equally talkative! She showed me upstairs to my bedroom, but we spent about thirty minutes in conversation at the doorway. She was genuinely interested in my walk and informed me that a few other End to End walkers had stayed with her in the last year – she had even printed off copies of their blogs for her guests to enjoy. I read one with amazement – one guy had walked the route in 2012 in 40 days, without taking any rest days, but more remarkably, most of his journey was undertaken in the rain. I admired his spirit, but I was thankful that I had chosen the hot, dry summer of 2013 in which to undertake my own journey.

Before dinner, I had a delicate operation to perform. Throughout my walk, I'd been using the charity monies I'd collected en route as a personal banking service. About once a week, I emptied out the contents of my Cancer Research UK plastic collection pot, counted out the funds raised and electronically transferred this sum into my JustGiving charity account. This enabled me to retain the notes and coins, which was a blessing as there had been very few banks or cash machines on my journey and I regularly needed cash to pay for my accommodation and provisions. Unfortunately, a ten pound note had become wedged at the bottom of the collection pot and, without any suitable tools in my kit, I had been unable to retrieve it. In the seclusion of my B&B room, I hatched a plan. I borrowed a piece of Blu-tack, which had been attached to a notice, carefully affixed it to the base of the narrow chair leg, and then slowly guided the chair leg into the collection pot. It worked a treat – I cautiously removed the chair leg and a crumpled ten pound note was duly attached!

I walked down the hill and opted to eat at Vines Pizzeria, which Ali had suggested. A pepperoni pizza and two large Peroni beers later, I ventured back up the hill.

Day 50 – Okehampton to Lewdown
Distance: 14.6 miles
Cumulative distance: 843.7 miles
Weather: Warm and sunny

A pleasant accompanied walk along the Two Castles Trail and an accommodation hiccup

After a delicious breakfast with extensive choices and equally extensive conversation with my delightful host Ali, I managed to depart and walked down the hill to the Tourist Information Centre to meet my two walking partners for the day. Ian, my brother-in-law arrived first, shortly followed by Lucie, the Area Volunteer Manager and my key contact at Cancer Research UK. Both would celebrate my fiftieth day on the road with me, which I would also mark with the receipt of three brand new Cancer Research UK tee-shirts to replace my profoundly weathered original ones.

Ian lives in Plymouth and had travelled by car and bus to join me for the day and was planning to do the same tomorrow. Lucie lives in London, but was visiting her parents in North Somerset for the weekend. I'd spoken to her by phone numerous times, but had never met her in person, so it was pleasing to be able to put a face to her voice – she was actually younger than I'd envisaged! She was accompanied by Diddie, her very well behaved terrier (named after the Chelsea footballer, Didier Drogba!).

Thanks to the generous contributions of family, friends, colleagues and people I'd encountered en route, I had raised nearly £12,000 for Cancer Research UK so far, but I had set a target of £15,000 and was desperately keen to reach this. Just before Lucie's arrival, I'd contacted my supporters to seek their help in getting me closer to my target in the final few days of my journey. I reminded them that the main purpose of the walk was, and remained, to raise as much money as possible for Cancer Research UK, whose work relied entirely on public donations to help to improve the survival rates for different types of cancer. Within minutes, the message had made an impact, as further contributions started to roll in.

For the next two days, my route would follow the Two Castles' Trail, which runs for 24 miles from Okehampton to Launceston. Apart from the major long distance footpaths, this was a rare occasion where an existing footpath exactly mirrored the route I was intending to follow. Conveniently, the trail started from the Tourist Information Centre.

In perfect walking conditions, we followed the trail across a golf course, then over rolling countryside and woodland, running parallel to the edge of Dartmoor to our left. We passed Longston Hill and Homerton Hill, then skirted around Sourton Tors and descended into the village of Sourton, passing the impressive tiny church of St. Thomas a Becket. On the main road in the village stands the Highwayman Inn, sometimes described as "the most unusual pub in Britain".

Originally built in the thirteenth century, it was acquired by the present owners' family in 1959. The pub has evolved into an Aladdin's cave of hidden treasures, artefacts and gothic architecture. A carriage forms the main entrance and the restaurant is an old sailing galleon. It is also said to be the most haunted inn in Devon.

It was too early for our refreshment break, so we crossed over the road and followed the footpath as it diverted towards the next village of Bridestowe, where we did visit the local pub for much-needed refreshments. A little further on, the trail skirted three sides of Burley Wood, the site of an Iron Age hill fort and also a Norman motte-and-bailey earthwork. Unfortunately, the signposts went into hiding in Burley Wood and we strayed slightly from the route, re-joining it after crossing several fields and climbing over a dry stone wall. In keeping with many of the official trails, we didn't pass a soul for the entire day.

We finally reached the small village of Lewtrenchard, where Ian had parked his car, and where Lucie and Diddie said farewell to us (well Diddie wagged his tail, actually) to retrace their steps all the way back to Okehampton. Ian drove me a few miles to have a welcoming beer (Timothy Taylor's Landlord) in the neighbouring village of Lifton, then he transported me to my farmhouse B&B back in Lewtrenchard.

Before I had time to knock on the door of East Raddon Farm, Sylvia, the farmer's wife, appeared in the yard. I could tell immediately from the perplexed look on her face that there was a problem. She confessed that she had not entered my booking confirmation into her accommodation book and consequently had double booked for the evening. She was very embarrassed and hugely apologetic, but I could see her brain working overtime as she tried to unearth a solution to the problem. In true British spirit, within five minutes she'd produced a delicious Devon cream tea and a tray of freshly baked cakes for me and then disappeared to start the process of relocating her daughter, so that I had a room for the night! It was a blessing, as the only other accommodation nearby was Lewtrenchard Manor, a luxurious country house hotel. Apart from being well beyond the accommodation budget for my journey, with my muddy boots and weathered walking clothes, I was hardly suitably attired for a night at an exclusive hotel!

Sylvia cooked a delicious dinner of pork in cider sauce, with a selection of vegetables (including Swiss chard, courgettes and peppers fresh from the garden). Afterwards, the two children Charlie (11) and Chloe (10), who were both very artistic, entertained me with tales of life on a farm – Chloe had already taken me up into the field to be introduced to her pet lambs, every one of which had a name! The children insisted on playing some of their board games with me and managed to defeat me each time. The other guests, who were also family friends, then arrived, Sylvia's husband Robert joined us and we all chatted until nearly midnight.

Day 51 – Lewdown to Launceston
Distance: 10.8 miles
Cumulative distance: 854.5 miles
Weather: Cloudy with sunny intervals

Rolling countryside, butterflies, arrival in Cornwall, and a whinging woman

Sylvia (not the whinging woman!) explained the history of Lewtrenchard to me over breakfast. It was here where the famous Victorian, the Reverend Sabine Baring-Gould, was both squire and parson for many years. He wrote a selection of books on Devon, especially Dartmoor, collected and published an exhaustive list of Devon folk songs and stories, and wrote the famous rousing hymn 'Onward Christian Soldiers'. He lived at Lewtrenchard Manor (before it became a hotel), which was originally a small 16th Century manor house, but was later enlarged by Baring-Gould at the end of the 19th Century.

I had a fine farmhouse breakfast, then Ian phoned me at the farm to apologise that he wouldn't be able to re-join me for today's walk after all. Unfortunately, he had retained my only copy of the trail guide, so I would have to navigate the rest of the route with just my standard map. I bade farewell to my most welcoming farmhouse hosts and set off across farmland and woods. To my relief, the route was clearly marked on the map and adequately signposted on the ground, so I need not have worried.

I walked along footpaths and minor lanes through rolling countryside, passing the villages of Lewdown and Stowford. At a nearby hunt kennels, the hounds were noticeably excited as I approached, raising the volume of their barking in unison. The trail followed a minor country lane, where I spotted a signpost for Dingles.

The Dingles Fairground Heritage Centre houses the National Fairground Collection. It proclaimed itself as a "unique facility", designed to "capture the magic of a bygone age through exhibits, vintage engineering and stunning artwork displays". Dingles is a sizeable indoor visitor attraction that provides a rare opportunity to view Britain's fairground heritage in a beautiful rural location. The collection comprised ten major rides, including the Victorian Rodeo Switchback (the only spinning top switchback still in existence), examples of 1930s Dodgems, Noah's Ark and Skid rides, and a 1940s Ghost Train. Unfortunately, I did not have time to experience the attractions for myself, but the regular flow of vehicles turning into the well-signposted car park provided evidence of a busy day ahead for the centre's proprietors.

The secluded country lane transformed into a bridle path and I was immediately struck by the large number of butterflies in the neighbouring hedgerows. The volume and variety of butterflies had increasingly become a feature of my journey, but the numbers and diversity here surpassed everything I'd encountered to date. It was now abundantly clear that the warm and sunny summer of 2013 had enabled farmland butterflies to recover dramatically from the worst year on record for butterflies in the previous year, when almost all of the 56 British species monitored had suffered declines as a result of very wet weather.

The trail meandered through the bucolic Devon

countryside until I arrived in the village of Lifton, where I had enjoyed a post-walk beer with my brother-in-law on the previous day. It was here in his home village that the Ambrosia creamery was founded in 1917 by Albert Morris. The company originally produced nutritious food for infants, but this was soon acquired as a source of nourishment for First World War soldiers. Prior to the Second World War, the company began to create creamed rice pudding in a tin, with most of the production placed in Red Cross food parcels, but after the war Ambrosia re-launched the product, together with a creamed macaroni pudding. The business expanded rapidly and, after being bought out by several major companies, was latterly acquired by Premier Foods.

At Liftondown, the trail offered splendid views of Launceston, my next destination. After a mile, I left Devon behind and entered Cornwall, the final county of my journey. Land's End beckoned, but the weather forecast was not encouraging.

Bradshaw was not particularly enamoured with Cornwall and described it as "one of the least inviting of the English counties." He continued "A ridge of bare and rugged hills, inter-mixed with bleak moors, runs through the midst of its whole length, and exhibits the appearance of a dreary waste." He clearly overlooked the spectacular beaches, the dramatic, craggy coastline, the attractive valleys and the captivating fishing harbours.

At the 'Welcome to Cornwall' road sign positioned in the grass verge close to Launceston Rugby Club, I took a photograph of myself with my smartphone camera (otherwise known as a 'selfie') and later posted it in my blog. A number of people later complained that I had looked miserable in the picture and, given that I was nearing the completion of my walk, commented that I should have at least offered a smile. What the complainants did not fully appreciate was that the sign had been left to nature and was completely encircled by dense, towering nettles. I had managed to trample on some of the nettles, but ultimately, with nobody around to take the photograph for me, I had to lean across awkwardly to align my face with the wording on the sign and, in doing so, I could barely make out the resultant image on my phone. The end product was a picture that clearly showed me at the Cornish boundary, but without a smile.

My route passed through St Leonard's Equitation Centre, a riding facility which brimmed with activity on this Saturday morning in late July. I watched in deep fascination as a group of young riders carefully steered their horses over a cross country course, watched and encouraged by admiring parents.

I battled determinedly up the steep Ridgegrove Hill and finally reached the market town of Launceston, the "gateway to Cornwall" and once the ancient capital of the county. It was early afternoon, so I located a vacant bench in the busy main square and consumed my packed lunch.

I had time to wander around the centre and viewed the impressive 11th century Norman castle. My lasting impressions were of a very hilly town but, unfortunately, my B&B was situated near to the bottom of the hill on the north side of town, which would mean a long and steep climb back to the town centre the following morning.

After a shower and a snooze, I walked a short distance down the road and dined at the White Horse Inn, where I was entertained by two middle-aged women who were seated at a neighbouring table. Sat less than two yards away, I couldn't avoid overhearing their conversations as we dined but, whatever the subject, one of them was relentlessly critical. She complained quite vocally about her demanding mother, her indolent sister, her unreasonable ex-husband, her interrupted holiday, her unrewarding job, her boisterous neighbours, the intolerable hot weather and even her gossiping hairdresser. Surprisingly, she didn't find time to complain about her meal, but I sensed that, in different company on another day, she would probably have a host of critical comments to make about both this evening's meal and her dining partner.

CHAPTER SEVEN

The final stage to Land's End

Day 52 – Launceston to Mount
Distance: 19.3 miles
Cumulative distance: 873.8 miles
Weather: Heavy rain showers

Wet weather, waterproofs, Wayne, and warm welcomes

After another fine breakfast, I checked out and climbed the hill up to the town centre. There I waited to meet Wayne, an IT consultant and former work colleague, who was joining me for today's walk.

Wayne is an Aussie who was born in Launceston, Tasmania, so he had deliberately selected this day to meet me in Launceston, Cornwall. He is a cricket fanatic, having formerly partnered Australian Test player David Boon, and still plays occasional first team cricket for his local team. Wayne had chosen potentially the wettest day to walk with me, while the rest of his family visited the nearby Eden Project visitor attraction.

For the first time since Beattock in Scotland (day 21), I wore my waterproofs – that was a whole month ago! We immediately sheltered from the first shower under a shop canopy in the town centre, then headed towards the outskirts, stopping on the way to take Wayne's photograph outside Launceston College.

Today's route would largely be on quiet country lanes around the edge of Bodmin Moor, one of the major obstacles facing many End to End walkers. Most choose a route to the western side of the Moor, but I needed to follow the eastern side to be convenient for an appointment on the following day.

Our second rain shelter was a conveniently located church in the secluded hamlet of Trebullett – this was despite the fact that the Sunday morning service was still in progress! Some of the congregation beckoned us in, but we had our own mission for the day, our own prayers, and even our own collection pot. The neighbouring church hall provided timely toilet facilities for the wet hikers.

The tranquil, undulating country lanes afforded fine views of the ever changing rural landscapes in this mostly unpopulated area.

At Rilla Mill, we stopped for an iced Coke at the village pub, but the enticing smell of the Sunday roasts nearly stalled us for longer. An elderly gentleman wandered over to our table and enquired where I'd purchased my hat – he'd recently been diagnosed with skin cancer and had been looking out for a light floppy hat to protect his head from the sun's rays. I wasn't quite certain whether he was hoping that I would donate my hat, but I really needed it for the sunshine that would surely re-appear during the final few days of my walk.

We journeyed on until Minions, the highest village in Cornwall. The village is dominated by Caradon Hill, standing at 371 metres high, whose summit boasts a TV transmission mast. Minions was created for industry from a virgin moorland site, the three major activities being tin and copper mining, quarrying and railways. None of this industry remains now, but many of the pump houses and spoil tips can still be seen today and the nearby Minions Heritage Centre, located in a Cornish engine house, celebrates the history of the landscape from the Stone Age, through the eighteenth and nineteenth century mining, right up to the present day.

We passed by the village shop ("Open most hours for most things"), but we were lured into the village pub for another refreshing Coke. This proved to be most lucrative on the fundraising front. The pub was brimming with Sunday diners and drinkers, locals and tourists alike, but they were most welcoming and gave very generously at the sight of my collecting pot.

One particularly heavy downpour provided a complete soaking, the fiercest rain I had encountered during my entire journey. Fortunately, the subsequent light breeze enabled us to dry off quickly between showers.

We finally reached St Neot, national village of the year in 2004, where Wayne's feet decided that it was time to call his chauffeur. I had noticed what appeared to be a tree growing from the top of the church tower in the village, so I questioned a local man who was sitting outside the village pub.

It transpired that it wasn't an actual tree, but a large oak branch, which formed a key part of an annual ceremony in the village. Oak Apple Day was a formal public holiday celebrated in England on 29th May to commemorate the restoration of the English monarchy in May 1660. During the English Civil War, St Neot was staunchly Royalist and the village still commemorates this event today. Each year, the Vicar leads a procession through the village and is followed by the Tower Captain holding the oak bough, which symbolises the historical allegiance. The history of the event is explained to the audience and the Vicar blesses the branch. The Tower Captain then throws the old branch down from the top of the tower and the newly blessed branch is hauled up to the top, where it remains until the following year.

I continued alone, jogging intermittently for the remaining few miles to Mount, where tonight's B&B was located. After a rapid shower, I joined up with Wayne and his family (wife Nicky and daughters Lauren and Cassie) and we drove back to the London Inn at St Neot for dinner. I opted for the sea bream, served with cherry tomatoes and olives and sampled the local multi-award winning brew, Betty Stogs from the Skinner's brewery in Truro.

Day 53 – Mount to Roche
Distance: 13.6 miles
Cumulative distance: 887.4 miles
Weather: Cloudy, rain showers, sunny later

A leisurely morning stroll, danger on the A38, a station reunion and a walk to an industrial estate with rural views

I ate breakfast with Wayne and family, then they set off back to their home near to Windsor. The B&B owner kindly allowed me to stay long beyond the normal departure time as, for once, I was in no hurry to leave. It wasn't the frequent, heavy showers which deterred me, but the fact that I had only 6 miles to walk before meeting my son Daniel at Bodmin Parkway station after lunch. I relaxed in the conservatory and browsed through a collection of Cornwall Life glossy magazines, each overflowing with stunning pictures of the county's fine scenery and delightful properties. When I spotted a temporary gap in the rain clouds, I resolved to make my exit.

I followed a quiet country lane which descended steeply towards the A38, the main highway from Plymouth to Bodmin. My arrival at the junction of the main road coincided with a sudden heavy shower so, for a second successive day, I was forced to don my waterproofs.

I had no choice but to walk along the A38 for about a mile and a half to the station junction, but it soon became the most difficult road I had encountered during the entire journey. There was no pedestrian footpath, but a very narrow verge in some parts and no verge at all in others. Heavy goods vehicles thundered by at speed on this very busy major highway, made even more demanding by the spray which resulted from the recent downpour. My only option was to jog along the roadside when there were occasional breaks in the traffic and to seek refuge in the roadside bushes when it became too dangerous to proceed. I eventually reached the junction, but not without nearly slipping over a narrow bank into a ditch.

Crossing the main road to reach the station road proved to be another challenge, as the junction was positioned between two bends in the road. The station evidently did not cater for pedestrians arriving from an easterly direction. I listened for a break in the traffic flow and sprinted across the A38, risking life and limb. I made it safely, much to my relief, and was soon striding down the quiet lane towards the station.

Bodmin Parkway station is situated in a remote location, several miles from Bodmin town centre. When the railway was originally opened in 1859, there were plans to construct a branch line to the town centre, but the railway company could not raise sufficient funds, so Bodmin Parkway became the main station (the branch line was eventually opened nearly thirty years later). The station is on the mainline between Penzance and Plymouth, and provides direct services to and from London.

The station itself was a floral delight, with colourful displays along the length of each platform. I sat on a damp bench and ate my packed lunch, watching with interest as the steam hauled passenger train of the neighbouring Bodmin and Wenford heritage railway arrived at the opposite platform.

Daniel's train pulled in impressively on time. He had boarded at Reading, so it was quite a thrill for him to be able to travel on his own as far as Cornwall. Being a remote station, I'd anticipated that perhaps a handful of passengers would disembark here, but I was amazed to see several hundred people pour out of the carriage doors and it took me a few minutes to identify Daniel in the crowd. I greeted him for the first time in nearly eight weeks and welcomed him to the final stages of my journey. He'd come to join me for the final five days of the walk, but I silently hoped that he'd done sufficient training while I'd been away.

We left the platform and took a much more pedestrian friendly route to the south west of the station, as I tried to catch up on all the events at home. Being a typical teenage boy, Daniel's responses to my enquiries were mainly monosyllabic, so it did not take long for me to be fully briefed.

We walked at a fair pace, taking a short cut through the National Trust's Lanhydrock estate, with its ancient woodlands and tranquil pathways. The short cut took us well away from the popular walking routes through the estate and at times we wondered whether we had ventured onto private land, but before long we arrived at a pedestrian exit gate close to the estate office, having sliced a considerable corner from the longer alternative route.

We followed a country lane which ran parallel to the busy A30 highway and near Fenton Pits we spotted a quirky homemade finger signpost, which was situated just inside a field at the roadside. The Cornish flag flew from the top of the sign and the three fingers pointed to "Bodmin 3m ish", "Trevs Pub" and "Fentonpist just up the road". A retired electrician had made his own version of the sign after an official, but dilapidated, council sign had been removed. The council had subsequently removed his original sign, but it appeared that he had now replaced it just off the road.

After an 8 mile trek, a gentle introduction to long distance walking for Daniel, we finally reached an industrial estate in Roche, where our Travelodge accommodation was located. Despite its industrial base, our room offered rural views, including the local donkey sanctuary. We dined next door at the Victoria Inn, where a wide choice of food and efficient service was provided.

Day 54 – Roche to Truro

Distance: 18.7 miles
Cumulative distance: 906.1 miles
Weather: Morning drizzle, dry and brighter later

Cornish country lanes in the rain, danger on the A39, 900 miles completed and delightful accommodation in Truro

We each swiftly consumed the contents of our Travelodge breakfast box (orange juice, cornflakes and milk, croissant and muffin), but I really missed my customary morning cup of fresh coffee. We then set off in light drizzle to the centre of Roche, where we purchased a selection of items for lunch from the Co-op store.

The light rain persisted and, dressed in our waterproofs, we plodded on relentlessly, trying to be oblivious to the weather conditions. We followed a minor road, passing through the villages of Nanpean, Goonamarris and St Stephen, before joining the main 'A' road for a brief distance.

We were in the heart of Cornish china clay country, evident from the impressive peaks, known as the Cornish Alps, which dominated the surrounding landscape. In 1745, a Plymouth apothecary called William Cookworthy had discovered a rare type of decomposed granite nearby and found a way to separate the material, using water to remove impurities. Over a twenty year period, he developed a way of manufacturing porcelain and began making fine china. By the early nineteenth century the china clay industry grew rapidly and formerly tiny villages were soon developed, to the point where the Cornwall deposits had become the largest in the world. Throughout the 19th century the industry employed around seven thousand men, often forced to work in difficult and dangerous working conditions. Railways and tramways were soon built to transport the material to the coast and it was exported all over the world. Today, the St Austell deposits, which have produced around 120 million tonnes of china clay, have largely been abandoned.

We stopped at the village of Ladock, where we sat on a bench next to the thriving Portakabin shop and post office to have lunch. Soon afterwards the rain ceased and the sun gradually saw off the clouds.

Ladock and the neighbouring village of Grampound Road had joined forces to become the 75th transition town in 2008. The Transition Towns' movement began in 2005, when a group of friends launched Transition Town Totnes as the first step in a move towards a low carbon future for their community. They designed a number of steps that residents could take to prepare themselves for energy scarcity and a changing climate. Ladock and Grampound Road successfully applied for a government grant and were awarded half a million pounds to install low carbon technologies in the community. The monies raised from feed-in-tariffs for electricity generated by the wind turbine and photovoltaic cells are returned to the community to be spent on further low carbon installations. Ladock and Grampound Road had also established a range of other initiatives, including a group oil buying scheme, local food markets, a community orchard and allotments.

After passing by the fringes of the village of St Erme, we had to join the busy A39 road. Unfortunately, we could not locate the footpath which should have led us to St Clement Woods, so we were forced to continue along the road for another half a mile. Despite being a major road, there were no cycle or pedestrian paths and the grass verges were either too narrow for us or non-existent. This only confirmed my observation that Cornwall's major roads were the least pedestrian and cyclist friendly of all the roads I had experienced over the last two months.

It was a relief to join a minor country lane which followed a pleasant, peaceful wooded valley and eventually led us to the outskirts of the fine city of Truro. We managed to navigate our way under the railway arches and through a complex array of streets to locate our accommodation for the evening.

Inevitably, our B&B was situated at the top of a hill, just outside the town centre. The Townhouse Rooms provided a friendly welcome, a very comfortable room and a refreshingly hot shower, but additionally it offered complimentary hot drinks and delicious homemade cakes in the residents' kitchen.

In bright sunshine, we wandered down the hill to explore

the centre of Truro, passing by some fine Georgian buildings on the way. The shops were closed, but we did spot the Christmas shop (only 147 days to go!) and the impressive cathedral, which dominates the skyline.

The bustling city of Truro is the centre for administration, commerce and tourism for the County of Cornwall. There has been a town here since the 12th century when a castle was built, the remains of which were found during excavations for the cattle market. By the 14th century Truro was an important inland port, but the arrival of the Black Death later that century led to a mass exodus and the town was neglected. This was resolved by a petition to Parliament which excused residents from paying rent and, in the 18th and 19th centuries, Truro flourished as tin prices increased and wealthy mine owners built elegant town houses – the town was known as the "London of Cornwall". Queen Victoria granted Truro city status in 1877 and, thirty years after the laying of the foundation stones on the site of the 16th century parish church of St Mary the Virgin, the city's cathedral was completed in 1910.

We dined at Pizza Express, housed in the former Coinage Hall, an imposing Victorian building. The Coinage Hall dates back to a time when Truro was chosen as a Stannary Town, where smelted tin was assayed before being exported.

I celebrated reaching the 900 mile landmark today, but it dawned on me that the days and the miles were now running out. I felt a tinge of sadness at the prospect and vowed that, henceforth, I would savour every remaining moment, as my epic journey neared its inevitable conclusion.

Day 55 – Truro to Porthleven
Distance: 21.2 miles
Cumulative distance: 927.3 miles
Weather: Light drizzle

A day of country lanes and footpaths in the drizzle, a few missing signposts, the seaside and a family reunion

After breakfast, we set off in drizzle and soon reached a scenic country lane which took us away from civilised Truro and around the delightfully named Nansavallan Wood, but the road was also a popular short cut for local motorists. A footpath across farmland enabled us to avoid road traffic and to keep our route as direct as possible, as we reached the hamlet of Bissoe in the Carnon valley.

Bissoe, in the heart of a former tin mining area, was the site of an early arsenic extraction works, the second such commercial works in Britain. Point Mills Arsenic Refinery was famous for the high quality of its arsenic, a by-product of tin smelting. Its main market was the expanding Lancashire cotton industry, which used arsenic in pigments and dyes, but it was also exported for use in cotton plantations. The British Arsenic Company, later to become the Cornwall Arsenic Company, ran this factory for around one hundred years until it closed in 1939. The site remained unused until it was landscaped to form a public leisure area in 1986. Ironically, a contaminated industrial area that was once littered with mines, arsenic works and associated industries, now sits adjacent to Bissoe Valley Nature Reserve.

We continued along narrow, tree-lined lanes, then followed the road which gradually made the long ascent of Tubbon Hill, until we arrived at Stithians, where we stopped at the post office and general stores to purchase an early lunch – our first Cornish pasty, which we ate whilst sat on a bench outside in the rain. It still tasted good, even if we departed somewhat more sodden than we had arrived.

The village had recently held the annual Stithians Show, one of the largest one-day agricultural shows in the UK, with an attendance in excess of 20,000. The show was established in 1834 and has been held continuously since then, apart from during the two World Wars and in 2001, when the outbreak of foot and mouth disease resulted in cancellation.

We followed a couple of footpaths which provided shorter routes, but came unstuck on a later footpath due a complete lack of signposts. We found ourselves next to Stithians reservoir, having deviated from the scheduled route, but quickly found an alternative route, which traversed the top of the dam wall and skirted the reservoir itself. It was here in 2009 that a golden eagle was spotted – only the second observed in Cornwall in two hundred years.

Unfortunately, another missing signpost resulted in a further deviation and we were soon walking across a field in the mist, not quite sure how to re-join our route. With the assistance of GPS, we navigated our way back on track, but time and miles had been expended unnecessarily.

At Porkellis, we stopped for a Coke and a welcoming sit down at the Star Inn. We relaxed on the comfy sofa, and could happily have stayed for hours, but we had more mileage to cover. As we left, the landlord came running down the road after us to tell us that we were heading in the wrong direction for Land's End, so I had to explain that we would be walking via Porthleven along the scenic coastal path, rather than taking the direct road route to get to Land's End.

We passed Poldark Mine, an early eighteenth century tin

mine made famous by the BBC drama Poldark, which was based on the books of Winston Graham. In the year 2000, the mine was rescued from the receivers by local mining heritage enthusiasts and today operates as a popular heritage site, with local crafts people running workshops.

After a longer than planned walk, which Daniel's legs did not much appreciate, we skirted the town of Helston (the most southerly town on mainland Britain), crossed over the River Cober, then ascended the hill and followed a narrow, winding lane back down again until we finally arrived at the bustling harbour of Porthleven. Within minutes, we'd tracked down my wife Carole and my daughter Hannah and we were reunited as a family for the first time in two months.

Our hotel, the An Mordros (meaning 'sound of the sea'), was located up the hill, but offered superb views across the harbour. This was the first time I'd been so close to the sea since the early days of the walk in Scotland, when I had walked alongside the seals on the beautiful, deserted beach at Brora. It was uplifting to smell the brine and to hear the sound of the gulls flying overhead. With my family around me, the music of the sea to revel in, and the end of my immense journey just two days' away, I was back in holiday mood for the first time since I arrived in Wick on Day Zero.

I went for a leisurely stroll around the picturesque harbour with my daughter Hannah, then we called in for a drink at the wonderfully situated Ship Inn, a true Cornish pub built into the rocks at the entrance to the harbour. Unsurprisingly, back in the eighteenth century, it was renowned as a smugglers' inn.

We had an enjoyable family dinner at the Blue Haze fish restaurant in the harbour. The meal was excellent and there were splendid views over the harbour. My drink? A bottle of Porthleven ale from Skinner's brewery – what else?

Day 56 – Porthleven to Mousehole

Distance: 16.5 miles
Cumulative distance: 943.8 miles
Weather: Cloudy

A day on the South West coastal path – an exhilarating cliff-top hike, followed by a sea front walk through Penzance and Newlyn

After a family breakfast, and once Daniel had packed his rucksack and was finally ready to depart, we set off along the footpath to the opposite side of the harbour, passing the Ship Inn on the way. Hannah joined us for the first few minutes, then returned to the prospect of her other love, shopping.

We joined the South West coastal path and, within minutes, we were walking along the undulating, honeysuckle clad cliff-top track, with magnificent views along the rocky coastline and down to the crashing waves below. We encountered a number of old industrial ruins along the path, as well as wild ponies and a peregrine falcon.

We were intrigued by some of the handwritten signs which appeared periodically along the footpath. One warned "Beware of adders", while another located on a private road read "Drive slowly – deaf dog". Needless to say, we encountered neither.

We passed by a party of young people engaged in coasteering. This is a physical activity that involves traversing the rocky coastline by a mixture of swimming, climbing, scrambling, jumping or diving, without the assistance of boats, surf boards or other craft. Judging by the shouts of delight emanating from the waters below, they were evidently enjoying themselves.

We were surprised by the number of helicopters which flew past us along the coast, with one seemingly passing by every couple of minutes. Royal Naval Air Station (RNAS) Culdrose is situated just outside Helston on the Lizard Peninsula and is the largest helicopter base in Europe with some 75 aircraft and 3,000 personnel, so we concluded that they were undertaking a training exercise around us.

Occasionally, the coastal footpath was diverted inland for a short distance. This was presumably due to coastal erosion, where the existing path had been damaged, or was now closer to the cliffs than was considered to be safe for walkers. In contrast to most of the other long distance footpaths I had followed during my journey, the South West coastal path was well populated. In the warm summer sunshine, with a pleasant breeze, and dry ground underfoot, these were perfect walking conditions.

After rounding the headland at Cudden Point, we were treated to our first view of St Michael's Mount, a small castle-topped tidal island which sits impressively in Mount's Bay. The island is managed by the National Trust and is accessed at low tide by a causeway and at other times by a fleet of small boats.

We stopped for lunch at Marazion, where the cliff-top path gives way to a flat track along the sea front and from where the causeway to St Michael's Mount begins. We treated ourselves to a freshly baked Cornish pasty each, which we consumed in some terraced gardens overlooking the Mount, then enjoyed a pint of Trelawny ale (well, Daniel enjoyed a Coke!) at the King's Arms.

Daniel and I had briefly visited the town in the previous summer and were about to retrace in reverse the steps of a walk we had undertaken then. We'd travelled on the overnight sleeper train from London to Penzance, from where we walked along the coastal path to Marazion to visit St Michael's Mount, before taking an open-top bus tour around the western tip of Cornwall to St Ives and Land's End. Maybe that was part of the inspiration for my journey from John O' Groats to Land's End.

The coastal footpath from Marazion was bustling with day trippers, who were enjoying a leisurely stroll in the salty air. Deceptively, we could just make out our final destination of Mousehole far across the large horseshoe bay, but the distance on foot would keep us walking for several more hours yet. We were soon hemmed in between the railway line and the coast, as we reached Penzance, the most westerly town in Britain.

In 1595, Penzance, together with the neighbouring villages of Newlyn and Mousehole, was invaded and burned by a Spanish raiding fleet carrying around four hundred men. Known as the Battle of Cornwall, it remains the last time that England was invaded by hostile forces. Life around Penzance was traditionally focused on agriculture, fishing and mining, but as employment in these industries declined, many people emigrated overseas. Penzance's most famous son is probably Sir Humphry Davy, who invented the miner's safety lamp in 1801. His statue sits in Market Jew Street in the town centre, close to his birthplace.

The coastal route alternated between roads and footpaths as we passed through the vibrant fishing town of Newlyn, whose harbour is the largest fishing port in England. We climbed out of Newlyn and passed by some disused quarries, before turning in a south westerly direction at Penlee Point.

It was from here that the Penlee lifeboat disaster happened in December 1981. The Solomon Browne lifeboat had been launched at night to assist the MV Union Star, a mini bulk carrier, after its engines had failed in stormy seas and hurricane force winds. The lifeboat initially managed to rescue four people from the carrier, but both vessels were then lost in dangerous seas, resulting in the death of sixteen people, including eight lifeboat volunteers. Within a day of the disaster, enough local people had volunteered to form a new lifeboat crew and a major appeal subsequently raised almost ten million pounds.

We joined a quiet lane for the final descent into the pretty fishing village of Mousehole (pronounced 'Mauzl'), where we had a family room booked at the Ship Inn, situated right in the heart of the village, overlooking the harbour.

We had a delicious meal at the Ship (I opted for the wonderfully fresh mackerel) and I sampled the HSD ale from St Austell brewery. Afterwards, in the narrow street right outside our bedroom window, we were treated to a stirring display from a troupe of Morris dancers.

I caught up with events on the first day's play of the 3rd Ashes Test Match from Manchester. Australia had dominated, scoring 303 for 3 by the close, leaving England with much to do to maintain their 2-0 lead in the series.

For me, the end was nigh. After months of planning and training, followed by eight weeks of strenuous walking, the final day was about to dawn. It was difficult to believe that this mammoth journey was nearly over, but I really had run out of country, so Land's End was an appropriate final destination.

Day 57 – Mousehole to Land's End

Distance: 11.0 miles
Cumulative distance: 954.8 miles
Weather: Warm and sunny

The final day. A gentle stroll with the children, one last missing footpath, arrival at Land's End and, eventually, back home.

We had a late family breakfast as, somewhat unusually, the Ship

Inn did not start serving until nine o'clock. Laden with a full English breakfast, Daniel, Hannah and I then set off in glorious sunshine to complete the final ten or so miles of my journey.

I'd calculated that we didn't have sufficient time to follow the coastal path for the entire walk. This was due in part to its more circuitous route, but also because I wasn't certain how Hannah would have coped with the undulating coastal path. I was also anxious to reach Land's End at around lunchtime, since the weather forecast for the day indicated heavy rain showers from early afternoon onwards and to finish my journey in a storm would be an unfitting anti-climax.

Instead, we walked along desolate minor country lanes. We had planned to cut a corner by following a short footpath after a mile, but when we located it we discovered that it was completely overgrown. I was pleased to have witnesses, given my previous experiences of such paths during my journey.

We pressed on to Lamorna, then joined a track which climbed steeply out of the valley, before passing the Tregiffian Burial Chamber, a Neolithic or early Bronze Age chambered tomb with a walled and roofed stone entrance passage, which led to the central chamber.

Fate had decreed that there should be one final detour due to a disappearing footpath. The initial signpost was prominent and we followed the path around the edge of a field for a few hundred yards. The map clearly set out the route between two farms, but reality led us to a field of wheat and another field blocked by wire mesh netting. I'd managed to walk for 950 miles from the tip of Scotland, but now, just an hour from the end of my journey, we were lost! I adopted my usual approach – keep calm, head in the right general direction and cross fingers and toes. Daniel and Hannah were not quite as confident and started to panic as we clambered over a couple of stone walls, but fortunately it worked again as we re-joined a minor road, resulting in only a relatively small detour.

Hannah's feet had started to give her discomfort. In truth, she had ill-advisedly left her walking boots at home, so was today wearing her athletics shoes, which were not really designed for hiking. She attended to her feet at the roadside and vowed to complete the walk to Land's End.

We were all rather thirsty, so when a traditional Cornish village pub appeared out of the blue in the small village of Treen, we readily agreed to stop for final refreshments. The Logan Rock Inn is named after a large granite boulder which stands on the cliffs nearby and which was well-known for its ability to rock back and forth without falling.

Back on the road, a diminutive stall selling homegrown strawberries was an offer we could not refuse. We consumed a punnet between us and, nearby, noticed another bizarre homemade signpost, which read "Caution please – deaf white cat". After identifying similar signs on the previous day's walk, I was beginning to wonder whether this area of Cornwall was a permanent sanctuary for visually and aurally impaired pets, but perhaps this was just a ruse initiated by the locals to tease the countless tourists speeding by in their vehicles.

We walked the final few miles along a 'B' road, then joined the A30, which covers the final half a mile – unusually, but fortunately, this section of a Cornish 'A' road actually provided a pedestrian footpath. The A30 runs all the way from Land's End to London, a distance of 284 miles, and ironically, passes just a couple of miles from my house. Carole joined us for the last few hundred yards to Land's End, so we finished my journey as a family. Due to the detour and a few additional stops, I was one hour later than planned, but it didn't matter.

Crossing the official finish line in front of the main Land's End entrance was, to my surprise and disappointment, not an emotional experience. There was no immense excitement, no great sense of relief, and no tears, just a sense of sadness that the journey was over. The sun was shining in a cloudless sky, which felt like a really fitting end after two months of remarkably good weather.

We walked to the reception at the Land's End Hotel, where I had my official record card stamped, then strolled over to the official signpost to have the obligatory finishing photo taken. My privilege for having completed the journey from John O' Groats was two prints for the price of one – it seemed like a hard earned discount! As the photographer snapped away, a crowd of onlookers gathered around the roped-off signpost and spontaneously burst into applause.

Land's End is one of the most beautiful, naturally wild and unspoilt corners of Cornwall. The landscape is rugged and barren, but it offers magnificent views of coastal rock formations and animated seas. However, the Land's End site is owned and managed by a company called Heritage Great Britain plc, whose portfolio also incorporates John O'Groats, the Snowdon Mountain Railway in North Wales, the Lightwater Valley theme park and country shopping village in North Yorkshire, and The Needles Park on the Isle of Wight.

At Land's End, there are various attractions to tempt the visiting day tripper. Apart from the hotel, there is the West Country shopping experience, The First and Last House (offering refreshments and souvenirs), Penwith House (selling gifts and souvenirs, but originally a temperance house for Victorian visitors seeking soft drinks only), Greeb Farm (a children's farm and craftwork centre), Arthur's Quest (an interactive experience), 20,000 Leagues under the Sea (a 4D family cinema show), Air Sea Rescue (a motion theatre show), and the End to End Story (a family exhibition).

We didn't have the time (or the inclination!) to indulge ourselves in such frivolities, but after I had sent a few texts and emails to confirm my arrival in Land's End, we walked across to the hotel restaurant to have lunch. I celebrated with a simple Greek salad and a pint of Tribute ale. Daniel took a photograph of me as I held my pint of Tribute in front of me – just a few days later, I was amused to see Prime Minister David Cameron repeat the exact same pose during his family's holiday in Cornwall. We just had time to enjoy an ice cream, then it was time to depart for home. Job done!

The weather forecast turned out to be completely accurate. Shortly after we drove away from Land's End, storms clouds blew in from the West and released their contents over Cornwall. As the rain drops were being catapulted onto the car's windscreen, I reflected that I'd timed my final day's walk to perfection. Avoiding the rain at the finish seemed to reflect the good fortune I'd been blessed with throughout my entire journey.

Approaching Okehampton, we took a short detour and called in very briefly at East Raddon Farm to visit Sylvia and her family. Unsurprisingly, her kind hospitality stretched to tea and freshly baked cakes and, without the weight of my rucksack to worry about, I was able to purchase a few jars of her tasty homemade marmalade.

Apart from visiting East Raddon farm, our route home through the South West briefly re-united me with several places that I'd visited on my journey. The M5 passes within a mile of Sampford Peverell and the Grand Union Canal, then we stopped for refreshments at Bridgwater Services, a stone's throw from North Petherton, where I'd taken sanctuary in Tesco on a baking hot day. The motorway ran parallel to the road in Sydenham, where I had been offered a bottle of beer by a complete stranger, then finally we passed by the pedestrian footpath which ran alongside the southbound carriageway on the Avonmouth bridge, which had marked my entry to Somerset on a busy, hot Friday afternoon. These landmarks had featured on my journey over a two week period, but today they all flashed by within a few hours.

We travelled along the motorway at relative speed and covered the 300 mile journey home in around five hours. I had become accustomed to covering this distance in about two and a half weeks on foot, but it now seemed that the pace of life with which I had become comfortably familiar was accelerating out of control before my eyes. It felt like a film that, until now, I had watched at normal speed, but which was suddenly being fast-forwarded in front of me.

We finally arrived home at 11 o'clock in the evening. Tonight's accommodation was one with which I was well acquainted. I wouldn't need to check what time breakfast would be served in the morning, nor would I need to set my alarm for the next day's walk.

With the excitement of my own day's events, I had not been able to follow proceedings in the Test Match. For the second successive day, Australia were in command, having declared on 527 for 7 wickets. In reply, England had succumbed to 52 for 2, having lost two wickets just before close of play. However, the meteorologists had provided hope for England with the prospect of divine intervention from the ever dependable Manchester rain, leaving a drawn match as the most likely outcome.

I climbed into my own bed for the first time in two months and promptly fell into a deep sleep.

CHAPTER EIGHT

Back home – time to reflect

After completing my walk, I had a few days to re-adjust to life at home, prior to taking a family holiday in Wales. I had expected to adapt very easily to my normal routines at home – after all, two months is not a particularly long time to be away. In practice, however, it took me much longer than I'd imagined.

The first issue I had to face was the simple matter of getting dressed in the morning. On the walk I had worn hiking trousers and a Cancer Research UK tee-shirt every day, putting on a clean tee-shirt each day from my stock of three. On my first morning at home, however, I was confronted with a wide choice of polo shirts and tee-shirts, and of chinos or shorts, each offering a range of colour options. To make it worse, I had to select footwear as well. I was now forced to make decisions, where for two months, no decisions had been necessary.

After breakfast, which was not of the full English, Scottish or Welsh variety, I no longer had to go through my daily routines. Changing into outdoor footwear was now a simple activity, which no longer involved carefully pulling on my walking socks, tenderly placing each foot inside my walking boots, and skilfully fastening the laces to the precise tension. Leaving the house no longer necessitated packing all my belongings into my rucksack and checking fastidiously that I hadn't left any items behind. I no longer needed to have my official record sheet for my walk stamped by my accommodation provider. Most noticeably, I no longer had to lift my rucksack onto my back and carry it around with me for the day. For a few days, I felt as if part of my body was missing and, at frequent intervals, found myself unconsciously feeling my back for the attachment which was no longer there.

During the walk, it had been important to carry plenty of drinking water, but during the heat wave in particular, I'd spent time at the start of each day's walk assessing the options en route for buying refreshments and re-stocking supplies. For a few days back at home, I struggled to comprehend that there was always a well-stocked fridge and water on tap, or that shops stocking plentiful supplies were widespread.

Another difficult concept to grasp in my new life was that I no longer had to reach a daily destination. I could just about manage with a trip to the shops or a visit to friends, but staying at home for the entire day was an alien concept initially. This brought with it the related issues of being in the same place in the evening, having dinner in the same place and sleeping in the same bed. I had lived a peripatetic existence for two months and had become accustomed to the nomadic lifestyle, so it was inevitable that a sudden end to this way of life would leave its mark.

The hardest challenge I faced was not spending most of my day engaged in the act of walking. My body had quickly adapted to the physical demands of walking between fifteen and twenty five miles each day. From the initial winter training walks to the daily distances to be covered on the walk itself, walking had become my daily routine, my raison d'etre. Perhaps I had become addicted to the act of walking and this more sedentary existence was my cold turkey. I even found it difficult not to stand up while I consumed my lunch at home!

Not only did I really miss the walking, but I felt profoundly guilty for not walking. Part of this stemmed from the fact that if I was not walking, I was no longer out there promoting my mission and no longer raising funds for Cancer Research UK.

During my subsequent holiday, I gradually adjusted to my new existence and, by the time I had returned home again, I was finally able to start reverting to most of my pre-walk routines. However, the guilt from not walking still remained.

Now that the dust had settled and I had meticulously unpacked my rucksack, put away my walking boots and cleared my mountain of mail, I had a chance to reflect fully on my two month journey and to offer some initial observations.

I had set off from John O' Groats in early June with three main objectives: to survive, to raise as much money as possible for Cancer Research UK, and to enjoy myself. With the journey completed, it was now time to assess my performance against my objectives.

I had survived! After I'd resolved the issues with my right boot in the first week and had recovered both from the minor injuries I had sustained from falling over near Dornoch and my temporarily swollen shin, I was completely untroubled for the rest of the walk, apart from a few bramble scratches and nettle stings. I was genuinely quite surprised at how well my mind and body had coped with the daily onslaught. I didn't wake a single day with any doubts about walking and I felt fitter than I had felt in many years. My feet were in good condition and bore no scars from almost a thousand miles of action. What's more, there were countless other reasons why I could have been struck down during my two month expedition, with perils lurking around every corner. Thankfully, I had not experienced any illness, I hadn't suffered from food poisoning, exhaustion, heatstroke, hay fever or hypothermia. I hadn't slipped on any remote mountain tracks or rocky cliff-top paths or fallen into any rivers or canals. I didn't suffer from any panic attacks and I was mentally strong throughout my entire walk. Nor had I been trampled by cows, attacked by a ferocious dog, assaulted by seagulls, mugged by opportunists, or hit by a motor vehicle. Survival had not been guaranteed and any one of these hazards could have visited me, but with good fortune, I had indeed survived.

On the fundraising front, I had every reason to be extremely grateful to everyone who donated to the cause. People I know well, such as family, work colleagues, friends and neighbours, gave generously. What truly surprised me was the kindness extended by hundreds of complete strangers, whether stood in a crowded pub, walking along footpaths, shopping in the high street or simply sharing breakfast at my accommodation. With Gift Aid included, I raised nearly £18,000 for Cancer Research UK, which was significantly more than my initial target of £10,000, and a meaningful sum from a research spending perspective.

I never did receive a response from Premier Inn or Whitbread plc, the parent company, to my several written requests for sponsorship. However, ever the optimist, I live in hope that there might be a happy ending one day. After all, I was very upbeat about the quality of their accommodation and I have made numerous bookings with them since my walk.

In terms of enjoyment, my immediate reaction is to declare that I did enjoy most of the journey. Yes, there were moments (ok, minutes, perhaps even hours!) when blisters or excessive heat caused discomfort, but these periods of pain were an important part of the overall experience. Those moments were completely overridden by the wonderful scenery, the companionship of fellow walkers and the daily sense of achievement. In truth, my level of enjoyment increased as the walk progressed, perhaps as my body adapted to its daily routine and the prospects of completion increased. The off-guard moment, when I accidently referred to my journey as a 'holiday', probably reflected my feelings more closely. It wasn't quite a holiday, but it undoubtedly wasn't anything analogous to being sentenced to two months' hard labour.

I had invested much time into route planning and accommodation booking prior to starting my journey, to the extent that I treated it like a military operation, so I was delighted that my efforts paid off with interest. With the exception of a few footpaths which did not materialise, the routes were a great triumph, often managing to balance the conflicting objectives of the shortest route and the most scenic. The short cuts, which usually originated from Google Street View, had a very high success rate, and saved me both time and mileage, often when I appreciated it most. I did get mildly lost a few times but, in truth, the walk would not have been as much fun without losing my way on a number of occasions, even if I wouldn't have admitted it at the time.

My accommodation exceeded all expectations, not only in terms of providing a comfortable bed, a hot bath or shower and a filling breakfast, but particularly with regard to the friendly and open-hearted hospitality offered by my hosts. Despite my frequently dishevelled appearance and my occasionally muddy boots, I was never made to feel unwelcome within any home, hostel or hotel. It was a major advantage to have booked my accommodation early, thereby securing the best choices for location and quality, but also, on occasions, the very lowest available rates. I'm convinced that checking some of the feedback websites in advance really contributed to the success. Indeed, I was so impressed by some of my accommodation that I immediately composed a series of favourable reviews and submitted them to the same feedback websites.

Most of all, my decision at the outset not to opt for the camping option was entirely vindicated. Whilst I have full admiration for any long distance walker who carries a tent and associated equipment for such a journey, for me the additional weight to be carried and the loss of the enticing home comforts offered by my accommodation would have been too great a challenge.

My equipment served me well. My walking boots had to be stretched, then eventually replaced due to wear and tear, but my second pair had no opportunity to be broken in, yet remained completely comfortable to the end. My rucksack accommodated everything with ease and, though quite heavy, fitted well and was trouble-free throughout. My waterproofs had very limited use, but performed well when called upon – I had researched intensively for a waterproof jacket which was both light and effective, so I felt slightly cheated that I'd worn it so infrequently! Without any doubt, the star item on my kit list was my smartphone, which incorporated a wide array of services, including phone, text, email, internet, GPS mapping, camera, weather alert, blog provider and pub locator – all from a device which fitted neatly into my trouser pocket. The walk would have been an altogether different experience without the use of such technology and I often wonder how End to Enders in previous generations coped without it.

My approach to the entire journey was to take each day at a time. While this sounds like a banal sporting cliché, it allowed me to focus on the current day's walk and not be overwhelmed by the daunting prospect of the bigger picture. I found that this approach worked well for me and I took immense pleasure out of ticking off each day's completed mileage. This way, the days disappeared and the miles accumulated almost unnoticed, and it was always reassuring to set off each day with an increasing mileage bank already under my belt.

I had expected the first week or so of the journey from John O' Groats to be lonely, knowing that it was a sparsely populated area, but I probably underestimated the scale and duration of this solitude. However, I had anticipated that any solitude would evaporate as soon as I reached Inverness, where I would join the Great Glen Way and subsequently the West Highland Way long distance footpaths. Both trails were less busy than I'd envisaged, but I particularly hadn't expected that most walkers would be travelling in the opposite direction to me, which severely limited the opportunities for meaningful conversation. Perhaps that is the compelling reason for the long distance paths to be walked from south to north!

My lasting impression of the walk is that Britain is still very much a green and pleasant land. Scotland is infinitely greater in length than most people appreciate, but this helps to make it one of the last great wildernesses in Britain, where it is possible to walk for miles without confronting any civilisation. My cross-sectional route through Scotland, England and Wales, however, included so few urban or industrial areas (only Glasgow, Preston, Liverpool and Avonmouth), that it is difficult not to perceive almost the entire walk as rural. As a consequence, I encountered an ever changing variety of landscape, including remote hills and hidden valleys, tranquil lochs, nature-laden rivers and canals, fertile farmland and dense forests, wild marshland and stunning coastlines. Long may Britain remain this way!

Through extended exposure to this rural environment, I gratefully discovered a slower pace of life and developed a closer relationship with nature and a heightened sense of community, history and tradition. From games of shinty in northern Scotland to celebrations of Jubilee Day in North Wales, from the authentic way of life on a Devon farm to commemoration of Oak Apple Day in Cornwall, I was given an insight into a world that is markedly different from the one that most city dwellers inhabit.

One of the truly bizarre and thought provoking features of my chosen route was that it skirted so many scenes of tragedy and disaster, encompassing a period from hundreds of years ago to more recent times. This was acutely remarkable as my route was predominantly rural and therefore didn't border many heavily populated areas. I was aware of less than a handful of such events when I plotted my route initially, with the Lockerbie aircraft disaster being the most notable, so I was astounded to discover the volume, scale and diversity of these incidents as my journey across Britain unfolded. It seemed an inconceivable contrast that the tranquil rural idyll through which I was journeying had previously witnessed such carnage and extensive loss of life. Whether they were due to nature, disease, industry, or war, or whether they were accidents involving aircraft, ships, or trains, these events were all tragedies for the communities involved and many still bear the scars.

One of the lasting highlights of my journey was meeting up with family and friends at different stages of the route, although practically this was mainly restricted to England and Wales. It was fantastic to meet up with people I hadn't seen for a long time (some for over twenty years) and to re-kindle friendships, even if it was only a fleeting visit. Similarly, it was immensely enjoyable to walk with companions for a day, even if some (probably most!) left in greater pain and a worse physical condition than they had arrived! I did bear a heavy burden of guilt, knowing that I had been responsible for the physical injuries suffered by those people who had given their time generously to join me. Please forgive me!

Another overarching memory is of the kindness of strangers, not just in donating to my cause, but in frequently going way beyond the normal boundaries set by humanity. This extended to accommodation providers, walkers, pub landlords, shop owners and complete strangers – the man who invited us to join his family for a drink when the local inn was closed, or the young girl who donated her pocket money to my cause, are not isolated examples.

I can't review my journey without mentioning the weather. I read a few blogs from people who'd undertaken the same journey in the summer of 2012 and they regularly described heavy rain showers and made consistent references to waterproofs, mud, puddles and trying to dry damp boots and clothes. I duly planned for similar conditions – after all, I would be walking for two months in the British summer! At first, I was pleasantly surprised that northern Scotland provided sunshine and would happily have accepted that, in return for standard British weather for the rest of the journey. What I didn't expect was the extended heat wave, from the northern fringes of Lancashire, across the entire length of Wales and into the heart of Somerset. This provided an additional challenge, especially during the hilly, unsheltered Offa's Dyke section of the walk, in ensuring that sufficient liquids could be obtained en route. The rain I experienced was pitifully little, so my waterproofs barely made a handful of appearances in 57 days, with a whole month elapsing from Beattock in Scotland to Launceston in Cornwall, while they were consigned to my rucksack.

My gripes are few and insignificant. Some footpaths were

poorly signposted or significantly overgrown (some were both!) but, in general, I was able to locate and negotiate most of the paths I encountered. Of more concern were some of the 'A' roads I had to use, particularly those in Cornwall, which did not appear to make any allowance for pedestrians and cyclists, to the extent of being dangerous. In a country which promotes cycling and walking, it seems that we have to do more to safeguard their wellbeing.

More frivolously, I was frustrated by the number of pubs which closed their doors at lunchtime, when there was clearly demand, not just from one thirsty hiker, but also from numerous other potential customers I met outside their locked doors. In an era when pubs are closing down for good on a regular basis, it doesn't make economic sense to miss out on valuable opportunities for business.

My final complaint, based on nearly one thousand miles of walking across Britain, is that there is a dearth of seats or benches on which the weary pedestrian can rest his or her limbs. Whether on a road, a long distance footpath or a canal towpath, I really would have appreciated somewhere to sit down to enjoy my lunch or snack break, instead of being forced to stand up or sit on the ground.

A number of people have asked if I would repeat my journey from John O' Groats to Land's End. My straight answer is that I would in theory, with minimal changes to my original route. However, in truth, I simply couldn't replicate the novelty, the unique atmosphere or the circumstances of undertaking the walk for the first time, such as the prospect of a journey into the unknown, the challenge of fundraising, or meeting up with family and friends. Above all. I certainly could not re-create the exceptional weather I experienced.

My journey had been an astonishing experience which

would provide treasured memories for years to come. But the experience was much more than just the walking. What made it special were the other ingredients; the people, from family and friends who walked with me, met me en route, or kindly accommodated me, to the complete strangers who provided boundless hospitality; the remarkable weather, which undoubtedly played a role in shaping my experience; and even external events, such as Andy Murray winning the Wimbledon title or England's cricketers winning The Ashes. All of these ingredients were blended throughout my journey to create a magical experience in a golden summer.

That aside, I'm sure there's another adventure in the making…

POSTSCRIPT

As I write, some eight months after crossing the finishing line at Land's End, the walk is now a fading memory. The long, hot summer of 2013 seems even more remote when viewed from the perspective of the exceptionally wet weather of the winter which succeeded it. The walk itself seems like a distant dream and I regularly have to prove to myself that I really did undertake and complete the journey by flicking through my photo book and reminding myself that I was actually there. I miss the walk intensely and would relish more than ever to re-live my journey, but, as I have explained already, it just wouldn't be the same experience second time around.

I felt markedly fitter in the months following completion of my walk. Visibly, my body had reacted favourably to being treated to an extended daily walk and many hours spent in the fresh air. This point was specifically hammered home to me a couple of months after finishing at Land's End, when I took my son Daniel to visit the Pompeii and Herculaneum exhibition at the British Museum in London one evening. Afterwards, we travelled by the underground to Waterloo station, from where we would catch the train back home. We realised that if we really hurried, we might just catch the imminent train, thereby avoiding a long wait for the next one. Like fully trained athletes, we sprinted from the depths of the underground platform and up the steep and interminable escalator, through the ticket barrier and along the length of the station platform, reaching our carriage with seconds to spare. It dawned on me that, in my state of fitness prior to preparing for the walk, we would have missed the train quite comfortably.

During the October half term holiday, Daniel and I drove up to Scotland to spend a few days walking in the Highlands. We stayed at the Crianlarich Hotel, which had been my accommodation for one night on my journey. The weather was mixed, but we completed a couple of walks on the West Highland Way. The first took us up Conic Hill and around the village of Balmaha, while the second incorporated a walk to the King's House Hotel and a section of the barren wilderness known as Rannoch Moor. A small herd of deer was feeding just beyond the King's House and, in one brief moment, I spotted more deer than I'd observed during my entire End to End journey! On another day we caught the train to Glasgow, an idyllic journey which passed through wonderful mountain scenery and provided a continuous panorama of trees coated in glorious autumn colours. Glasgow was not bathed in sunshine on this occasion, but we took the opportunity to visit a few tourist attractions, which time had prevented me from doing, even on my rest day.

Despite the fact that I'd taken early retirement, I did spend a few unplanned days working in the run up to Christmas. I had received a call out of the blue, enquiring whether I would be interested and available to undertake a short piece of work with my former employer. After some deliberation, I accepted, on the basis that it was short term. It was good to have the opportunity to catch up with former colleagues and to thank them personally for the monetary and moral support they had provided throughout my walk, but it was a surreal experience to be working in the same office again. Despite having been absent for eight months, by the end of my first day, I felt as if I had never been away.

I was delighted to be invited to an official cheque presentation at Cancer Research UK's London offices. Lucie, who joined me on the Okehampton to Lewdown section of my walk in Devon, had subsequently left CRUK to join the British Heart Foundation, so Giorgia, a vivacious Italian, became my new Local Fundraising Manager. Giorgia later arranged for me to visit their research laboratories in London as a guest of Cancer Research UK, which gave me a fascinating and uplifting insight into the extraordinary work being undertaken by truly committed staff. I left feeling very satisfied that the funds I had helped to raise would be put towards a worthwhile project.

Having successfully completed my End to End walk, I became eligible to become a full member of the Land's End John O' Groats Association, which was established in 1983, following the inaugural journey from Land's End to John O' Groats and then back to Land's End again. This event raised in excess of £10,000 for various charities and the participants went on to form the first Committee.

Members of the Association have completed the journey in a variety of ways, and although cyclists, walkers and motorists are the most familiar, the more obscure modes of transport include a motorised supermarket trolley, a push scooter, various traction engines, unicycles, horse drawn carriages, a Phantom fighter jet, a microlight and a yacht. Most participants travel from one end to the other in a fairly direct route, but some include the four extremities of the United Kingdom, or the highest peaks in England, Wales and Scotland and a few extend their journey into Ireland and even the near continent.

Most impressively, a few months after I had finished my journey, Sean Conway ("Endurance Adventurer, Blogger, Author & Speaker") became the first person to swim from Land's End to John O' Groats, completing this remarkable endurance test in 135 days. Born in Zimbabwe, Sean had an adventurous upbringing in a National Park with his conservationist game ranger father and spent his early years climbing trees and chasing elephants out of his garden.

Sean's list of other achievements is truly extraordinary; a mini cycle adventure to the Alps, joining Team GB for the Strongman Run in Germany, walking from Cheltenham to London for less than the price of the train ticket (£48.50), competing in the Midmar Mile in South Africa (the world's largest open water swimming event), and cycling from London to Paris in 24 hours. Impressive enough, but that only covers his activities during the last year! Prior to this, Sean has cycled around the world (a pick-up truck crashed into him in the USA, fracturing his spine and destroying his bike – his helmet saved his life – but he still managed to complete the journey), cycled from John O' Groats to Land's End, and completed the Three Peaks Cycle Challenge. He had also climbed Mount Kilimanjaro dressed in a penguin suit! Throughout these adventures, he has raised funds for his favourite charities, Saving Rhinos, Solar Aid, and War Child. He's a truly inspirational adventurer.

My family recently joined me to attend the Land's End John O' Groats Association's annual dinner event at a hotel in Torquay, where I was presented with my certificate for successfully completing the journey on foot. I was also privileged to be presented with the Committee Cup, in recognition of the monies I had raised for Cancer Research UK. Some weeks later, my daughter Hannah cooked a delicious three course dinner, my prize for achieving my increased funding target, despite her protestations that I had set the threshold too high!

Having survived all the pitfalls placed before me over my

955 mile journey, I succumbed to injury while undertaking the most innocuous activity within a half mile of home. I was helping out with the local Scout Christmas Post one Sunday morning, delivering Christmas cards to a collection of houses in the village. Weather conditions were perfect (in previous years we had delivered in snow and sheet ice), but after depositing a couple of envelopes through one letterbox, I turned quickly, without realising that I had been standing on an uneven paving stone. Before I could react, I span on my ankle and found myself lying on my backside on the front lawn. My ankle immediately swelled up like a balloon, but I hobbled to deliver my few remaining cards, before returning home. I was out of action on the walking front for nearly three weeks.

The major weather event of recent months was indisputably the flooding which impacted many areas of southern and western Britain. My own village near to the River Thames was particularly badly affected, with much of the ground covered by several feet of water and many homes evacuated. The village was the focus of the national news for an entire week, attracting senior politicians and news reporters in their dozens, while the local flood wardens worked tirelessly, with support from the fire services, police, army and a variety of other agencies.

Most of the walking routes I had adopted during my training period just one year earlier were now completely inaccessible. The Thames towpaths had been entirely submerged, most of the other local footpaths were flooded, and the few unscathed by water had effectively become mud-baths. Had the same conditions been present last year, my training programme would have been severely disrupted.

However, the floods also seriously impacted some of the

areas which formed part of my journey from John O' Groats to Land's End. In Wales, the Offa's Dyke path around the River Severn valley near Buttington, north of Welshpool, was completely submerged, and the section alongside the River Wye near Hay-on-Wye was flooded. Part of my route around the Somerset Levels was inaccessible and I have also seen news footage of the extensive damage caused by extreme high tides at Porthleven and Newlyn in Cornwall. These events only highlight the fragile and changeable nature of the British weather, to the extent that the bone-dry, rock-hard paths I was walking on less than nine months ago had become, for the foreseeable future, spongy, mud-strewn tracks.

On the subject of fragile and changeable, England's cricket team, which I had been following attentively during the latter stages of my walk, experienced the same dramatic transformation, from basking in golden sunshine to being completely submerged a few months later. The England team went on to retain the Ashes with a convincing 3-0 series win on home soil against Australia (it would have been 4-0, but for some petty rulings on bad light in the final Test) and hopes were high that this success would be carried forward into the winter series in Australia. Unexpectedly, Australia rediscovered form with bat and ball, England capitulated physically and mentally, and the Aussies regained the Ashes with a resounding 5-0 series victory.

As the flood waters recede, the days start to become longer, and the mercury begins to rise, my mind has turned towards walking again. I've booked to walk the 73-mile Cumbria Way across the Lake District with Daniel for a week in the summer, but I'd like to do something more challenging. There are no concrete plans yet, but I have acquired a long distance footpath map of Britain and a couple of guidebooks for the Camino de

Santiago walk, which runs for 800 kilometres (a mere 500 miles!) across northern Spain. I've also developed an unhealthy fascination for the 870 mile Wales Coastal Path – 1,047 miles if you add the Offa's Dyke footpath to make a full circular walk!

Before I undertook my JOGLE adventure, I was warned by several people that long distance walking would be both addictive and life changing. At the time, I wasn't convinced, but left my mind open to such a possibility. Fast forward one year and, having completed 955 miles, I am now left in no doubt that it is indeed addictive. I still feel a compelling need to walk, in part fuelled by a continuing interest in reading about long distance journeys undertaken by others. But, as addictions go, walking long distances in the fresh air is a healthy activity and must rank fairly low down in the league table of harmful dependencies!

Was it life changing? I now regard my walking adventure as one of the major events and achievements of my life and I will carry forward the resultant memories of it forever. The walk has given me the confidence to consider undertaking other long distance walking routes, but it has also taught me to respect those who undertake much more difficult physical challenges, whether on these shores or in other parts of the world. Above all, the adventure reinforced my love of the natural world and reminded me that a simpler, slower-paced lifestyle can often be more satisfying than the complicated, fast-paced way of life that many of us lead.

It hasn't changed my life yet, but my voyage has become a defining part of my life. It has rekindled my spirit of *carpe diem*, seizing the moment, when translated from the Latin. Or, as Gandhi decreed so succinctly, "Live as if you were to die tomorrow. Learn as if you were to live forever."

I did achieve what I set out to do. I completed the walk, I survived, I raised money for Cancer Research UK, and I rather enjoyed myself. I wasn't the fastest End to End walker; others carried heavier loads, followed more strenuous routes, endured more extreme and uncomfortable weather conditions, suffered more severe physical injuries and bore more mental scars, tolerated more challenging sleeping, washing and eating arrangements, adopted a more carefree approach to planning and raised greater sums for charity.

I did it on my own terms, at my pace, with a high degree of planning, following my own individually tailored route, staying in my varied choices of accommodation, and accompanied by an eclectic mix of walking partners.

But I did it. I did it my way.

ACKNOWLEDGEMENTS

- Jeff, my former boss, for allowing my crazy idea to germinate.
- Mark Moxon, for a really informative website (landsend johnogroats.info).
- The Land's End – John O' Groats Association, for invaluable route guidance.
- Abigail, Lucie, Giorgia and Jenny at Cancer Research UK, for fundraising ideas and enthusiastic support.
- Family, friends, colleagues, acquaintances and complete strangers who donated very generously to my cause.
- All of my many accommodation providers, especially family and friends.
- Calum at Craigdon Mountain Sports (Inverness) and Donna at Cotswold Outdoor (Liverpool), for services to my walking boots.
- Everybody who accompanied me on the walk (especially those who suffered for the cause!) and those who met me somewhere en route.
- Christine and Jeff from Preston, 'professional' long distance walkers, for valued friendship.
- Complete strangers who regularly went far beyond the call of duty.
- The many well-wishers who emailed and texted me during the walk.
- Mum, John, Carole, Daniel and Hannah, for ongoing family support.
- Rosie, my niece, for being an inspiration throughout.